Developing the Underdeveloped Countries

Developing the Underdeveloped Countries

EDITED BY

ALAN B. MOUNTJOY

WILEY-INTERSCIENCE
A Division of John Wiley & Sons, Inc., New York

First published in Great Britain 1971

Published in the U.S.A. by
WILEY–INTERSCIENCE DIVISION
John Wiley & Sons, Inc., 605 Third Avenue
New York, N.Y. 10016

Library of Congress catalog card no. 77–163461

ISBN: 0 471 61958–2

Printed in Great Britain

Contents

6 *Contents*

Acknowledgements

'Profiles of the Third World', by Keith Buchanan, *Pacific Viewpoint*, v 2 (Sep 1964) 97–126.

'The Third World and Beyond', by Keith Buchanan, *Outlook* (Feb 1966).

'The Economic Impact of Colonialism', by G. Myrdal, *Development and Underdevelopment*, © National Bank of Egypt (Cairo, 1956) pp. 51–6.

'The Expansion of Exports and the Growth of Population', by H. Myint, *The Economics of the Developing Countries* (Hutchinson, 1967).

'Natural Resources and Tropical Development', by B. W. Hodder, *Economic Development in the Tropics* (Methuen, 1968).

'The So-called Social Aspects of Economic Development', by V. L. Urquidi, *The Challenge of Development in Latin America* (Pall Mall Press, 1964) U.S. © Frederick A. Praeger Inc.

'The Take-off into Self-sustained Growth', by W. W. Rostow, *Economic Journal* (Mar 1956) 25–48.

'The Theory of Development and the Idea of Balanced Growth', by R. Nurkse, *Problems of Capital Formation in Underdeveloped Countries* (Blackwell, Oxford, 1953) U.S., copyright Oxford University Press.

'Unbalanced Growth: An Espousal', by A. O. Hirschman, *The Strategy of Economic Development* (Yale University Press, New Haven 1958).

'Balanced v. Unbalanced Growth: A Reconciliatory View', by Ashok Mathur, *Oxford Economic Papers*, XVIII (1966) and by permission of the Clarendon Press, Oxford.

'External Capital and Self-help in Developing Countries', by W. B. Reddaway, © *Progress: The Unilever Quarterly* (1966) 50–7.

'Agriculture et développement en Afrique Occidentale', by H. Isnard © *Cahiers d'Outre-Mer* (1963) 253–62.

'Land Consolidation in the Kikuyu Areas of Kenya', by G. J. W. Pedraza © *Journal of Administration Overseas* (1956) 82–7.

'New Railway Construction and the Pattern of Economic Development in East Africa', by A. M. O'Connor © *Transactions of the Institute of British Geographers*, XXXVI (1965).

'The Form of Industrialisation', by Alan B. Mountjoy, *Industrialisation and Underdeveloped Countries* (Hutchinson, 1968).

'Rural Industries', by E. F. Schumacher, *India at Mid-passage* © Overseas Development Institute 1964.

'The Economic Expansion of Jinja, Uganda', by B. S. Hoyle, *Geog. Review*, LIII (New York, 1963) © American Geographical Society of New York.

'An African Labour Force', by W. Elkan © *East African Studies*, no. 7 (1956).

'Planning and Industrial Developments in Apulia', by Alan B. Mountjoy © *Geography* (1966) 369–72.

'The City in the Developing World and the Example of South-east Asia', by D. J. Dwyer © *Geography* LIII (1968).

'The United Nations Development Decade at Mid-point', by U Thant © *United Nations Monthly Chronicle* (New York, 1965) 16–19.

Introduction

WE are all concerned in one way or another with the problems of the developing world and their solutions. Involvement is now world-wide, and international efforts and agencies play an increasing part in gathering and publishing information, in preparing development projects and plans, in raising and allotting aid in many forms. Interest in the 'Third World', as the less developed countries have come to be called, has never been so great. Much of this interest has been created and stimulated by the United Nations Organisation, and this year, 1970, marks the end of the United Nations Development Decade. This has been a valiant but somewhat disappointing period, launched at a time when aid was becoming publicised, respectable and, in the light of East – West relations, desirable. It began at a time when public interest within the rich countries had become stirred, when the colonial era was nearing its end, and progress in economic theory roused optimism and hope and seemed to clothe with reality President Truman's Point Four:

> Fourth, we must embark on a bold new programme for making the benefits of our scientific advances and industrial progress available for the improvement and growth of underdeveloped areas. More than half the people of the world are living in conditions approaching misery. Their food is inadequate. They are victims of disease. Their economic life is primitive and stagnant. Their poverty is a handicap and a threat both to them and to more prosperous areas. For the first time in history, humanity possesses the knowledge and the skill to relieve the suffering of these people.

The growing self-confidence in post-war thoughts on growth economics, fostered, or at least aided, by the agreeable dynamism that advanced economies began experiencing after the war had ended, coincided with a growing awareness of the world-wide inequality of economic development. The designation of the sixties as a Decade of Development sought to underline the gap between the minority of rich nations and the two-thirds of humanity existing in poverty.

The aim was to stimulate the new awareness of the situation into remedial action. Member-states were to co-ordinate their efforts in trade, capital investment and technical assistance in order to increase the transfer of resources to the less developed countries with a view to their attaining a 5 per cent growth rate. A significant step was the suggestion of the General Assembly that the annual flow of capital and assistance might reach approximately 1 per cent of the combined national incomes of the economically advanced countries. Thus a concept of shared resources between states and not merely between citizens within states has come into being. Further, the economic prospects of the poorer countries have become factors in international relations.

It is wrong to write off the Development Decade as a failure, but few of the initial high hopes have been fully realised, partly because expectations were pitched too high. Theoretical models that seemed to indicate orderly progress to a 'take-off' within one or two five- or seven-year plans have been proved imperfect under the test of reality. The Development Decade has at least injected greater realism into economic planning, and 'development in half a century' may now be a more certain appraisal. Bluntly, it is easier to make further economic progress in a developed country than it is to prise from rest a stagnant underdeveloped economy, and economic growth in the leading developed states has been more substantial than in the underdeveloped lands, although a few exceptions must be noted.

A fact much publicised, but not unexpected, has been the widening of the gap between the annual per capita income of the rich and the poor states. What should be remembered is that the gap will get wider even if the rate of increase is the same in both developed and less developed countries, simply because the existing base is so much greater in the one than the other. If the rich get richer they can afford more aid; the important thing is that absolutely the poor do not become poorer.

It has been unfortunate that over much of the Decade the annual flow of official assistance and capital to developing countries did not increase but hovered at around £2,200 million (in fact, in real terms it decreased). To this should be added private long-term capital investment which showed some increase over the Decade, bringing the average annual total capital aid to about £3,250 millions. This falls short of the 1 per cent of income target of the richer countries (one estimate is 0·9 per cent in 1967), but nevertheless, whether on target or not, it is a massive amount. More serious is the servicing and repayment situation. Much capital aid has been in the form of loans, and rates of interest have varied considerably, from nominal rates to as much as 6 or 7 per cent. As a result interest repayments increase, and in recent years most of the increase in aid has gone straight back to service debts or repay old loans. In 1960, $2,300 million was paid back in interest by the major developing countries, by 1965 their repayments had reached $3,500 million, and the capital has yet to be repaid. It is possible that 12–15 per cent of the developing countries' foreign exchange earnings are being paid back in debt servicing. The effects of this growing burden of debt were becoming appreciated by the end of the Decade and led to low-interest loans and a greater number of outright grants being made.

The effectiveness of this massive transfer of resources is difficult to assess, but generally the results have been far below the early over-optimistic expectations. The knowledge that much aid was being misused, poorly used or wasted has led to a general tightening-up of aid conditions and their supervision. These measures have sometimes been regarded with mistrust by recipient countries, who fear neo-colonial overtones. The truth is that we enter the seventies with confused ideas about the place and value of aid. Variously it seems to be a prop, a lubricant and a catalyst. It is distributed widely among about forty states at various levels of development; a concentration of aid upon the few states nearing or capable of attaining the 'take-off' is one view that gained support as the Decade neared its end.

The experience of recent years has underlined the fact that economic development does not depend on capital alone. Development demands and produces far-reaching changes in societies; the fabric of social life becomes altered, social attitudes change. Institutional arrangements and political conditions can make or mar development plans, as indeed can adverse terms of trade. Perhaps more than anything else it is the human factor that is most underdeveloped, and it is upon improvement in the quality and condition of the human factor that in the first instance other material development depends. Obstacles to development that are not easily quantified or incorporated in planning models include the inequality of income distribution; conditions of land ownership and tenure; character, organisation and efficiency of the various levels of government; degree and rigidity of tribal organisations; and social customs, such as the prevalence of the extended family system (that acts against labour mobility and

removes individual incentive for progress). Also there are psychological obstacles, not easily removed, such as in many parts of Africa
'a lack of flair for mechanics, lack of a sense of maintenance or
belief in mechanics, so that clocks, telephones and typewriters are
left unmended more through apathy than absence of skill'.[1]
Perhaps we should not be surprised that adjustment from simple
traditional economies and ways of life to the fast-advancing technologies and the feverish pace of life in the developed world in the
second half of the twentieth century is slow. The process, however,
seems inexorable; aspirations once lifted cannot be suppressed.

Despite disappointments, the Decade of Development accomplished a great deal, and although the full balance sheet has yet to be
drawn up (and then it can only be in imprecise terms), some account
of achievements is needed to balance the much publicised short-
comings. Taking the less developed countries as a whole and allowing
for the accelerating rate of population increase in most of them, it
seemed that near the end of the period this group of countries were
becoming richer at a rate of between 2 and 3 per cent a year. On this
basis, current standards of living would be doubled in about thirty
years. Unfortunately in most cases the current standard of living is so
low that the prospect even of doubling it within thirty years seems
unacceptable. In a few countries much more substantial progress has
been made. In this category come Formosa, South Korea, Mexico,
Pakistan, Thailand and Kenya. All have received above-average aid,
all have authoritarian governments that have made economic
development their goal.

Further, great strides have been made in what are often unexciting
but essential infrastructure projects: roads, railways, ports, health
and education. Gradually skills and aptitudes in administrative and
managerial abilities are being fostered. It is upon the success of these
measures that future progress depends: their cost may fall within the
Development Decade, their fruits will accrue in a later period.

Institutional impediments to development are gradually being
removed. This is particularly evident in the spread of land-reform
measures, aimed variously at reducing the power of large landowners, removing 'feudal' mentality from the peasantry and
distributing the national income more equitably. From within our
urbanised society the difficulties and pitfalls facing these land-reform

[1] J. Ardagh, 'Africa's dilemma: facing the modern world', *The Times*,
27 Mar 1969.

measures are not readily appreciated, and apparent tardiness in execution is seized upon as evidence of insincerity. In the developing countries economies are based almost entirely on agriculture; consequently land is the prime source of wealth. The land-owning system and the customary usages of land are part of the countryman's life and of national tradition. Changes here do not come lightly. Further, it is doubtful whether land reform in itself promotes economic development, for a more equal distribution of incomes may reduce savings and investment. Success with such measures appears to come where the organisation of farming is adjusted to benefit from economies of scale, despite small-scale ownership of the land. Egypt has been in the van with such schemes which are proving extremely successful in raising both agricultural productivity and the standard of living of the fellahin.[1]

Inevitably development strategy has varied over the years with the gaining of experience, and a new emphasis upon agricultural development was becoming clear as the Development Decade progressed. Much of the poverty in the less developed countries is not due to a lack of manufacturing industry but rather to traditional, inefficient and poorly productive agriculture. Any efforts to develop the industrial sector must rely upon increased productivity from agriculture – to feed the increasing population, to feed the growing urban-industrial populations, to supply agricultural raw materials to industry, to decrease the need for food imports and, where possible, to provide surpluses for export and the earning of foreign currency; and above all to increase farm incomes and create an expanding market for the new industries. These views are not new but were first treated with suspicion in the developing world. Agriculture has always been with the poor countries; what they felt they needed were visible signs of change: the factory chimney rather than the denser paddy field was more in keeping with earlier moods. Foreigners harping on agricultural development suggested to them continued economic subjugation to the industrialised states, and thus opposition to these views meant that many plans allotted too few resources to agricultural modernisation. Changing views here are gradual but convincing. India, a major country with appallingly low yields from the land, in recent planning has increased the proportion of investment in agriculture and irrigation, and towards the end of the

[1] G. S. Saab, *The Egyptian Agrarian Reform, 1952–62* (Oxford University Press, 1967).

Development Decade there came the indication of greater agricultural returns as the result of the increasing provision of fertilisers, selective seeds, water supply, etc.

Variations in strategy also reflect changing views in economic thought. Leibenstein's population blockage, where population increase absorbs the fruits of modest economic development and a treadmill pattern becomes envisaged, led to the 'big push' view and to Nurkse's 'balanced growth' approach. This in turn has lost ground to the disequilibrium view of Hirschman, who suggests that productivity can be promoted by judicious and selected use of resources even where infrastructure shortages exist. Rostow's 'stages of economic growth', imaginatively phrased in aeronautic language, and deceptively lucid in exposition, have lost some support through a suggested lack of mechanism linking the different stages and because other economic historians of present-day advanced countries fail to discern the investment pattern that Rostow cites.

Turning from the journals of the economists, one searches in vain for magisterial papers in this field from geographers. One reason for this is that the character of his contribution differs: it is more frequently down to earth, micro rather than macro. Another reason is that the geographer has been slow in putting forward his case for participation in this domain.[1] Now the geographer is increasingly being called upon to take part in social and resource surveys in developing countries. His studies of population, settlement and land use and their mapping provide valuable basic data for both social and economic planning. His expertise is now sought in the three stages of resource surveys (the exploratory stage, when the physical environment is described and mapped; the appraisal stage, when the resources offered by the environment are evaluated; the development stage, involving the drawing-up of plans to utilise the resources),[2] and his training equips him to view sets of facts in a regional setting, to appreciate interdependence and interrelationships.

The foregoing serves to demonstrate some of the many interdisciplinary facets to development studies. Economists, demographers, geographers, sociologists all have parts to play in an exercise that now transcends in size and complexity any previous

[1] R. W. Steel, 'Geography and the developing world', *Adv. of Science*, 23 (1967) 566–82.

[2] A. Young, 'Natural resource surveys for land development in the Tropics', *Geography*, 53 (1968) 229–48.

world activity. Indeed, imperfect though the many single operations may be, these activities represent the first real global mobilisation of energies and resources in a fight against poverty and backwardness. Increasingly information from detailed investigations and studies is becoming published, thanks mainly to the work of such bodies as the United Nations Organisation, the Food and Agricultural Organisation, the World Health Organisation and UNESCO. The more we know about the developing world in all its aspects, the better position we are in to diagnose its ills and prescribe remedies.

The selections of twenty writings for this book from the substantial volume of literature now available was carried out with the breadth and diversity of the activities in the field of development in mind. Aspects of economic theory that have left their mark in development planning are included, as are views and discussions on trade, population, social infrastructure, agriculture, industrial developments, transport and urbanisation. Contributions have been chosen therefore to offer a comprehensive view of problem, theory and practice. This means a volume of breadth rather than depth, one that is designed to stimulate further reading. Most of the articles are reproduced as originally published; in a few cases small excisions have been made where the main argument is unaffected. Thanks are due to the authors who have made their work available for this anthology, and the editor hopes that provision of such varied fare will give further stimulus to the study of developing countries, their economies and their problems.

A. B. M.

1 Profiles of the Third World

KEITH BUCHANAN

THE maps presented here,[1] with a brief commentary, give a series of
profiles of the social and economic geography of the Third World.
This 'immense community of newly or imminently independent
nations' forms the third element in a world power structure dominated
up to the present by the technologically more advanced nations of the
Atlantic bloc or the European Communist bloc. Its muted or passive
role in world affairs has been due to its technological backwardness,
and to the colonial control, overt or concealed, which was both a
cause and a consequence of this backwardness. This passive role is
increasingly a thing of the past for, among at least the elites of the
Third World, there is an emerging and increasingly focused awareness of their potential strength. This awareness is not entirely the
product of an opportunism which has flourished in the genial climate
provided by the manœuvres of two opposing power blocs, each
desperately striving to win friends and influence nations; it is
ultimately much more solidly based. For two out of every three men
on our globe are citizens of a Third World country (and by the end
of the century it will be three out of every four) and these countries,
in spite of present poverty, have a rich resource endowment. They
have the immense resource represented by two thousand million
human beings, often technologically undeveloped but capable of
acquiring all the skills and the techniques to build great cities, convert
bushland into farmland, to convert matter into energy – and maybe
destruction. Many of them are heirs of rich and complex cultures,
cultures which perhaps have been less gutted of human content and
purpose than has our own; this psychic wealth may be their greatest
asset. In spite of stark and abject poverty they yet possess, collectively,
great riches – for this Third World contains much of the world's
metallic minerals, its water power and oil and coal, its timbers and its

---

[1] The base map used in this series is purely diagrammatic, with the size of the
countries proportional to their population in the mid-1950s. Certain smaller
island territories are grouped together.

potential cropland. . . . Because of this wealth these countries have in the past been an important source of strength to the colonial countries of the West; the drive towards total national independence, involving real economic independence and a possible withdrawing of many of these resources from the unfettered control of the West, could, under these conditions, significantly change the world power pattern. In the next decade or so we may therefore expect a continuing drive to win over the hearts and minds of these dwellers in the world's slums, and, perhaps even more important, the weaving of 'subtler nets to enmesh the new countries'[1] to counter this potentially disastrous loss of an extremely important resource base. Whichever way we look at it,these Third World countries are going to be of critical importance in the years ahead. . . .

DEFINITION

The congealment of political blocs resulting from the Cold War has given us a clear picture of the location, on the world's political map, of the crevasse which separates the Western bloc from the Soviet bloc. The unremitting and indefatigable industry of the propagandists may, indeed, have resulted in a dangerous and misleading exaggeration of the differences which divide the two great groups of developed countries; we tend too easily to overlook the increasing similarity of conditions of material life, even of details such as industrial organisa- tion,[2] between the affluent nations of the West and those of the socialist bloc. And while we are vaguely aware of the *other* split in our world society – of the Iron Curtain of poverty which separates the 'haves' and the 'have nots' – we are not always aware of the content, in terms of countries or hundreds of millions of human beings, of the world behind *this* Iron Curtain.

We are aware that this shadowy world of half-life exists, just as in the past it was possible to be aware of the squalid and shadowy slums in which many millions of citizens of a wealthy and imperial Britain lived and died. We know that from time to time desperate groups rise in despair against the desperate conditions of their day-to-day life – the Rastafarians in Jamaica, the Africans in Angola, the peasants of South Vietnam or Brazil or Peru – but we see these as merely isolated

[1] Worsley (1960, p. 139).
[2] See, for example, Granick (1961). The same topic is dealt with by F. Zweig (1957, esp. p. 70–1).

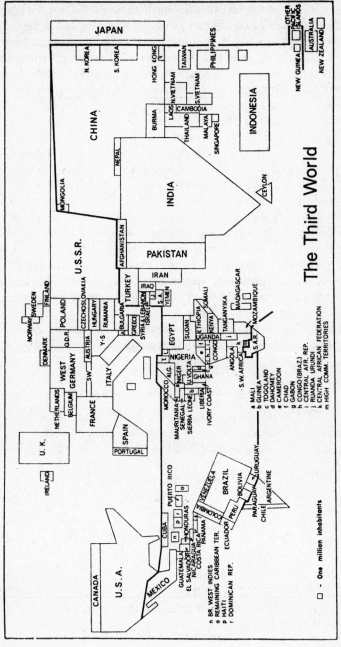

Fig. 1.1

episodes, not as the first twisting birth-pangs of the world's hungry and half-human masses as they struggle to be born as full men. Yet, if over the years we plot on a map these peasant uprisings, guerilla wars, anti-colonial struggles – if we plot all these we get emerging a coherent pattern, a geopolitical unity, which stretches from the Andes, across Latin America and Africa and South Asia towards the rain forests of Borneo and the tawny steppe lands of Mongolia. . . .

We can define this Third World, this 'commonwealth of poverty', then, by mapping the symptoms of its unease, by mapping the world's 'trouble spots'. We can dissect in more clinical fashion and map the individual conditions giving rise to unease, to the rapidly festering tensions. The contours of poverty, for example, define it clearly, for in contrast to the affluent nations of the 'white north', most of the rest of the world's peoples exist on incomes of under £100 a year; if we reduce the other social and economic conditions of the world's population also to a series of indices, we get emerging again and again the same pattern of shading, the same shadowed world of poverty and deprivation, contrasting sharply with the neon-lit garishness of the other world – the world of those who are prosperous or who are attaining prosperity.

The Third World, within the boundaries shown on the map, contains two-thirds of the world's population.

'A UNIVERSE OF RADICAL SCARCITY'

'The Third World is a universe of radical scarcity. Defining and determining every dimension of men's relationship to each other . . . the inadequacy of the means of livelihood is the first and distinguishing truth of this area.'[1]

We can measure this scarcity, and map its areal pattern in several ways. In Fig. 1.2 the real G.N.P. per capita is shown; over much of the Third World it is under $200 per capita; only in one or two areas does it exceed $500 and here the wealth is a precarious one, based either on a highly specialised export economy (Malaya) or the feverish exploitation of fugitive resources such as oil (Venezuela). Per capita income figures follow the same general pattern; over much of Africa and Asia they are below $100 per capita; this is the *annual* income and it is an *average* figure inflated by the incomes of the affluent

[1] *New Left Review* (1963) p. 4.

few.[1] And, as Robert Heilbroner observes, 'This is a standard which in fact defies numerical treatment: it means existence at the borderline of animal needs.'[2]

This 'borderline' quality of life for hundreds of millions of human beings is emphasised by the extent of the dark-hatched areas on Figs. 1.3 and 1.4; these indicate, in the impersonal language of statistics, how heavily hunger weighs on the world's peoples. While in the developed areas of the West food intake exceeds requirements by about 20 per cent, while tens of millions of Europeans or Americans are endangering their health by overeating, while millions of tons of unsaleable food grains accumulate in the United States, hundreds of millions of people in South and East Asia, in parts of Africa and in the Andean republics of Latin America (and in *relatively* wealthy Venezuela) are existing on diets whose calorie content is below the critical minimum, *for the average adult at rest*, of 2,200 calories. Just what the total of the world's hungry is, is difficult to establish; a recent evaluation of the food situation by Professor Michel Cépède states: 'more than one-third and no doubt nearly one-half of mankind suffers from under-nutrition due to lack of calories, that is, hunger in the strictest sense of the word'[3] – in short, perhaps between one billion and one and a half billion people. Moreover, in addition to this generalised hunger, there are the 'specific hungers', resulting from the shortages of essential food elements such as vitamins, minerals or protein, which may sap the health of those whose diet, measured in energy-giving (calorie) terms, appears adequate.[4] Protein deficiency, in particular, has been described as 'without a doubt the most serious of all the diseases which afflict mankind'; in its acute form, *kwashiorkor*, it affects some four-fifths of the children in

[1] For example, Malaya's per capita income was $ U.S. 275 in 1957, which was among the highest in Asia. The country's wealth, however, is highly concentrated in the hands of a relatively small and in part non-resident group. Tjoa Soei Hock (1963) comments: 'If $ M. 1,500 (approximately $ U.S. 500) per year is taken as a subsistence level for Malaya, then the great majority of the Malayan people (about 98 per cent) – Malays, Indians and Chinese – live on the verge of subsistence' (p. 77). He adds: 'The concept of per capita income should be scrutinised more, especially in the so-called underdeveloped countries where income is much less equally distributed than in Western countries.'

[2] Heilbroner (1960, p. 84).

[3] Cépède (1962, p. 20).

[4] To produce one calorie of animal products, 7 calories of vegetable origin must be fed to the animal. A diet of 2,200 calories, of which 600 come from animal products, corresponds thus to a figure of 5,800 'initial' calories (1,600 calories + 600 calories × 7) (Cépède, 1962, p. 22).

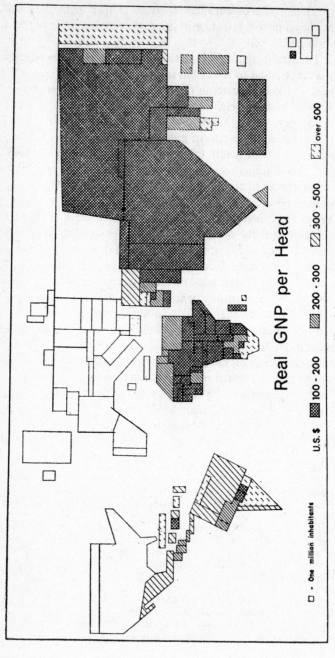

Real GNP per Head

□ - One million inhabitants

U.S. $ ▨ 100 - 200 ▨ 200 - 300 ▨ 300 - 500 ▨ over 500

Fig. 1.2

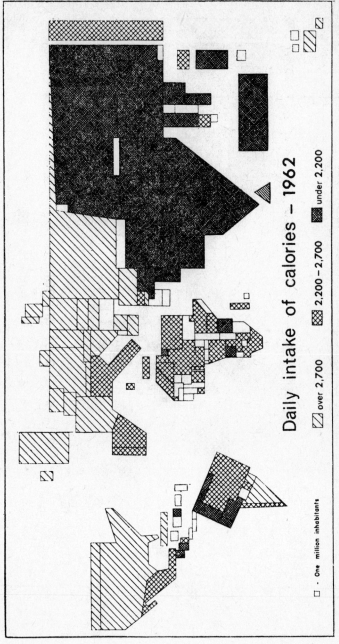

Daily intake of calories — 1962

□ - One million inhabitants

⬚ over 2,700   ⬚ 2,200 – 2,700   ◼ under 2,200

Fig. 1.3

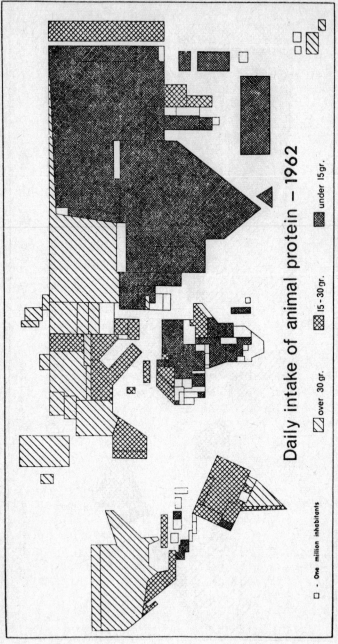

Daily intake of animal protein – 1962

◻ – One million inhabitants

▨ over 30 gr.   ▩ 15 - 30 gr.   ▨ under 15gr.

Fig. 1.4

parts of the tropical world, killing, or leaving those who survive crippled for life.

It will be seen from Fig. 1.4 that low protein intake is more widely distributed than low calorie intake, but these two indices define clearly the shape of the Third World, overlapping on to the poorer countries of southern Europe and the Balkans. These hungers, as Michel Cépède rightly affirms, 'are the scandal of our time for which ignorance is responsible and not the ungenerosity of nature or the number of people on earth – ignorance and the problems of economics' – and this scandal, as the maps show, is one with a clearly defined pattern. . . .

A LEGACY OF WARPED ECONOMIES

The hunger of so great a proportion of the world's population is not in any way predestined, determined by a relentless and hostile environment. Many countries of the Third World *do* face environmental difficulties – poor soils, erratic climatic regimes which bring drought or flood, devasting human diseases and pests and predators which ravage the food crops. But the control exercised by these influences is by no means absolute, rather does it depend on the level of technology and the material resources of the groups concerned; many tropical diseases, which are killing or crippling diseases to the African, are of minor importance to immigrant groups possessed of the means, in the shape of prophylactics or immunisation, effectively to counter them. Poverty and underdevelopment give rise to a vicious circle in which poverty means helplessness in the face of the problems posed by a particular environment – and this helplessness leads to ill health, inefficient farming, hunger, and back to poverty. And this poverty and underdevelopment has been perpetuated, even aggravated, by generations of Western exploitation which have distorted and twisted the economies of the dependent territories.

Over most of the Third World over one-half of the population is engaged in agriculture (Fig. 1.5), and over most of Africa and southern Asia the proportion is between 70 and 90 per cent; this compares with under 30 per cent in most of the advanced countries of the West, dropping to under 15 per cent in countries such as the United States or the United Kingdom. Over wide areas the agriculture remains a grubbing subsistent type; in Africa such subsistent economies occupy between one-quarter and four-fifths of the land, according to territory, and even in the case of a relatively market-oriented economy such as that of Nigeria, subsistence crops represent three-quarters of the agricultural output by value. Export production takes the form of small islands of market-oriented production set in the midst of a sea of stagnating peasant economies; it is, moreover, highly specialised in terms of crops grown – three-fifths of Ghana's exports consist of cocoa, nine-tenths of Gambia's exports of groundnuts, three-fifths of Malaya's of rubber. . . .

The economies of the Third World countries are thus misshapen, with a grossly inflated agricultural sector (Fig. 1.5) polarised between inefficient production of food for local consumption and the production of export crops for a world market. Moreover, given the stagnation (or in some territories the actual deterioration) in levels of food production, these countries, in spite of the size of their agricultural sector, are heavy importers of foodstuffs. In the cases of Malaya and Pakistan, Indonesia and Egypt, to mention only a few, the proportion of total imports represented by foodstuffs is higher than in some of the industrialised nations of north-west Europe. This fact helps to set China's recent grain imports into something like a correct perspective; it also underlines the precarious character of the Third World economies, especially when seen against their rapid rates of population increase, and emphasises the difficulties they face in reaching the point of economic 'take-off' (for the necessity to use scarce overseas funds to purchase food means a corresponding reduction in the amount available to purchase capital equipment for industry).

The warped, and consequently highly vulnerable, character[1] of the economies of the Third World countries is highlighted by Fig. 1.6 which shows the dependence of their export trade, and thus of their overall prosperity, on the sale of a very limited group of primary products. This degree of export specialisation, as Beguin remarks, 'constitutes a supplementary index of dependency'.[2] In some countries, such as Malaya, most of West Africa and the Andean republics of Latin America, over 90 per cent of their exports are accounted for by three commodities, and in the case of certain smaller countries, such as Jamaica, Panama and Fiji, this specialisation has increased in the last decade. A high degree of specialisation and hence of

---

[1] To take a single example, the drop in coffee prices in Latin America over the last ten years has cost the continent $10 billion – which more than cancels out all aid received.

[2] Beguin (1963, p. 85).

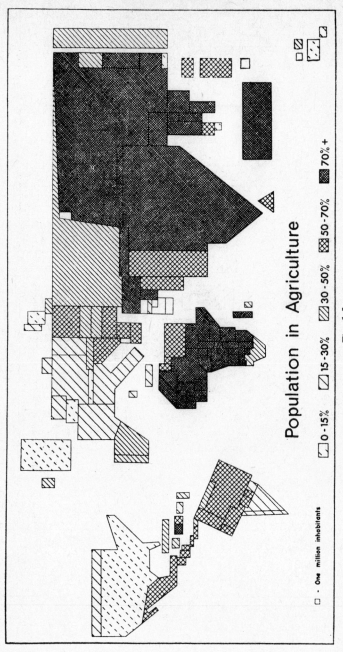

Population in Agriculture

☐ - One million inhabitants

☐ 0 - 15%   ▨ 15 - 30%   ▧ 30 - 50%   ▩ 50 - 70%   ▦ 70% +

Fig. 1.5

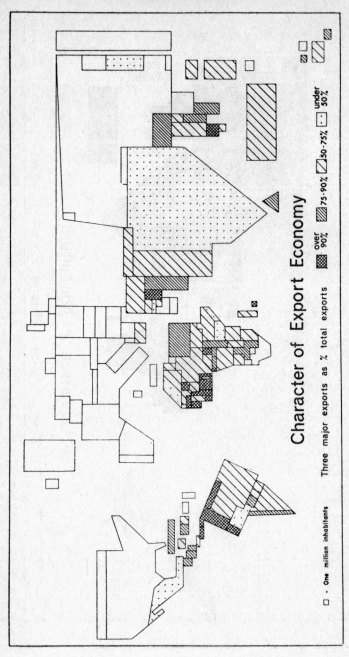

Character of Export Economy

□ - One million inhabitants   Three major exports as % total exports

over 90% 75-90% 50-75% under 50%

Fig. 1.6

vulnerability is especially typical of oil-producing countries such as Iraq and Venezuela. Such patterns of specialisation are the result of the abnormal development of certain sectors of the economy which complement the industrial economies of the West,[1] and this 'colonial hangover' seems likely to be perpetuated by agreements which tie in the economies of the emergent countries to neo-capitalist groupings such as the E.E.C.

The import trade of the Third World countries shows an equally distinctive quality. Some 70–80 per cent of the imports consist of manufactured goods, especially consumer goods; in contrast to the developed countries the imports of primary products and fuels represent only a small proportion of total imports. As far as imports of capital goods are concerned, the contrast between the developed and underdeveloped countries is less clear-cut though it may be noted that in the case of countries in the first group the imports of capital goods are on a small scale because these countries supply most of their own needs; in the case of underdeveloped countries such as Afghanistan or Niger they are negligible simply because these countries are not equipping their economies to any significant degree.[2]

The dependent character of these 'semi-economies' in the Third World countries is underlined by the 'polarisation' of trade on a limited group of developed countries and particularly on the former metropolitan power. Beguin has attempted to measure this 'polarisation of trade' between what he terms the *pays-foyers* and the *pays-affiliés* (dependent countries). It is strongest in the case of the French African colonies, and the trading agreements which create this 'polarisation' are excellent examples of the 'subtler nets' which are being woven to enmesh the newer countries. The formerly British colonies and the countries of South and South-east Asia show a more diversified pattern of trade, with a higher Third World component. The Latin American countries are 'polarised' largely on the United States, the degree of 'polarisation' increasing northwards; it has tended to decrease in recent years as a result of the swing of trade towards the Common Market countries. Summarising the trade

[1] Thus Carlos Fuentes observes: 'A good part of the Latin American economy is not serving its own development, but is nothing more than an extension of foreign economies. . . . Iron and oil in Venezuela, copper in Chile, Peruvian minerals . . . are a possession of the American economy and benefit only that economy' (Fuentes, 1963, p. 13).
[2] Beguin (1963, p. 91).

situation, it is clear from the maps that there is a sharp contrast in the composition and character of trade between the Third World and the countries of the 'white north'; it is also clear that within the Third World a certain regional diversity can be discerned, a diversity due to factors such as proximity, colonial history or the heterogeneity or complementarity of certain regions.[1]

The distortion of the economies of the Third World countries manifests itself in another significant fashion – the gross inflation of the tertiary sector. This is due to many factors: to the proliferation of the bureaucracy which has been one of the infantile disorders of new nationalism,[2] to the high profits offered by commerce as contrasted with the lower, less certain, profit offered by secondary industry, to the migration of the unemployed and underemployed from the rural areas towards the cities to find semi-employment as white-collar workers, petty traders, servants and the like. The result is that those employed in the tertiary sector outnumber those employed in secondary industry by 2:1 in many parts of the Third World, and the ratio exceeds 2·5:1 in parts of Central America, in some of the newly emergent countries of Africa and parts of South-east Asia. It is largely this rapid expansion of the tertiary sector of the economy which explains the rapid growth of the capital cities and large towns of the Third World. Great-city growth rates have been considerably higher than the growth rates of the population as a whole, and this has been due, not to any great increase in the productive sector of the city's economies, but rather to an accentuation of their 'parasitic' function. The city is a centre of consumption rather than of production, and the misery of the stagnating countryside siphons off into the cities to create an impoverished and explosive *lumpenproletariat*. Lack of structural change in agriculture is thus intimately related to the mushroom growth of parasitic *megalopolises* in which 'the gulf between excess of luxury and excess of misery shatters the human dimension'.[3]

'ULTIMATES IN POVERTY AND DEGRADATION...

The long, and continuing, exploitation of the colonial and semi-colonial territories led to what have been aptly described as 'the ultimates in poverty and degradation'. It produced a world (a world

---

[1] Examined more fully by Beguin (1963, pp. 114–16).
[2] Dealt with by Cheverny (1961) and Dumont (1962).
[3] Lévi-Strauss (1962, p. 6).

containing two-thirds of humanity) whose existence was that of, at the best, half men, living poorly and living briefly, living in the twilight world of the illiterate, living in the brutalising certainty that half of their children would perish of hunger or preventable disease before adolescence. . . . Living alongside the West somewhat as Dickens, in *A Tale of Two Cities*, describes the Parisian crowds faced with the Marquis: 'So cowed was their condition, and so long and hard their experience of what such a man could do to them, within the law and beyond it, that not a voice, or a head or even an eye was raised. . . .'

China, Vietnam, Cuba, these countries and others suggest that this long nightmare of humanity is drawing to a close and, indeed, perhaps the most striking feature of the contemporary world is not the much talked-of emergence of *new nations* as the emergence of *humanity* – as two-thirds of mankind struggle upwards to assert themselves as full men. Such a full human stature is not acquired automatically as a result of the granting or the winning of political independence; this may be only the first and possibly easiest step forward. Far more important is the wiping out of the conditions which political dependence created or prolonged, such as illiteracy and the short and brutish quality of life for the majority.

The size of this problem, and the gradients between the countries of the Third World and the 'white north' in such fields as literacy, infantile mortality or death rates, are illustrated in Figs. 1.7–1.9.

Except in limited parts of Latin America and South-east Asia illiteracy rates in the Third World are everywhere over 50 per cent; even in these countries cited which have a lower figure, whole groups, such as the Andean Indians or the hill tribes of South-east Asia, remain largely illiterate. Over much of Black Africa and much of colonial South Asia over four-fifths of the population were illiterate in 1950. It is scarcely necessary to stress that any real economic breakthrough is made immeasurably more difficult if to the purely economic barriers there are added the deadweights of illiteracy and ignorance. The vulgarisation of even simple agricultural techniques must then depend on word of mouth, the creation of any real political awareness is hampered and the masses exposed to the influence of rumour and of demagogues, the problem of enlarging a group's awareness beyond the limits of the clan, the tribe or the village is almost insuperable. The mass education drive is thus of critical importance in consolidating any real national unit in an emergent

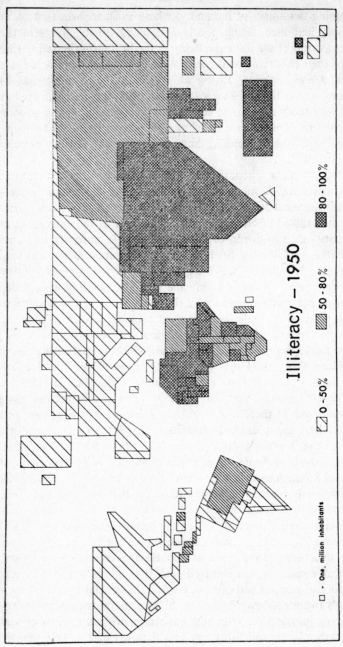

Illiteracy – 1950

□ 0 – 50%   ▨ 50 – 80%   ▦ 80 – 100%

□ - One million inhabitants

Fig. 1.7

country; moreover, it not only removes a major obstacle to modernisation but also offers, as in China and Cuba, a field in which the idealism of the young, and of the student group in particular, can find expression. . . .

One of the greatest resources of the 'underdeveloped' countries is their people, and as China has illustrated, the mass mobilisation of millions of hands can be used as a partial substitute for machinery and capital to begin the leap from poverty to decency; this 'turning of labour into capital' is, indeed, one of the lessons of Chinese experience most widely applicable to other countries of the Third World. But this population resource is at present only partially utilised. Preventable disease leaches away the energies of hundreds of millions of people; death rates are often higher than in the West, in spite of the fact that the Third World's population is demographically a much younger one; reduced expectation of life means for hundreds of millions a working life of fifteen to twenty years as against a working life of thirty-five to forty years in the advanced countries. The most savage losses are in the younger age groups. In Brazil 'every 42 seconds a child dies, that is 85 every hour, 2,040 every day. Every year, 6 million Brazilians aged under 16 are taken to the cemetery. Of each 1,000 children, 350 and even 400 die before reaching one year of age. . . .'[1] In many of the so-called 'underdeveloped' countries, more than one-half of the child population dies before adolescence and the infantile mortality rate is between five and eight times that of the developed countries of the West. And, while we may attempt to assess the economic wastage, the wastage of a precious human resource, which these cold and impersonal statistics convey, it is fitting that we should not lose sight of what is ultimately of much greater human significance – the anguished deprivation, the shattered hopes and personal sufferings which lie behind the statistical measure. . . .

THE SEARCH FOR IDENTITY

The Third World countries are differentiated from the old-developed countries of the 'white north' not only in economic terms but also in socio-political terms. Most of them are engaged in a search for identity – national identity in the shape of an integrated and purposeful national structure, international identity in the sense of a place in relation to the great power blocs which dominate the world scene.

[1] Julião (1963, p. 106).

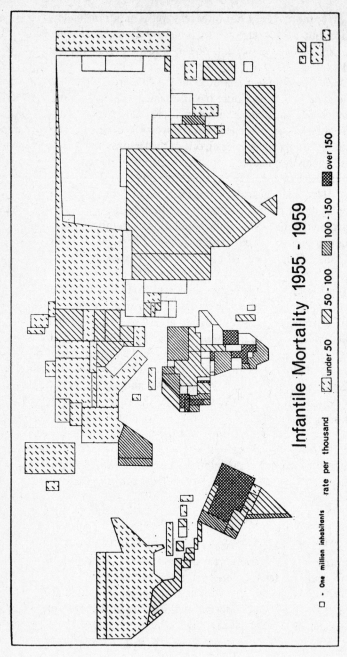

Infantile Mortality 1955 - 1959

☐ - One million inhabitants   rate per thousand   ⬚ under 50   ⬚ 50 - 100   ⬚ 100 - 150   ⬛ over 150

Fig. 1.8

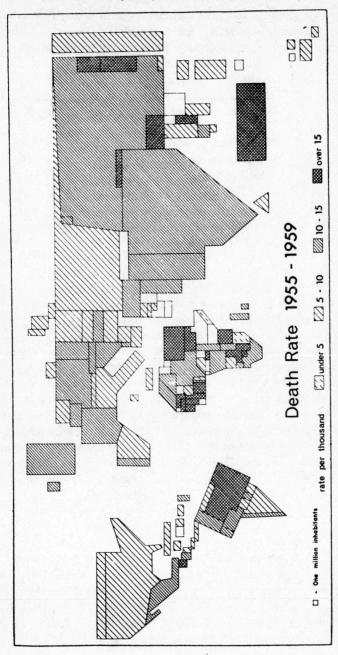

Death Rate 1955 - 1959

□ - One million inhabitants   rate per thousand   ▨ under 5   ▨ 5 - 10   ▨ 10 - 15   ▦ over 15

Fig. 1.9

And given the shifting balance of classes or even of ethnic groups within national boundaries, given the shifting pressures of the international scene, this search for identity may be accompanied by protean changes in the world's political map.

The striving towards an integrated national structure is closely bound up with the whole process of economic development, for, as Robert Heilbroner points out, *economic development is not primarily an economic process in the Third World but a social and political process*. In the Euro-American world (and including, to some extent, the U.S.S.R. in this context) economic development took place within existing societies which had been created over a relatively long period of time. In the Third World, by contrast, such national societies do not exist and here a prime essential is the 'creation, forcibly or otherwise, of workable institutional structures'.[1] Such a process must inevitably be revolutionary in character, for the necessary reorganisation involves, in a backward nation, a reorganisation of its class structure. The extent of the problem posed is indicated by Fig. 1.10, which attempts to show, in the very broadest of terms, the degree of national integration. In contrast to the developed nation-state of Euro-America the Third World shows a range of national structures: the traditional societies of Black Africa consisting of a loosely-structured aggregate of tribal groups set within often arbitrary colonial-inherited boundaries; the colony-derived states of Latin America, controlled by a small 'white' elite, with a dominantly *mestizo* population and with large and compact Indian communities existing largely outside the political or social framework of the state; and the new nations of southern Asia which contain uncomfortably within their frontiers advanced 'lowland' cultures and backward hill peoples, together with sizeable Asian immigrant groups (such as the Chinese) whose role in the country's economic life may be out of all proportion to their numbers. The Communist nationalities policy, as exemplified by China, or North Vietnam, offers one solution to this problem of integration; the alternatives are the nation-wide political party as in Guinea, or the charismatic ruler as in Cambodia.

THE GEOPOLITICAL PERSONALITY OF THE THIRD WORLD

Speaking of the Afro-Asian bloc, Samaan Boutros Farajallah says: 'Elements of both an objective and subjective character ... the fruits

[1] Heilbroner (1963, p. 24).

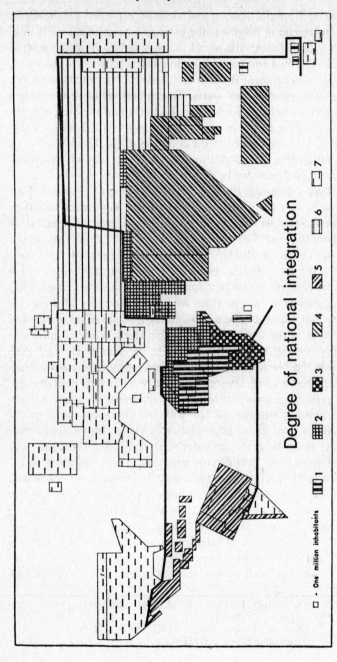

Fig. 1.10 Key: 1. Traditional societies lacking political integration. 2. Partially-integrated traditional societies. 3. Traditional societies with considerable settler groups. 4. Asian societies with substantial indigenous minorities. 5. Colony-derived societies with marginal indigenous populations. 6. Socialist multi-national states. 7. European-type national states.

of a long and painful history and skilfully exploited by the Great Powers, intervene to fragment the emergent geopolitical unity constituted by the Afro-Asiatic world . . . they reduce it, at the best, to more or less limited and unstable regional structures . . . at the worst, they threaten to pulverise it into a multitude of 'micro-nations' which take the form of miniature states, fiercely jealous of their nominal independence, the latter freshly acquired at a period when only the large units have a chance of survival and progress'.[1] These remarks are no less valid if extended to the countries of the Third World as a whole; within this extended grouping the same play of centripetal and centrifugal forces can be discerned.

Two themes dominate the policies of the emergent countries: their refusal to be any longer the *objects* of world diplomacy and their aspirations to assume a positive role, the role of *active subjects*, on the international scene.[2] This twofold, negative and positive, aspect of their policies expresses itself clearly in their role in the United Nations; together with the pressures exerted by the United States and the other great powers[3] on these economically vulnerable 'micro-nations', or, more precisely, on the elites who hold the reins of power, it explains what appears to be a bewildering mixture of principles and opportunism in the voting pattern of the Third World countries.

The cohesion of the group varies. On the general issue of anti-colonialism the Third World countries, and especially the Afro-Asian bloc, have shown a high degree of solidarity as far as *general declarations of principle* are concerned. On *specific issues* in this field many of the countries with special ties with the colonial powers or the United States have shown themselves very vulnerable to great-power pressures; these became particularly marked after the Cold War extended to Asia in 1949–50 and produced a fragmentation of the Third World bloc in the United Nations.[4] In the socio-economic field there is the same solidarity with regard to many of the general measures discussed by the Economic and Social Committee of the United Nations (indeed, largely because many of the suggested measures were the result of extensive compromises, they were often adopted virtually unanimously); discussions on the allocation of financial and technical assistance, however, revealed cleavages

[1] Farajallah (1963, pp. 413–14 freely; translated).
[2] Farajallah (1963, p. 417).
[3] See, for example, O'Brien (1962, esp. pp. 22–9).
[4] Farajallah (1963, pp. 433–4).

between the African bloc and the Latin American and Asian blocs who feared increased aid to Africa would reduce the aid they were receiving. On the relative merits of the policy of channelling all such aid through the United Nations or seeking bilateral or multilateral aid outside the machinery of the United Nations there has again been little unanimity; certain states, such as Thailand and the members of the U.A.M. (Union Africaine et Malgache), for example, expressed a strong preference for the latter policy. Most of the Third World countries are agreed on the vital need for stabilising the prices of raw materials, more especially for prices determined not so much by the operations of world markets but by reference to the price of manufactured goods; on the need for freedom of trade there is much less unanimity, for countries such as the African states associated with the E.E.C. show little inclination to forgo any advantages such association may bring in order to present a united front to those who seek tropical raw materials. As Farajallah observes: 'Their reactions, indeed, are those of underdeveloped *countries* and not those of an *organised group;* national egoism and competition between countries have not yet given place to an Afro-Asian solidarity (and not even to any real *regional* solidarity).'[1]

As a geopolitical entity, then, the Third World demonstrates an inchoate quality. This derives in part from the very number of nation-states which it comprises, but more powerful influences are the diversity of political regimes, the economic orientation of the component states, the variety of conditions under which they attained national status (and thus the strength of ties which still bind them to the former metropolitan power), the character of dedication of their elite groups and, above all, the susceptibility of these groups to outside pressures. . . . Under these conditions, while the coalition of the Latin American and Afro-Asian blocs gives the countries of the Third World an *ad hoc* unity when confronted by socio-economic problems in the United Nations, the achievement of any wider unity, of any unifying sense of purpose, among the proletarian nations is dependent upon internal political changes. Such changes and such a realignment are likely to be slow; the process is likely to begin in the U.A.M. group of states whose pro-Western orientation is largely determined by the francophile character of the elites and the personal influence of de Gaulle; it is likely to be delayed longest in the Latin American satellites of the United States. But whatever its timing,

[1] Farajallah (1963, p. 448; free translation, emphasis mine, K.B.).

this 'revolution of the Third World' will decisively transform the character of the United Nations; for this reason alone, it will mark a turning point in human history.

THE DEMOGRAPHIC LEAP

The contrast between the unintegrated 'primitive' political structures of the countries of the Third World and the developed nation or multinational states of the 'white north' focuses attention on the fact that one of the outstanding features of the underdeveloped world is retardation in a historical sense. Largely because of the degree of outside control which irradiated it, the Third World was by-passed by many of the great economic and socio-political changes which transformed the rest of the globe. The fluid conditions within it today are thus in large measure the result of the sudden involvement of its countries in a series of changes which in Europe were spread out over generations or even centuries, but which in the Third World are being compressed into decades. The outstanding example of this is the demographic revolution.[1]

In eighteenth-century Europe the expectation of life did not exceed thirty years and one out of every two men died before the age of twenty. The revolutions in hygiene and medicine which accompanied the Industrial Revolution in Europe gradually eliminated the epidemics and infectious disease which each year had erased millions of lives; Europe went through a period of explosive population increase. This 'demographic revolution' has, after a delay of a century or so, reached the countries of the Third World. Moreover, it has reached them in an accelerated form, for the new techniques of death control make possible a much more rapid drop in mortality rates; in Ceylon, for example, the elimination of malaria resulted in a drop in the death rate of from 22 per thousand to 12 per thousand in seven years – the achievement of a comparable reduction in England and Wales took a century. And, what is even more important, this explosive growth of population in the Third World is not being accompanied by any great expansion of the economy, as was the case in Western Europe during *its* period of greatest population growth. Such a rapidly expanding economy (based in part on the exploitation of overseas territories and the possibility of relieving population

---

[1] See, for example, Lenica and Sauvy (1962).

pressure by migration) just does not exist in the case of the Third World countries. . . .

While the world's population is growing at the rate of 1·8 per cent annually, growth rates in many parts of the Third World are as high as 3·5 per cent, which means the population is doubling every twenty-one years – and with increasing control over infantile mortality rates and the gradual increase of the at present shockingly low expectation of life, we may expect this rate to increase rather than diminish. It is hardly necessary to add that this increase is greatest in those countries which at present are the most impoverished and marginal. . . . By the end of the century the underdeveloped countries,

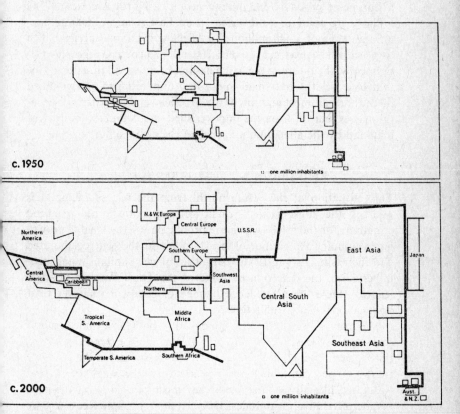

Fig. 1.11　*The size of the various countries or groups of countries is proportional to the population at the appropriate period. The massive population increase of the Third World is dramatically highlighted by a comparison of these two maps.*

most of which already have a large 'surplus' or underemployed population, will have increased their total population from the present figure of 2,000 million to some 4,900 million; of these, some 2,000 million will be in the under-fifteen age group, so the Third World's age structure will be a relatively 'young' one, with potentialities for continuing rapid growth. . . .

The shape of the world our children will live in is suggested graphically in Fig. 1.11; here the size of countries is proportional to area, and both maps are constructed on the same scale. If, instead of the medium growth assumptions used here, we adopt the United Nations 'high' assumption (which seems increasingly the most likely), a Europe of probably 592 million people, a North America of 544 million, are going to be dwarfed by an East Asia of 2,000 million, a South Asia of 1,440 million, by Africa and Latin America which together will have a total of over 1,200 million people. Geographically, politically, the future of the white nations of the north threatens to be that of a wealthy but small minority group cramped and confined on the northernmost margins of the American and Eurasian continental masses, cut off from the impoverished and coloured majority of mankind by the alienating influence of their own affluence. . . .

'REDUCING EVEN THE IRREDUCIBLE...'

This alienation of the 'white north' from the rest of mankind is perhaps the most critical challenge confronting the advanced countries, for the forces which are producing it – the lagging growth and continuing exploitation of the Third World, the swiftly elaborated and increasingly sophisticated strategies of neo-capitalism and neo-imperialism, the defection of some of the Third World's political leaders – these are a challenge to men of goodwill whatever their political or religious affiliations.

The maps presented here are intended to bring this challenge into some sort of focus; the *size* of the problem, and the *increasing* size of the problem, is suggested in Fig. 1.12. These estimates of the probable trends in per capita income are based on the work of Robert Fossaert;[1] like all such estimates they must be used as, at the best, a scale of relative magnitudes. Detailed analysis is unnecessary; we have only to ask ourselves what sort of world solidarity is likely if Fossaert's projections prove accurate, if the ratio between the living

[1] Fossaert (1961).

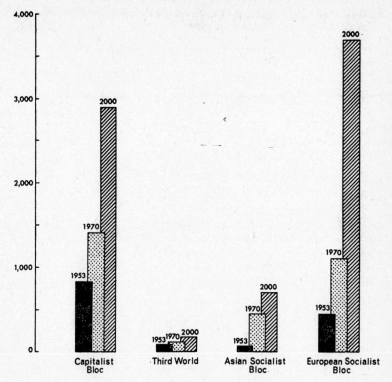

Fig. 1.12 Estimated per capita income in dollars.

levels of the 'white north' and the great mass of the underdeveloped countries – *even after almost half a century of 'development'* – is of the order of 20:1, on a world increasingly crowded, a world in which wealth is white and poverty wears a dark skin. . . . What *is* the answer of our affluent societies to the problems thus posed . . . ?

REFERENCES

BEGUIN, H. (1963) 'Aspects structurels du commerce extérieur des pays sous-développés', *Tiers-Monde*, Paris, Jan-June 1963.

CÉPÈDE, M. (1962) 'Hidden Hunger', *Courier* (UNESCO) Paris, July-Aug 1962.

CHEVERNY, J. (1961) *Éloge du colonialisme*, Paris.

DUMONT, R. (1962) *L'Afrique noire est mal partie*, Paris.

FARAJALLAH, SAMAAN BOUTROS (1963) *Le groupe afro-asiatique dans le cadre des Nations Unies*, Geneva.

FOSSAERT, R. (1961) *L'Avenir du capitalisme*, Paris.

FUENTES (1963) 'The argument of Latin America', in *Whither Latin America?*, ed. P. Sweezy and L. Huberman, New York.

GRANICK, D. (1961) *The Red Executive*, New York.

GEUVARA, CHE (1961) 'Cuba: exceptional case', *Monthly Review*, New York, July-Aug 1961.

HEILBRONER, R. (1960) *The Future as History*, New York.

—— (1963) *The Great Ascent*, New York.

JULIÃO, F. (1963) 'Brazil: a christian country', in *Whither Latin America?*, ed. P. Sweezy and L. Huberman, New York.

LENICA, J., and SAUVY, A. (1962) *The Population Explosion*, New York.

LÉVI-STRAUSS, C. (1962) 'Crowds', *New Left Review*, London, xv, May-June 1962.

O'BRIEN, C. C. (1962) *To Katanga and Back*, London.

SAPIR, M. (1958) *The New Role of the Soviets in the World Economy*, New York.

TJOA SOEI HOCK (1963) *Institutional Background to Modern Economic and Social Development in Malaya*, Kuala Lumpur.

UNITED NATIONS ECONOMIC AND SOCIAL COUNCIL (1960) *Economic Development of Under-developed Countries* (E. 3395).

WORSLEY, P. (1960) 'Imperial Retreat', in *Out of Apathy*, ed. E. P. Thompson, London.

ZWEIG, F. (1957) 'The use of models for social economic structures', *Sociological Review*, Keele, v 1, pp. 65–73.

The Third World – and Beyond

KEITH BUCHANAN

THIRD WORLD: DOUBLE-TALK?

IN spite of the wide acceptance of the term 'Third World' by French social scientists, it has been strongly criticised by French left-wing writers, notably the economist Pierre Jalée,[1] who claims: 'This expression is more than confused, it is a mystification.' Jalée rests his argument on what he sees as an implication of the term – that there is a group of countries which belongs neither to the socialist bloc nor to the capitalist bloc; 'objectively,' he comments, 'such a group of countries does not exist'. He adds: 'at present only two economic systems divide and dispute the world: capitalism and socialism. The so-called third ways are never more than a camouflage for the first.' Yet it is not easy to understand the violence of his attack; few writers, except the most myopic, would challenge his dynamic concept, adopted from the Chinese, of the Third World as a series of 'storm centres'; few would quibble with his insistence that these countries 'constitute a special zone within the imperialist camp' or that this dependent relationship as 'underlings of imperialism' is anything more than a transient phenomenon. Indeed, as we shall see later, while this Third World *can* be characterised in dynamic terms, in terms of the 'earthquakes of change' shuddering through it, while even a perfunctory analysis of the internal situation in the component countries emphasises the striking uniformity in the problems they confront, the most important key to understanding these countries lies in their *external* relationships, in the warping effects of long decades of colonial exploitation and in the dependent and hence vulnerable economies they have inherited. . . . And the sociologist Georges Balandier recognises clearly that the progress of these countries is ultimately dependent on 'mutations' in the so-called 'developed countries'.[2] In short, while not all geographers or socio-

---

[1] Pierre Jalée, 'Third World? Which Third World?', in *Révolution* (Paris)
I 7 (1963) 3–9.

[2] Georges Balandier, in *Le Tiers Monde*, ed. Alfred Sauvy (Paris, 1961), p. 132.

logists employ the rigorous Marxist approach of Jalée, their interpretation differs little if at all from his own interpretation and is
based on a clear awareness of the fact that development and underdevelopment are two sides of the same (imperialistic) coin.

THE INTEGRATION AND SHATTERING OF GLOBAL SOCIETY

While human society might be *objectively* a single coherent unit, it for
long consisted *subjectively* of a series of more or less isolated 'culture-
worlds' – those of China and India, those of Black Africa and Meso-
America, those of the Islamic Middle East and the Christian West.
The unification of the globe as a single social system was, as Peter
Worsley has pointed out, the achievement of European imperialism.
As the critical date in this process of unification he selects 1885, the
year of the Congress of Berlin; this represents the high tide of imperialism, and imperialism, he stresses, is not just 'the highest stage of
capitalism' but an entirely new phase in human social development:
'*Imperialism brought about the consolidation of the world as a single
social system.*'[1]

And, by a paradox, in the very act of achieving this unity it brought
about a new and more significant division of the world into the rich
nations and poor nations, into a developed Euro-American core and
an impoverished, because exploited, zone of tributary states, of
colonial dependencies. This simple duality created in the process of
achieving unity was shattered in 1917, then further shattered in the
years following the Second World War, by the withdrawal of the
socialist states of the U.S.S.R. and Eastern Europe, themselves
formerly semi-colonial appendages, from the world created by
imperialism and by their forced march which has created a second –
and socialist – group of developed and industrialised societies. Three
worlds – and suspended over the Asian socialist states a great question
mark: a Fourth World, a pole of attraction around which many of
the emergent nations will cluster, or merely a variant on the theme
first orchestrated by the U.S.S.R. almost half a century ago? It is in
the outcome of the 'great debate' being carried on currently by the
Societ Union and China that we shall have to seek the answer to this
question.

That the geographer is often unwilling to recognise that the
impact of Western imperialism on its colonial or semi-colonial

[1] Peter Worsley, *The Third World* (London, 1964) pp. 14–15, 50–1.

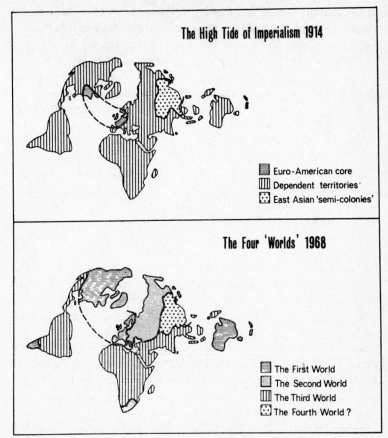

The High Tide of Imperialism 1914

- Euro-American core
- Dependent territories
- East Asian 'semi-colonies'

The Four 'Worlds' 1968

- The First World
- The Second World
- The Third World
- The Fourth World?

Figs. 1.13, 1.14

dependencies resulted in the conversion of 'pre-developed' societies into 'underdeveloped' societies is perhaps due to the fact that in his analyses he has been greatly concerned with *resources* but little concerned with *men*. Yet, as Worsley reminds us, 'to utilise or valorise resources, colonialism has to exploit men'.[1] It was this exploitation which reduced previously developed societies to the condition we now describe as 'underdeveloped',[2] it was this exploitation

---

[1] Ibid., p. 47.

[2] The concept of 'pre-development' is derived from Jean Chesneaux, *Le Viet Nam* (Paris, 1955); the theme is taken up by the present writer in 'South-east Asia: pre-developed or under-developed?', in *Eastern Horizon* (Hong Kong) Nov 1964, pp. 6–16.

which created – and is widening – the gap between the affluent nations and the proletarian nations; it is on this exploitation that the well-being of the Western worker – and of Western left-wing groups – ultimately rests.[1] Expressed in sociological terms: 'The centres of power [i.e. the Euro-American nations] ... can maintain their dynamism only by accentuating the 'depressed' character of the weaker zones to which they are related; this is evident within the limits of national frontiers where there emerge regions whose backwardness is increasing, and in the field of relationships between nations of unequal power.'[2] It is against the background of this process that we must see Frantz Fanon's claim that 'Europe is literally the creation of the Third World'.[3]

OF SUPERORDINATION AND SUBORDINATION

As a result of this process of exploitation 'a relationship of subordination and dependence of the underdeveloped areas has been created with respect to those that are developed, a structure of superordination and subordination that is typical of a system of social stratification'.[4] This 'satellite'[5] quality of their economies and societies is the major distinguishing feature of the countries of the Third World and it is in this satellite status that most of their geographical problems are rooted. The writer has elsewhere[6] dealt with the manifestations of this condition; here attention may be focused on some of the broader international implications.

First, the countries of the Third World must confront not only a colonially-induced retardation of their technical progress but also the fact that their attempts at accelerated development are conditioned by the capitalist system within which, with few exceptions, they operate.

---

[1] See, for example, Pierre Moussa, *The Underprivileged Nations* (London, 1962) esp. pp. xiii–xiv, and *Science and Technology for Development*: vol. I, *World of Opportunity* (U.N., New York, 1963) p. 31.

[2] Free translation from Balandier, *Le Tiers Monde*, p. 121.

[3] Frantz Fanon, *Les damnés de la terre* (Paris 1961) p. 76. (Trans. into English under the title of *The Wretched of the Earth* (London, 1965; Penguin ed., 1967).)

[4] Gustavo Lagos, *International Stratification and Underdeveloped Countries* (Chapel Hill, N.C., 1963) p. 6.

[5] Bert F. Hoselitz, *Sociological Aspects of Economic Growth* (Glencoe, Ill., 1960) p. 93.

[6] See pp. 17–44 above.

Aid is conditional and must be devoted largely to building up the free-enterprise sector of the economy; the development of this sector may prejudice attempts to create a viable state sector, as in India; may, indeed, be diametrically opposed to the real interests of the emergent country. Moreover, the effectiveness of technical or financial aid can scarcely fail to be reduced by the Western fear that massive development of their economic satellites 'would in effect be creating a future world in which their own peoples would become progressively smaller minorities, and possess a progressively smaller proportion of the world's wealth and power'.[1]

Secondly, coming relatively late on to the international scene, the emergent nations face the problem of establishing themselves within a structure of trading relations (and a system of prices) created and now controlled by the affluent nations. The discussion of price levels for primary produce at the Geneva Conference on world trade in 1965 revealed the extent of the cleavage between the views of the affluent nations and the proletarian nations; it emphasised the solidarity of the former when it came to defence of their own interests; above all, it underlined the extent to which the prospects of self-sustaining economic development in the Third World countries (which depends to a considerable extent on the level of export earnings) were, and are, controlled by the affluent nations of the white north.

Thirdly, even though the conditions under which a breakthrough from stagnation and squalor to at least minimum levels of human decency and comfort can be achieved are becoming increasingly clear (these conditions include a high degree of central planning, a restructuring of society including real and not token land reform, and a massive mobilisation of a country's human and material resources to obviate a crippling dependence on external aid), this path can be adopted only at the risk of the hostility and probable active intervention of the West. The bitter opposition to the East Asian countries who have chosen this path (China, North Vietnam, North Korea); the economic blockade and the armed invasion which aimed at preventing Cuba's restructuring of her society; the massive military intervention designed to prevent the South Vietnamese from reshaping their society: all these drive home the determination of the affluent nations to maintain the countries of the Third World in a

---

[1] Frank Notestein, in *Demographic Studies of Selected Areas of Rapid Growth* (New York, 1944) p. 156.

subordinate – and exploitable – status.[1] To repeat an earlier quotation: 'The centres of power ... can maintain their dynamism only
by accentuating the "depressed" character of the weaker zones to
which they are related.'

BEYOND THE THIRD WORLD...

I have stressed the aspects of stratification, of subordination, partly to
correct what appears now to have been excessive emphasis in some of
my earlier papers on the *internal* characteristics of the countries of the
Third World. This emphasis on *relationships* is critical: just as the
colonised exists, and defines his personality, largely in relation to,
or in reaction against, the colonist, so, too, do the peoples of the
Third World see themselves, *whatever their class*, in relation to the
wealthy nations of the white north, as subordinate, as an external
proletariat, as less-than-men. ... The bitter memory of past subordination, the bitter taste of a new political freedom rendered empty
and useless by continuing economic dependence, the bitter awareness
of the continuing deterioration of their living levels by comparison
with those of the affluent nations – these things, negative though they
may be, are among the strongest factors of unity in the Third World.

And, at the same time, they are powerful factors working towards
the ultimate transformation of the Third World ... and perhaps the
emergence of a Fourth World.

Gustavo Lagos, as we saw earlier, compares the system of superordination and subordination which today characterises the relations
between 'developed' and 'underdeveloped' nations to 'a system of
social stratification'. Our own Western societies show us how few
such systems can preserve their stability once hunger and poverty in
the lower strata reach a certain point; this point was reached in

---

[1] The issue in South Vietnam, as seen by Leo Huberman and Paul Sweezy,
is 'can a country fight its way out of the "free world" – that is, the free-enterprise
world, the world open to exploitation by American capitalism ...?' They
continue: 'If South Vietnam can do it, why not Brazil or Nigeria, or Turkey or
Iran? Would it not be the end of the free world, that indispensable *Lebensraum*
of American capital?' (*Monthly Review*, New York, Apr 1965). That Western
military experts are in fact expecting a progressive erosion of the West's special
position in its economic dependencies is suggested by the increasing number of
studies of 'special warfare' (counter-insurgency); in this context cf. Stuart
Alsop's comment 'The American commitment in South Vietnam ... is only
the beginning of the story...' (Foreword to James E. Cross, *The Conflict in the
Shadows: The Nature and Politics of Guerrilla War* (London, 1964).)

France in 1789 and was followed by a drastic transformation of French society. Today, objective and subjective pauperisation of the great majority of humanity are proceeding apace,[1] and this is creating, as it did in France before 1789, a pre-revolutionary situation throughout much of the Third World. The critical point at which men fear death less than hunger and the continuing denial of their humanity was reached in China in 1949, in North Korea in 1950, in South Vietnam in 1954, in Cuba in 1956. . . . It is being approached in parts of southern Asia, of Africa, of Latin America; in the words of the Senegalese writer Abdoulaye Ly 'a girdle of fire is flickering through the length and breadth of the Tropics'.

[1] Projecting present trends forward, and excluding the Asian socialist societies, the Third World's share of total world product, which was 15 per cent in 1953, will drop to 9 per cent by 1970 and to 5·5 per cent by the year 2000 (*New Left Review*, no. 18 (Jan–Feb 1963) p. 4).

2 The Economic Impact of Colonialism

GUNNAR MYRDAL

MANY of the underdeveloped countries were until recently under the political domination of a metropolitan power; some are still. Almost all of the underdeveloped countries that were not colonies were, and many are still, economically dominated from abroad with effects in the economic field which are closely similar to those under colonialism.

In judging the economic results of colonialism, I think it would contribute to avoiding an irrational heightening of the resentments of these nations if the main thesis of these lectures were constantly borne in mind, namely that because of circular cumulative causation a tendency towards inequality is inherent in the unhampered play of the market forces, particularly when the general level of development is low. Nationally, this tendency will be countervailed by the spread effects of expansionary momentum when once a country has reached a high average level of economic development and by national integration policies; internationally, for reasons just given, the spread effects are much weaker and the cumulative process will be more unhampered in unfolding itself in the direction of inequality, if the forces in the markets are given their free play. Keeping the commercial advantages of this tendency of the play of the market forces and also of the political and economic power position inherent in colonialism does not presume any sinister design on the part of the ruling country or its businessmen and politicians.

This should not be implied to mean that what the metropolitan countries and their businessmen undertook in order to advance their own economic interests, always and necessarily was to the disadvantage of the dependent countries. In a very real sense the economic activities of the colonisers represented a measure of spread of economic expansion which without the peculiar power relations of colonialism would not have taken place. Thailand, which the jealousies between the colonial powers left in political independence, did not become more developed than Burma.

The colonial governments also built roads, ports and railways and invested in other forms of overall capital – or provided the conditions of political security and economic profitability without which they would have not been built by private business concerns. Even when, as usually was the case, these enterprises were motivated primarily by the colonial governments' own interests and those of their settlers and business groups, they represented important advances towards creating the conditions for general economic development.

The colonial government established law and order, a regular civil service, took measures for elementary sanitation and, in some cases, for popular and higher education on a limited scale. These generally beneficial activities of colonial governments and their business people took a larger scope in the cases where the political domination was a more complete institutional arrangement and endured for a considerable time, as in India or Indonesia, while they were of smaller consequence in the cases where the domination was less complete and durable, as in Egypt or in the Middle East.

More generally, colonialism implied contacts with the ideas and ideals of the world of the advanced countries and conferred higher education and training to administrative and professional responsibility to some whose number differed greatly as between the several colonial empires. When the former colonies now steer out on their own course as independent states they have this as their basis for their policies, including their economic development policies. But during the time of dependency, these positive accomplishments showed a persistent tendency not to result in much of economic development – even if, in most cases, the colonies had more of development than they probably would have had if they had been left alone. To explain this, we have to reach down to the cumulative mechanism of the play of the forces.

A metropolitan country had, of course, an interest in using the dependent country as a market for the products of its own manufacturing industry. If it took special measures to hamper the growth of indigenous industry – which often happened – this was a natural commercial policy of a country which had political domination over another country. Usually such measures, however, were not necessary, as its home industry had an incomparable lead and in surroundings of well-developed external economies could produce the products so cheaply that it easily could undersell any competitor in the dependent country – if only that country was prevented from protecting itself, which is the essential element of political colonialism. Likewise the metropolitan country had a clear and obvious interest in procuring primary goods from its dependent territory and even to invest in producing them in plenty and at low costs, thereby exploiting in its own interest the local natural resources and the indigenous cheap labour.

A metropolitan country had also a self-evident interest in monopolising so far as possible the dependent country for its own business interests, both as an export and an import market. In pursuing this interest it had at its disposal the trade and payment regulations as an important outflow of its political domination. But in a natural and normal way it got the protection of its monopolistic interests fortified even more by the whole structure of legislation and administration and the entrenched institutional system of business connections which was gradually built up. This 'enforced bilateralism', as I have called this phenomenon in another connection, characterised all colonial empires, though in different degrees. It was a natural result of political and economic dependency, and it now tends to retain its hold even after political liberation.

In the metropolitan countries this bilateral tendency was often idealised as 'close cultural and economic ties' to a mother country. And, as I said, there were very substantial advantages to the dependent country connected with it. But at the end of the process it must, of course, normally mean a considerable economic disadvantage to the dependent country, as it tends to worsen its terms of trade by restricting artificially the scope of the markets where it buys and sells. It gives an interesting sidelight on the power situation in the world to note, in passing, that when this enforced bilateralism was occasionally challenged, it was not from the interest point of view of the dependent countries, but from that of other industrially developed countries which demanded open access to their markets as sources of raw materials and as outlets for their exports of manufactured goods.

The capital, enterprise and skilled labour a metropolitan country sent to a dependent country tended for natural reasons to form enclaves cut out and isolated from the surrounding economy but tied to the economy of the home country. Racial and cultural differences and the very much lower level of wages and modes of living made even within the enclaves themselves strict segregation a natural consequence. Segregation hampered the transfer of culture to the indigenous population, including technical skills and the spirit of enterprise. It is one of the main reasons why these economic starts of colonialism remained enclaves and why the spread of expansionary momentum was extremely weak or altogether absent.

When employment opportunities were expanded in the mines and on the plantations, the new demand for labour was rapidly filled by population increase, which was also spurred by the unquestionably beneficial policies, referred to above, to preserve internal order and peace and improve sanitation, etc. As the colonisers had an interest in plentiful labour supply and low wages for their enclaves, rapid population increase and the lack of real development in the much larger subsistence economy outside the enclaves did not to them appear as an unfavourable trend of events.

A main interest of a metropolitan country was quite naturally order and social stability. By an almost automatic logic it therefore regularly came to ally itself with the privileged classes in the dependent country; sometimes such classes were created for this purpose. These favoured groups were, by and large, primarily interested in preserving the social and economic *status quo* under which they were privileged, and they would normally not press either for a national integration policy, aimed at greater equality within the country, or for progressive economic development in the main subsistence sector of the economy.

From one point of view, the most important effect of colonialism was related to the negative fact that the dependent nation was deprived of effective nationhood and had no government of its own which could feel the urge to take protective and fomenting measures in order to promote the balanced growth of the national economy. Lack of political independence meant the absence of a unifying and integrating purpose for the collectivity – except, at a later stage, the negative purpose to expel the foreign rulers. The country and the people were laid bare and defenceless to the play of the market forces as redirected only by the interests of the foreign metropolitan power. This by itself thwarted individual initiatives, at the same time as it prevented the formation of a public policy motivated by the common interests of the people.

For all these reasons, *colonialism meant primarily only a strengthening of all the forces in the markets which anyhow were working towards internal and international inequality*. It built itself into, and gave an extra impetus and a peculiar character to, the circular cumulative process. It had – and in some countries still has, not least in the dependent countries themselves – its close parallels in certain

institutional power structures within individual countries: the caste
system, the racial and religious chasms, the dependence of the rural
regions upon the richer city and, in the feudal or semi-feudal order,
the dependency of the peasants upon the landlord, the merchant, the
moneylender or the tax collector.

In the era of awakened nationalism in the underdeveloped world
the colonial system is now doomed and its liquidation is one of the
most important political avalanches taking place before our eyes.
The remnants of the system are bound to disintegrate within a period
of time which is very short in the annals of history.

The new nationalism is always, in a sense and to a degree, 'democratic' and, in any case, the old alliances with privileged groups
interested in *status quo* do not any longer assure social peace. In the
dependencies which still linger, the military and other expenses for
maintaining the regime and the costs and losses caused by the popular
revolts, and also the financial burden for social reforms and for
investments in economic development which are now thrown in, take
the profitability out of the colonial system and make it instead
increasingly a liability to the metropolitan countries.

There are special vested interests in these countries, sometimes able
to infect whole political factions in their parliaments. The settlers and
business corporations, who have profits, investments and a whole way
of life to lose, will of course resist giving up their privileges. The ideas
about this system as a vehicle for a national 'civilising mission' in
history, which under the epoch of colonialism had emerged and
become systematised with different ideological structure and
phraseology in the different metropolitan countries, will for a
considerable time be earnestly upheld by writers, statesmen and the
common citizens. Fundamentally, these ideas are, however, largely
rationalisations of economic interests, and when gradually the
profitability of the system is lost and it stands out as an increasingly
expensive political luxury, the colonial system is doomed and the
national ideologies will be readjusted accordingly. The intellectual
leaders in the great humanistic tradition in these countries will
instead increasingly be concerned with the eminently practical
problem of how with wisdom and foresight the liquidation of the
colonial system could be handled so as to cause a minimum of
incidental human sufferings and in any case to avoid tragedies on a
large scale.

When a poor and backward nation thus becomes politically

independent, it will find, if it did not know it before, that political independence most certainly does not mean that it is automatically on the road to economic development. It is still up against the circular cumulative social processes holding it down in stagnation or regression: the natural play of the forces in the markets working all the time in the direction of internal and international inequalities as long as the general level of development in a country is low.

It has to start where the colonial regime leaves off and, as I said, the overall investments and the civilisational accomplishments of that regime become its principal assets. It inherits a large subsistence economy with enclaves producing primary goods – to afford importing the capital goods it urgently needs for economic development it will have to press on with the production and exports along the same line. The 'enforced bilateralism' is firmly entrenched in the whole business set-up and can only gradually be transferred into a more profitable system of many-sided business relations with the entire world supply and demand markets. As it cannot offer the security of political colonialism it will initially have greater difficulties and not smaller to attract foreign entrepreneurs and funds from the international capital market. The one great asset its liberation from colonial domination has bestowed on it is its liberty to regulate its life according to the interest of its own people. And this new asset, its freedom to interfere with the play of the forces in the markets, will not be remunerative, except when put to use in an intelligent and firm manner.

Meanwhile, the very struggle for independence has in many cases released spiritual forces for national identification, this necessary first condition for a nation's ability to conceive a national development plan. India is, of course, an outstanding example of this birth of a nation through the fight for independence. Libya, on the other hand, which got its freedom by a decision of the United Nations as incidental to the defeat of fascist Italy in the Second World War, or several countries in the Middle East, which owe their existence as separate states mainly to the balancing jealousies of the West European colonial powers, when cutting up the Ottoman empire after the First World War, and have between them got artificial boundaries set by the interplay of the same foreign influences, now demonstrate the weaknesses concomitant with their having won their nationhood too cheaply and in a manner too haphazard from the point of view of their inner human forces.

3 The Expansion of Exports and the Growth of Population

H. MYINT

THE OPENING-UP OF THE UNDERDEVELOPED COUNTRIES

A popular idea of the underdeveloped country is of a closed society stagnating in traditional isolation, like Tibet before the Chinese annexation. Paradoxically enough, such a society in complete isolation would have few of the typical problems of the present-day underdeveloped countries. It would have a low and stagnant income per capita, but this would not matter if its inhabitants were blissfully unaware of the higher standards of living in the outside world. With no foreign trade, it would not have the problem of dependence on a few primary export commodities whose prices fluctuate violently in the world market. With no foreign enterprises operating within it, and no colonial rule, it would be free from real or imaginary grievances against 'foreign economic domination' and 'colonial exploitation'. And with a high death rate to match a high birth rate, it would not have to contend with the problem of population pressure as the population would be fairly stable or fluctuating around a constant size.

In contrast, the typical problems of the present-day underdeveloped countries arise, not because these countries are in the traditional state of isolation, but because they have been 'opened up' to outside forces, in the form of foreign trade, investment and colonial rule. The expansion of export production and the spread of the money economy have disrupted in varying degrees the economic self-sufficiency of the traditional 'subsistence economy'. The introduction of an orderly framework of administration by the colonial governments and the provision of basic public services, especially public health, have reduced the death rates, and caused a rapid growth of population. This has disrupted the traditional balance between population, natural resources and technology. Of course, the traditional society still persists in varying degrees in most underdeveloped countries in the form of the 'subsistence sector', and, as we shall see, this dominates the economic life of many countries, particularly in Africa. But it is still true to say that the typical present-day problems of these countries arise, not from traditional isolation, but from modern changes. In a sense all underdeveloped countries are at different stages in the long transition period (or the 'pre-take-off' period) in which they are having to adapt to a continuing process of rapid and disruptive changes. Their problems arise from their difficulties in making satisfactory adjustments to these changes.

In this chapter I shall make a preliminary survey of the two major forces of change which have had and still continue to have a profound impact on the economic and social life of the underdeveloped countries. The first is the expansion of primary exports and the growth of the money economy. The second is the growth of population.

EXPANSION OF EXPORTS

I shall begin by clearing up two points about the expansion of primary exports from the underdeveloped countries.

First, it is frequently described as the 'nineteenth-century' pattern of international trade. Those who use this epithet may merely mean that it is associated with the nineteenth-century belief in free trade, but the general impression created is that the expansion of primary exports from the underdeveloped countries was historically important only in the nineteenth century. This is rather misleading. It is true that this process started in the latter half of the nineteenth century and owed much to the nineteenth-century revolution in transport such as the railways, the steamship, and, in the case of the Asian countries whose exports expanded fastest during this period, to the opening of the Suez Canal. But what is not generally realised is that the greatest expansion of primary exports from the underdeveloped countries of Africa and Latin America has taken place in the first half of the twentieth century. Contrary to the general impression that primary export expansion slackened off in the inter-war period, P. Lamartine Yates has calculated that the African and Latin American countries have expanded the total value of their exports tenfold during the period 1913–53.[1]

Secondly, the primary exporting countries and the underdeveloped countries are frequently identified with each other, and the relative prices between primary exports as a whole and manufactured exports as a whole have been used to measure the gains from international

[1] P. Lamartine Yates, *Forty Years of Foreign Trade*, Table 102, pp. 160–2.

trade to the underdeveloped countries. This again is not accurate. While all underdeveloped countries may be primary exporters, not all primary exporters are underdeveloped countries. The high-income countries of Australasia and North America are also important primary exporters. As a matter of fact, in 1913 the share of Asia, Africa and Latin America in the total value of the world's primary exports (excluding Iron Curtain countries) was only about 35 per cent. It rose, however, to about 40 per cent by 1928 and was about 46 per cent in 1937. In the post-war year of 1953 it was about 47 per cent.[1]

Although the underdeveloped countries as a group contribute less than half of the world's primary exports, there can be no doubt that individually most of them are highly dependent on a few primary exports. Apart from exceptionally large countries such as China and India, exports form more than 10 per cent of the national income of most underdeveloped countries. In 1953, there were at least thirteen underdeveloped countries which had ratios of merchandise trade to national income above 33 per cent, and another six countries for which this ratio ranged between 20 and 33 per cent. Moreover, the degree of dependence seems to have been increasing in the last few decades – in 1913 there were only nineteen underdeveloped countries who obtained more than 50 per cent of their export receipts from one commodity; in 1953 there were no less than thirty countries in this situation.[2]

With this high degree of dependence on a few major exports, the underdeveloped countries are very vulnerable to the flucutations in the world market prices of these exports. A recent United Nations report has estimated that, making allowance for the trend, the year-to-year fluctuations in the export receipts of the underdeveloped countries during 1948–58 have averaged between 9 and 12 per cent, some countries having an average fluctuation of 18 per cent.[3]

The problem of the underdeveloped 'export economies' which has received widespread attention is the problem of economic instability, and vulnerability to the violent fluctuations in the world market prices

[1] Ibid., Table 19, p. 47.

[2] Ibid., Table A 104, p. 163, excluding South Africa and Japan. But one should add Northern and Southern Rhodesia and Kenya to the list of countries with ratios of exports to national income higher than 33 per cent. See also Tables 120, 121 and 122, pp. 179–81.

[3] *International Compensations for Fluctuations in Commodity Trade* (New York, 1961) pp. 3–5.

of primary products. In the short run, this is clearly the most serious problem facing many underdeveloped countries. It not only introduces a serious instability into the consumption and living standards of these countries but also creates formidable difficulties for maintaining a steady flow of investment for long-term economic development. But we cannot obtain a complete picture of the impact of the outside economic forces on the underdeveloped countries without going beyond this familiar short-term problem of overall economic instability to two further deepseated problems.

The first problem is the relation between the expansion of primary exports and the long-term economic development of the under-developed countries. Some of the orthodox economists were inclined to assume too readily that the expansion of international trade would automatically transmit economic growth to the underdeveloped countries, and the 'specialisation' in the production of those primary products most suited to their resources would automatically raise their general level of skills and productivity and lead to a more productive combination of resources. This would pave the way for further economic development. Nowadays, the pendulum has swung to the opposite extreme, not only among the political leaders of the developing countries but among professional economists also. It is now generally assumed that the expansion of primary exports is highly unlikely ever to provide a satisfactory basis of continuous economic growth for the underdeveloped countries. I shall examine not only the older generalisation but also the newer generalisation which is a reaction against the older view.

The second problem arises from the fact that the expansion of primary exports in the underdeveloped countries generally took place through the agency of foreign-owned enterprises operating within these countries and, until recently, under colonial rule for most of the Asian and African countries. The problem of the relationship between the expansion of primary exports and long-term economic development is therefore considerably complicated by the problems of subjective discontent concerning 'foreign economic domination' and 'colonial exploitation'. To study these problems I shall have to go beyond the overall values of the exports of the underdeveloped countries as geographical units, and analyse how the proceeds from these geographical exports were distributed between foreign domestic participants in export production. In the case of peasant export commodities, the participants were the foreign export-import firms and the domestic peasant producers. In the case of mining and plantation exports, the foreign participation covered not only capital investment and skilled labour but also in many cases unskilled labour from other underdeveloped countries; the domestic participation was mainly confined to such indigenous unskilled labour as might be employed in the mines and plantations. These different patterns and the differing extent of domestic participation in export production are important, not only from the point of view of income distribution but also from the point of view of long-term economic development. First, the distribution of incomes between the foreign and domestic participants would have some effect on the proportion of incomes reinvested locally and spent on domestically produced goods, compared with the 'leakages' abroad in the form of imports and remittances of the earnings of the foreign participants. Secondly, if we wish to find out how far the expansion of primary export production has affected the skills and productivity of the indigenous people of the underdeveloped countries, we shall have to go beyond the pattern of distribution of incomes to the distribution of productive activities and economic roles. We can then look for the particular features in the past pattern of primary export expansion that have been unfavourable for the maintenance of long-term economic growth, and consider whether these characteristic features are the inevitable concomitant of future expansion in primary export production for some of the underdeveloped countries.

With these questions in view, I shall devote the next three chapters to the study of the expansion of exports first from the peasant sector and then from the mining and plantation sector. I shall outline the typical patterns of the growth of the market economy, not only in the markets for commodities but also in the markets for labour and capital funds. I shall start from the early phase of export expansion and bring the story up to the present time when the reaction against the past economic pattern has led to various nationalistic policies of economic development being adopted by the governments of the newly independent developing countries.

THE GROWTH OF POPULATION

Let us now turn to the other major change which has affected the underdeveloped countries – the growth of population. An underdeveloped country in its traditional state of isolation tends to have a fairly stable population with a high birth rate and a high death rate balancing out over the long run. Although accurate information is not available, the most probable estimate seems to be that, before their contact with the West, many underdeveloped countries in Asia and Africa had high birth rates in the region of 4 per cent per annum matched by equally high death rates of about 4 per cent. Starting from the initial position of high birth and death rates, I shall describe the typical pattern of population growth with three stages or sets of factors that reduce the death rate while the birth rate continues at its high initial level.[1]

First, the introduction of a modern administration improving law and order and eliminating local warfare, and the introduction of modern transport and communication eliminating local famines and spreading trading in foodstuffs, can by themselves reduce the death rate of an underdeveloped country by as much as 1 per cent per annum. So if the birth rate remains unchanged, population will be increasing at 1 per cent per annum. Secondly, the introduction of public health measures controlling epidemic and endemic diseases such as plague, smallpox, cholera, malaria, yellow fever (and eventually tuberculosis) can reduce the death rate by at least another 1 per cent. So if the birth rate remains the same, the population of the underdeveloped country will be increasing at some 2 per cent per annum at the end of this second stage. Thirdly, the spread of individual medical attention and the increase in the number of doctors and hospitals can bring down the death rate by another 1 per cent, depending on the age structure of the population. In this final stage, therefore, if the birth rate remains the same at 4 per cent and the death rate is reduced to 1 per cent per annum, the maximum possible rate of growth in population will approach 3 per cent per annum.

Most of the underdeveloped countries have passed through the first two stages and are well into the final phase with the rate of population increase between 2 and 3 per cent per annum. Some have attained or even exceeded the 3 per cent rate of population growth, suggesting that the general assumption of 4 per cent maximum birth rate is too low for them. During the period 1950–60, the average rate of population growth for the underdeveloped countries as a group was 2·2 per cent per annum. The fastest rate of population growth was recorded for Latin America with the average annual rate of 2·8 per cent, while Africa and the Far East showed rates of growth of 2·2

[1] Cf. W. A. Lewis, *The Theory of Economic Growth*, chap. 6.

and 2·1 per cent respectively.[1] India, which until the last census
in 1961 had a population growth of 1·4 per cent per annum, now
seems to have passed the 2 per cent mark, mainly due to better control
of malaria. So when people speak of the 'population explosion' in the
underdeveloped countries, they mean that the populations of these
countries are not only increasing but increasing at a faster rate of
growth year by year with a high rate of acceleration. An extreme
example of this is the case of Ceylon where D.D.T. has wiped out
malaria, reducing the death rate from 2·2 to 1·2 per cent in seven
years from 1945 to 1952 – a fall which took seventy years in England
and Wales.[2]

Although the rate of population growth is clearly very important,
two other factors must be taken into account in studying the problem
of population pressure in the underdeveloped countries.

The first is the population density in relation to natural resources
and technology. Population density in a significant sense cannot be
measured simply by taking the number of people per square mile.
It will depend on a number of factors such as the quality of agricultural land, climate and water supply, the existence of mineral
resources, the possibilities of hydro-electric power, to name a few;
and also, very importantly, on the level of productivity and technology. Europe and Asia, for example (excluding U.S.S.R. from both),
are estimated to have the same amount of agricultural area per
person of 1·5 acres, but with widely differing standards of living or
'population densities' in the economic sense. But taking the level of
technology to mean the indigenous methods of agricultural production and making allowances for obvious differences in natural
resources, it is still possible to say that there are very significant
differences in population densities between the different parts of the
underdeveloped world. Compared, for example, with the agricultural
area per person of 1·5 acres in Asia, Latin America is estimated to
have 6·9 acres, and Africa 10·6 acres of agricultural area per person.[3]
In a relatively sparsely populated region like Latin America, even a
high population growth rate will not for the time being give rise to
the problem of population pressure. In fact, many would regard
it as a favourable factor for future economic development. In
contrast, with the dense population of China even a small popula-

[1] United Nations, *World Economic Survey 1963*, Part 1, p. 20, Table 2-2.
[2] P.E.P., *World Population and Resources*, p. 12.
[3] Ibid., p. 50, and chaps. 2 and 3.

tion growth rate will create formidable problems of population pressure.

There are two main types of underdeveloped country with high population densities. Firstly, there are the long-settled agricultural countries such as India, China or Egypt. In a sense, their present population problem is due to their successful development as agricultural countries in the past. This enabled them to support a dense population before it started growing in the modern period. Secondly, there are the island plantation economies, such as the West Indies, Fiji, Mauritius or Ceylon. Here, immigrant labour has been brought from outside to work in the mines and plantations to add to the indigenous population. Population pressure subsequently developed, helped by the relative ease with which diseases such as malaria can be wiped out from the islands. In general, the first group of countries tend to have a larger population base than the second – contrast India's 438 millions in 1961 with Mauritius's 0·6 million.

This brings us to the second important factor to be taken into account in studying the population problems of the underdeveloped countries, that is the absolute size of the population base. When giving aid, countries like India with a huge population base clearly present a more formidable problem than countries with a smaller population, even if the smaller populations are increasing at a faster rate. Even before 1951, when the rate of increase was relatively slow, India's population was increasing at the rate of 5 millions a year: with the new, higher rate of 2·15 per cent per annum shown by the 1961 Census, it will be increasing at the rate of 8 millions a year. The size of the population base, however, is also of great importance as it affects the total scale of the economy; this is relevant for the success of industrialisation programmes. Of course, the size of the domestic market of a country does not depend only on the numbers, but also on the income level of its inhabitants. But given the same low level of per capita incomes, a country like India offers a more favourable environment for setting up heavy capital-goods industries which depend so much on the economies of scale for their success. In contrast, a thickly populated country with a small population base such as Ceylon seems to be especially handicapped by the smallness of its market.[1] Finally, considering the absolute size of the population base serves to remind us that while the large populations of the advanced countries have grown up after, and as a consequence of,

[1] J. R. Hicks, *Essays in World Economics*, pp. 207–8.

economic development, the large populations of the underdeveloped countries exist before development: this makes development not only more desirable but also more difficult.[1]

In broad terms, the population problem of the densely populated underdeveloped countries is a vivid illustration of the Malthusian theory. On a closer analysis, I would add three qualifications.

(i) The Malthusian proposition that the growth of population will exceed the growth of food supplies underrates technological innovations in food production, including the opening-up of new territories and international trade. That was why the advanced Western countries were able to escape from its direful predictions. In a sense, the theories of economic development for the overpopulated underdeveloped countries are built on this qualification. They are based on the idea that while there is a maximum limit to population growth, say 3 per cent per annum, the possible rate of increase in output owing to technical innovation and capital accumulation can exceed this maximum rate of population growth, keeping the Malthusian Devil at bay until the birth rates in the underdeveloped countries begin to fall, as they have fallen in the European countries and are falling in countries like Japan.

(ii) The Malthusian theory is based on too rigid a causal connection between the rate of growth in food supply and population growth. According to the theory, population will not grow unless the food supply or the standard of living rises above the minimum subsistence level. But as we have seen, the population in many underdeveloped countries has grown very rapidly without any appreciable rise in per capita income, mainly owing to medical improvements reducing death rates. If the Malthusian theory has underrated the possibilities of technical improvements in food production, it has also underrated the medical improvements reducing death rates. The possibility that even a population struggling at a minimum subsistence level could grow in the short run simply by medical improvements entirely unconnected with the general standard of life adds to the seriousness of the problem in the modern setting. There is a gleam of hope, however, if we are willing to believe that the technical improvements in medicine which are at present reducing death rates only can be eventually extended to reduce birth rates by the invention of simpler and cheaper methods of birth-control.

[1] S. Kuznets, *Underdeveloped Countries and the Pre-industrial Phase in the Advanced Countries*, World Population Conference, 1954 Papers, vol. v.

(iii) The Malthusian theory is formulated in the setting of a more or less developed wage economy. According to it, with given natural resources and technology, the saturation point in a country's population will be reached when the level of wages, determined by the marginal product of labour, is equal to the minimum subsistence level. But in many underdeveloped countries, the problem of population pressure takes place in the setting of the subsistence economy before the development of the money and the wage economy. In this setting, with an extended family system, many people whose marginal product on the land is below the subsistence level can continue to exist at that level because the total output from land is shared among the members of the extended family. That is to say, with the same natural resources and technology, the saturation point of population in a subsistence economy is larger than that of a wage economy (without public poor relief) because it is determined by the equality of the average product of labour to the minimum subsistence level. Many people who would have been unemployed and starved in a wage economy are maintained in 'disguised' unemployment by their relatives as part of a traditional social security system. As we shall see, much has been made of this phenomenon of 'disguised unemployment' in the post-war theories of economic development as a concealed source of saving. But there is one point which is not always appreciated. In so far as we believe that economic development can take place only through the introduction of a modern money and wage economy which entails the dismantling of the traditional social security system of the subsistence economy, the overpopulated underdeveloped countries in a process of transition have to meet a double problem of population increase. In addition to their natural rate of increase in population they also have to find jobs for those who are displaced from the subsistence economy when the development of the exchange economy and economic individualism reduces the size of the 'family' as a social security unit.

To sum up, the problem of population pressure in the underdeveloped countries has three aspects: (i) the rate of growth of the population; (ii) the existing density of population; and (iii) the overall magnitude of the population base. In these terms, the population situation in the underdeveloped countries shows considerable variation. At one end of the scale there are the underdeveloped countries which are relatively thinly populated and are not yet suffering from population pressure. These include some of the

South-East Asian countries such as Burma, Thailand, Malaysia and the Outer Islands of Indonesia; many of the African countries with the notable exception of Egypt; and most of the Latin American countries. The magnitude of the population base in these countries is also small and is below 50 millions, with the exception of Brazil, which is, however, still thinly populated. At the other end of the scale there are the densely populated countries suffering from varying degrees of population pressure. These include islands with plantation economies such as the West Indies, Mauritius and Ceylon where the population pressure is acute although the magnitude of the population base is fairly small; and the thickly populated countries of Asia and the Middle East with much larger population bases. The population pressure problem is most formidable in countries like India and Pakistan which are not only densely populated, but have a large population base and are now entering into a phase of rapid population growth above the 2 per cent annual rate.

Post-war theories about the developing countries tend to be dominated by the model of the overpopulated countries. But large areas of the underdeveloped world such as Latin America, South-East Asia and various parts of Africa started with sparse populations in relation to their natural resources and are not yet suffering from population pressure. We need, therefore, at least two main theoretical models, one for the countries with no signficant population pressure, and another for the overpopulated countries. For certain purposes involving the analysis of the economies of scale, we shall find it useful to subdivide the overpopulated countries into two groups: those like India with a large population base, say over 50 millions; and those like Ceylon and Mauritius with a small population base.

4 Natural Resources and Tropical Development

B. W. HODDER

THE SIGNIFICANCE OF NATURAL RESOURCES

IN assessing the role of natural resources in economic development, a number of writers strongly criticise the 'geographical school' (by which is meant the 'natural resource' school) of economic development studies for its crude determinism, its tendency to discuss physical factors at length but non-physical and especially economic factors hardly at all, and for appearing to ignore altogether the theoretical framework of economic development studies. Examples of this 'natural resource' school of thought can be found in the work of Semple (1911), Huntington (1915) and Parker (1961).

Some authorities would go so far as deliberately to disregard the role of natural or physical resources in economic development. It is argued, for instance, that economic growth is determined by capital – 'the engine of growth' – and is thus largely the result of an interaction between savings and the capital–output ratio (Harrod, 1948). Analyses such as this leave nature out of explicit consideration and give little if any attention to the role of natural resources, either qualitatively or quantitatively. While natural resources may receive some mention in theoretical analyses, their explicit consideration is commonly believed to be unnecessary (Kuznets, 1959; Meade, 1961). It is argued not only that land is a fixed factor but also that the old Ricardian model in which economic growth is limited by land – and especially by the poverty of natural resources – has been completely disproved by the experiences of nineteenth-century Europe and North America. Increasing returns and technical progress have always upset the Ricardian model. Even where countries have resource deficiencies, it should be possible for them to draw upon the resources of other countries, for instance by trade. Trade clearly opens up the possibility of breaking through any constraints imposed by natural resource deficiencies and links growth more intimately and directly to population and capital accumulation, both of which leave a continuing potential for economic expansion (Barnett and Morse, 1963). Again, it is possible to compensate for lack of natural resources by the substitution of capital or labour skills and by social and economic improvements, including education – 'investment in human capital' – managerial capacity, and economies of scale (Kindleberger, 1966, pp. 53–4).

Even the most cursory glance at natural resources – water, forests, soils, minerals or power – reveals that there is indeed little correlation between the occurrence of these resources and the level of economic development in any particular tropical country. The presence or absence of naturally occurring material resources in no way immutably determines the economic development of a country. 'Since the changing fortunes of many countries and regions have not been connected with the discovery or exhaustion of natural resources within their territories, the fortuitous distribution of these resources certainly does not provide the only, and probably not even the principal, explanation of differences in development and prosperity' (Bauer and Yamey, 1957, pp. 46–7). High productivity and prosperity can be achieved without abundant natural resources. While their possession may give certain initial advantages, plentiful natural resources are not necessarily associated with prosperity, nor are they a precondition for economic development.

It is true that many analyses grossly exaggerate the role of natural resources in economic development; and this is perhaps especially true of the work of geographers. In spite of his interest in the physical environment and in the broader aspects of man–environment relationships in specific areal settings, the geographer cannot afford to argue the overriding importance of the physical factors in development; he cannot associate himself with the school of thought which puts the emphasis upon natural resources and claims that the level of economic development in a country is somehow causally connected with its natural resource endowment; nor can the geographer afford to view economic development simply in terms of how far the natural resources in a country are developed or utilised. To abstract the purely physical factors in applied development studies is to falsify as surely as is to abstract the purely economic, political or social factors.

On the other hand, it can be argued that there is no justification for ignoring natural resources altogether in any development analysis, and that there are real dangers in any tendency to underestimate the role of natural resources in tropical development. That any analysis of the applied problems of economic development cannot afford to accept natural resources as 'given' or 'fixed' is clear from the widely accepted need for the conservation of resources, both exhaustible and renewable: the problems of soil erosion and forest degeneration, for example, vividly illustrate the consequences of neglecting the utilisation and conservation of resources. Again, the theoretical arguments for giving scant attention to natural resources in tropical development studies may fall down in practice; for while in theory tropical low-income countries can make up for the lack of certain natural resources by trade, capital and skills substitution, in practice most of these countries do not have the external trading potential, capital or labour skills to enable them to make up for limited natural resources in this way (Barnett and Morse, 1963). Then again, a good deal of the available empirical evidence supports the contention that natural resources are by no means an irrelevance, especially in the early stages of development. In Venezuela the per capita income is higher than in most other tropical countries, and this fact is clearly and causally connected with the exploitation of rich oil resources in that country. Oil is generally believed to be a dominant factor in explaining the relatively high per capita income in Venezuela, though several writers point out that the lack of natural resources of this kind cannot in any way help to explain the low income levels of most other Latin American countries.

Thus while the relative lack or abundance of natural resources is never a determining factor in economic development; and while the natural endowment is usually less important to this process than is the human contribution; natural resources may constitute an important factor in planning and decision-making as far as economic development in low-income tropical countries is concerned. This, at least, is the standpoint taken in subsequent chapters. The importance of natural resources to developing countries is relatively greater than to the developed countries of the world. In low-income tropical countries rich natural resources can have great significance as sources of exports and foreign investments, while poor resources may form some limitation to growth. The quantity and character of natural resources may well have an important initial effect on patterns of production and levels of income (Chenery, in Berrill, 1965).

THE STUDY OF NATURAL RESOURCES

Perhaps the most striking impression received from any study of the natural resources of the tropical world is the urgent need for more information about those resources. Such an impression remains true, not only for the assessment of mineral and power resources but also for the quantitative and qualitative analysis of moisture resources, vegetation and soils. This point will be made several times in the following pages and is underlined by the reading of the current development plans of any tropical country. It is now widely realised that not enough is known about most of the natural resources of countries in the tropics, and that topographical, geological, hydrological, soil and ecological surveys are vital prerequisites to any successful attempt at resource utilisation. Though precise, accurate data are often very difficult and expensive to obtain, and though, also, it is true that these resources cannot easily acquire commercial value, further research into the various natural resources and their utilisation is an immediate and basic need everywhere. Without such information, as has been abundantly proved on a number of occasions over the last two decades or so, all development schemes can be undertaken only with a serious risk of failure.

Yet while it is clearly convenient for the purposes of analysis to treat particular natural resources separately, it is perhaps worth pointing out that this is a somewhat arbitrary and misleading procedure. In any particular applied problem of economic development the interdependence of natural resources may be so close that it is impossible ever to single out any one factor or element as the crucial one for study. Water supply and hydro-electric power; forests, soils and vegetation: these are particularly obvious cases where the various kinds of natural resources are intimately dependent on one another. Furthermore, in any consideration of the applied problems of development of any of these natural resources, non-physical elements – human resources, economic factors or political considerations of one kind or another – are necessary to any full understanding. While it is convenient to write of the natural environment and natural resources associated with that environment as being quite distinct from the non-physical environment and resources, the truth is that all applied problems of economic development demand the examination of the 'total' environment, with its complex of resources and factors – natural, human and capital.

Again, the quantity and quality of natural resources vary considerably from place to place, and it is perhaps not too much to say that every natural resource or group of resources poses a unique problem within the context of a specific area. This question of regional variation is of considerable geographical interest and is of great importance to development planning. The non-physical elements in the utilisation of any natural resource are numerous, and may well be determining, but they operate within the limits and possibilities set by the nature and location of that resource. Mineral exploitation may be limited by difficulties of access. And in developing hydro-electric power potential, many of the best areas from the point of view of rainfall regime – that is, with rain all the year round – are associated in the tropics with the most difficult forest vegetation, the lowest population densities and low economic activity generally; many of the best potential sites from the physical point of view are therefore limited by their location.

Such areal differentiation in natural resource distribution is relevant not only to a continent or region but also the political state within which the natural resources lie. In practice, the development of natural resources normally operates only within the context of a nation-state, and the uneven distribution of mineral and power potential among different states is a matter of serious concern to those charged with planning. Many tropical developing countries, notably in West Africa and Central America, encompass only very small areas, and so may possess a narrow range and, perhaps, some important omissions in their pattern of natural resources. The territorial state context is also of importance here because some natural resources may be partly or even wholly private property: in the case of minerals, it may well be that the country in which the mineral lies will receive little or no financial benefit from its exploitation by concerns operating from another country (Barnett and Morse, 1963).

It is, indeed, an important principle in the relationship between natural resources on the one hand and economic development on the other, that standards of world comparison are not necessarily relevant to the level of or prospects for economic development in a country. In this sense a map of the distribution over the world of any natural resource is almost an irrelevance in economic development planning. What matters more to a particular country is the occurrence of these resources relative to its own size, population and economy. This is most clearly illustrated in the case of mineral and power resources. In Asia, Brunei's economic development has been overwhelmingly the result of her production of petroleum which, though small by world standards, provides a large part of her national income. Similarly, although the production of natural phosphates in Togo (West Africa) is small by world standards, the discovery and exploitation of phosphates in Togo has proved to be probably the most important single event in that country's economic history, making it possible to add some 50 per cent to the value of its export trade within a few years.

While it is to some extent arbitrary to treat natural resources separately from the other factors of production in any analysis of the applied problems of economic development, there is perhaps more justification for doing this in the tropical world about which we still know very little and where the implications of natural resources for economic development have not yet been fully worked out. Yet even though it is necessary to emphasise our ignorance rather than our knowledge about the physical factors and natural resources of the tropics, it is also necessary to emphasise that there are no grounds for assuming that natural resources are anywhere a limitation to economic development or an excuse for the present relatively low standard of living in any part of the tropics: 'the Creator has not divided the world into two sectors, developed and underdeveloped, the former being more richly blessed with natural resources than the latter' (Bauer and Yamey, 1957, p. 46). The early traditional viewpoint of the tropics as having exceptionally rich natural resources and the 'modern' view of the tropics as poor or inferior in natural resources are equally false. The problem of natural resources is not that they are especially poor or inadequate in tropical countries but rather that the facts about these resources are little known and that their significance for economic development in any specific area is not fully understood. Any realistic analysis of an applied situation in tropical economic development must start from the assumption that the natural resource base is potentially adequate for substantial development, given sufficient knowledge about these resources and a ready adaptation of planning to the opportunities and limitations set by them.

REFERENCES

BARNETT, H. J., and MORSE, C. (1963) *Scarcity and Growth: The Economics of Natural Resource Availability*, Baltimore.

BAUER, P. T., and YAMEY, B. S. (1957) *The Economics of Underdeveloped Countries*, Cambridge.

CHENERY, H. B. (1965) *Economic Development with Special Reference to East Asia*, ed. K. Berrill, London.

HARROD, R. F. (1948) *Towards a Dynamic Economics*, London.

HUNTINGTON, E. (1915) *Civilization and Climate*, New Haven, Conn.

KINDLEBERGER, C. P. (1966) *Economic Development*, New York.

KUZNETZ, S. (1959) *Six Lectures on Economic Growth*, New York.

MEADE, J. E. (1955) *Trade and Welfare*, New York.

PARKER, W. N. (1961). Comment in *Natural Resources and Economic Growth*, ed. J. J. Spengler, Washington.

SEMPLE, E. C. (1911) *Influences of Geographic Environment*, New York.

5 The So-called Social Aspects of Economic Development

V. L. URQUIDI

IF it is granted that economic development is not an end in itself but a means to better human relations and well-being, then economic progress must be judged by its social results. Economic development cannot be considered a simple accumulation of productive capacity, nor can the standards of living of a population be measured in terms of steel ingots produced or electric power installed. However, social gains deriving from economic development are difficult to appraise accurately, for several reasons: First, there is no established pattern by which to evaluate them; then, economic development may bring social losses as well as gains; furthermore, by its very nature, development may result in long-term benefits which only become apparent after a period of relative sacrifice; finally, the concept of social progress, of the individual's personal welfare and his relation to society, varies according to ideological and philosophical beliefs.

Some observers argue that, in spite of its many failings and its recently slackened pace, Latin America's economic development in the past ten or fifteen years has produced great social improvement and made possible important advances towards a better future, or in any event, provided a base for such advances. Others are convinced that it has brought few advantages to the Latin American masses, particularly those in the rural section, and that it has created poverty-stricken urban concentrations. Some think that it has left large sectors of the population outside current concepts of welfare and progress, while permitting a small minority to attain a standard of living equal to that found in countries with the highest income. It is said that Latin America's economic development has not been directed towards achieving social objectives long considered fundamental by even the least progressive European countries or the world's most capitalistic country.

Nevertheless, Latin America has formulated lofty social aims, and several of its countries have made considerable social progress. It has been argued that, in some instances, objectives have exceeded a country's economic capacity, and that a shortage of resources, not indifference to social needs, explains why more has not been accomplished. If such is the case, it might be more to the point to speak of the economic aspects of social objectives rather than of the social aspects of economic development.

Although social progress may appear to be simply an objective or end result of development, it has recently been viewed as an indispensable part of the process of economic growth by which living conditions will be improved. It is increasingly evident that the allocation of resources to welfare – education, housing, changes in the system of land tenure, health, social security, better social relations – must be considered an economic investment that raises a country's capacity to develop and accelerate its achievement of social goals. Social and economic investment are today theoretically and materially inseparable.

It is, therefore, surprising that in many parts of Latin America only limited efforts are made to improve or change social conditions and that the supposed urgency of other objectives has relegated social programmes to a secondary level. In comparison with other countries in similar circumstances, a small proportion of available resources is allocated to education, housing, the assimilation of marginal population groups, rural improvement, etc. Situations, prejudices, social organisations, ways of life and collective outlooks persist that contradict the philosophy of progress and human dignity that Latin America has expounded so often and recommends so freely to other regions of the world.

Have the social problems of development been correctly identified? At times, sociologists enter into a maze of abstractions that economists find confusing. Perhaps these abstractions are valid if it is assumed that society is still governed by the automatism implicit in the economic liberalism that guided the development of Western Europe and the United States. But it is difficult to relate these abstractions to the problems of development in Latin America. Theories about motivations and attitudes, and about the rational or irrational behaviour of different sectors of society, fall within this category of ideas. These concepts are of little economic interest or urgency. The economist can easily name the social requirements for economic development; but he expects the sociologist and other social scientists to indicate how to surmount the social and institutional obstacles to growth and how to foresee the social consequences of given measures and to provide data and analyses that, added to his own knowledge of the possible economic consequences, will enable him to decide on the best solutions.

The economist believes that the social requirements for economic development include the following: improvement in the quality and extent of education; the individual's adjustment and dedication to a new, impersonal type of work in urban industrial and commercial employment; organisation and co-ordination of groups – co-operatives, associations, teams of technicians, public administration, trade unions, etc. – to undertake jointly certain economic tasks; acceptance and maintenance of higher standards of nutrition, health and hygiene; training of leadership in business, public administration, trade and professional groups; a change in the concept of property from one of unlimited private use and benefit to a more restricted one recognising the primacy of collective needs; honest administration of development activities and increased public support for holding government officials responsible for their conduct in office. Progress in these areas – and the economist is not equipped to indicate specific methods for attaining these goals – would help to accelerate economic development under the conditions peculiar to Latin America and, conversely, an increase in productive capacity would facilitate achievement of the objectives of general social welfare.

Education is a case in point. Without overlooking the economic causes of low educational ratios in the majority of Latin American countries, other more deeply rooted, neglected factors exist. According to one authoritative study,[1] in 1950 almost one-half of Latin Americans aged fifteen years or more had never attended school or had dropped out before finishing the first grade; 44 per cent had had some primary instruction; and only 8 per cent had completed primary school. Six per cent had had some secondary or vocational education, 2 per cent had completed or nearly completed these studies, and only 1 per cent had begun or completed any form of higher education. Thus, the great majority had had no educational opportunities, perhaps not even the chance to learn to read and write and do simple arithmetic. Of those few fortunates who reached secondary school, two out of three had dropped out before finishing their studies.

[1] Oscar Vera, 'The position of education in Latin America, including a discussion of educational requirements in the region', in UNESCO, *Social Aspects of Economic Development in Latin America*, ed. Egbert de Vries and José Medina Echavarría, I (Paris, 1962).

Even though this situation has improved in recent years – notwithstanding the rapid growth of the population – the economist is bound to be sceptical about education in Latin America. He suspects that it is based on erroneous concepts, and that educational programmes under which so many children drop out of primary or secondary schools are too long and are ill suited to the social and economic environment. Since development requires the creation of a labour force capable of learning practical skills in various activities that are certain to expand – agriculture, forestry, mining, manufacturing, etc. – as well as the formation of a professional and intellectual elite, should not systems of early selection be adopted? Under such systems, a high proportion of children could early be directed towards vocational training in agriculture or industry, and education could be programmed, scheduled and geographically located in a way that would take into consideration the pupil's economic and social background. In view of the high rate of drop-outs among pupils obliged to assume economic responsibilities early, would not shorter, less ambitious school programmes be preferable? Should not more emphasis be placed on preparing the student for work than on educating him for high cultural achievements? The economist knows that, to accelerate economic development, not only must investment be made in capital goods and the labour force increased in size, but the level of competence of the labour force must be raised continually. An educational system designed primarily to train men for the liberal and technical professions cannot possibly promote steady increases in productivity. More schools and more – and especially better – teachers are not the sole requirements.[1] Education must be oriented so that it will be instrumental in the rapid attainment of economic goals, which, in turn, will bring cultural and educational opportunities within reach of an increasing proportion of the population.

This approach makes it clear that education is an economic problem, although it is usually presented as a social one. Education and economic development must be dealt with jointly; otherwise, there is only a tenuous and indirect link between the two. If education

---

[1] 'Fifty per cent of the primary school teachers and an even higher proportion of secondary and vocational school teachers have no specialised training for their work' (O.A.S., *Planning of Economic and Social Development in Latin America*, Report of the Group of Experts, Topic 1 of the Agenda, Special Meeting of the Inter-American Economic and Social Council at the Ministerial Level, Doc. ES-RE-4, 15 June 1961).

is to be treated as a high-priority productive investment, those responsible for preparing and promoting economic development programmes in Latin American must make allocation of resources to education contingent upon adaptation of the educational systems to the needs of development programmes. It goes without saying that the resources referred to are not simply budgetary or financial, but real.

Similar situations exist in nutrition and health. The economist cannot object to better nutrition or a steady improvement in health and sanitation, which includes everything from disease prevention to construction of adequate individual and collective housing. Obviously, any programme of nutrition, sanitation or housing has various economic aspects, some of which may be limiting factors. But the economic value of this kind of social progress must not be under-estimated, and the resources allocated to these ends should be regarded as productive investments, just as in the case of educational programmes. From the standpoint of economic development, the problem is that social programmes of this type, which are also educational, are not always properly adjusted to the economic realities of the countries, regions or zones in which they are carried out. Ideal goals of great social value are established, but they may contribute very little to the economic development without which they cannot be financed, and they may actually hamper growth.

It is possible to illustrate the above with a few striking examples. For various reasons, in almost all of Latin America, there is a very large and increasing housing deficit, particularly in urban centres. It is estimated that 30 to 40 per cent of the population of the principal cities live in hovels or overcrowded slums and that the housing shortage increases annually by one million units.[1] Many of the technical solutions offered are predicated exclusively on construction of new housing and establishment of standards several times superior to present ones. Such solutions are doomed to failure in any under-developed country that must invest simultaneously in education, in other social programmes, and in increasing its overall economic capacity. From the economic standpoint, it would be far better to design and execute vast programmes simply to improve existing housing by introducing minimum sanitary facilities with the help of the present occupants, rather than to yield to the tempting alternative of razing entire areas in order to build great, low-rent apartment

[1] Ibid.

blocks that can satisfy only a small proportion of the needs. This is a strictly economic statement of the problem, and it does not indicate any lack of social feelings on the part of the economist. If Latin American countries had a greater immediate potential, they could permit themselves higher goals in housing and build the most elaborate projects drawn up by city planners. But meanwhile, Latin America should resign itself to more modest aims, secure in the knowledge that any slight improvement in existing housing conditions will result in increased productivity and general economic benefits.

Most Latin American countries do not have an adequately developed economic concept of public-health programmes. In spite of the humanitarian aspects of, say, the anti-malaria campaigns, it is hard to believe that the resources spent in these campaigns could not have contributed more to economic development if they had been used to expedite the introduction of drinking-water supplies,[1] which would have had far-reaching effects on health, or to construct clean market places. Clearly, as long as there exist poverty, poor health and the conditions favouring them, these grave social problems will have a negative effect upon economic development. However, as in education, the ideal technical solutions are not necessarily best suited to facilitiate important gains in economic capacity.

Latin American industrialisation must advance rapidly to make possible the attainment of higher living standards within a short span of time. The economist foresees that a social obstacle to industrialisation will be the excessive individualism characteristic of both labourer and entrepreneur. Although collective discipline may seem neither desirable nor pleasant from other points of view, industrialisation requires large groupings of workers willing to accept it. As Medina Echavarría says, the industrial worker must adapt 'to the social and psychological conditions imposed by modern industry in its three special dimensions – space, time and hierarchy'.[2] Latin American industrial growth cannot be based on small workshops or

---

[1] It is estimated that 23 million urban and 86 million rural inhabitants – more than half the total population – live without potable water. Between 1950 and 1960, this service was brought to 21 million people, but the population meanwhile increased by 30 million. See O.A.S., *Planning of Economic and Social Development in Latin America*, ibid.

[2] José Medina Echavarría, 'Relationships between social and economic institutions: a theoretical model applicable to Latin America', *Economic Bulletin for Latin America*, vi 1 (Mar 1961) 34.

artisans. There is really no inherent or intrinsic reason why the required adaptation cannot be made, but technical training and workers' education programmes must orient the outlook of labour as well as teach it skills. Although this is a matter for the sociologist, he must bear in mind the needs of economic development.

Very similar problems are encountered in organising co-operative action in both private and public economic undertakings. In view of the backwardness of agriculture in a large part of Latin America and the unfavourable conditions that frequently exist in foreign markets and in domestic distribution, there is an urgent need for co-operative or producer organisations in agriculture. The Achilles' heel of economic development is the inelasticity of food production. In many cases, larger investments in agricultural development will be fruitless unless such organisations are established. The economist is not convinced that adequate measures have been taken to organise agriculture, even though there are exceptions. The absence of a spirit of co-operation is a serious impediment to progress in other important activities, including public administration. As long as these conditions persist, uncorrected by techniques and methods that sociologists could provide, economic development will of necessity be slower and more costly.

The era of the Schumpeterian innovator has passed for Latin America. Economic development can no longer be left to the impulses of the entrepreneur, the public official or the empirical politician. It must be fully recognised that growth cannot be accelerated unless the educational system and the existing social organisations – trade unions, producer associations, public agencies and others – train in both the private and public sectors the professional managerial elements who will assume responsibility and make the decisions necessary for economic progress. To date, the type of leadership that has predominated in most Latin American countries is the political or accidental type of entrepreneur, whose fortune depends on the government in power. However, the professional entrepreneur is beginning to appear, along with the 'public manager'. These same comments might be made about the labour leader. The social task is to create professional leadership for those activities that are expected to expand most rapidly or to take priority, from the standpoint of economic development prospects.

There are other important social aspects of economic development that cannot be gone into here. However, the matter of property has transcended the purely social and economic domains and become the subject of the great political controversies of our time. At the risk of stirring up a commotion among philosophers and jurists and, to a much lesser extent, sociologists, the economist cannot help concluding that the Latin American concept of property is far from conducive to accelerated economic development. The few instances in which private property is subordinate to social or community welfare only confirm the need for Latin America to replace its traditional concept of property with one that will free the forces of progress for its people. The concentration of private property, particularly agrarian, its improper use or non-use in economic activity, and the resultant social and economic consequences are important obstacles to Latin American development. This situation exists not only in agriculture but also in the control of natural resources, urban zones and industrial and commercial property.

The realities of the land-tenure structure are disturbing to anyone concerned with economic development. Latifundia are still common in Latin America. It has been estimated that, in 1950, agricultural enterprises of more than 1,000 hectares comprised only 1·5 per cent of the total number of farms, but held 65 per cent of the land area. At the opposite extreme, farms of no more than 20 hectares made up 73 per cent of the total number, but occupied barely 3·7 per cent of the land.[1] This is the situation, even with the results of the Mexican agrarian reform included in the overall figures. Since 1950, basic land reform has been carried out only in Bolivia and Cuba, although it has had limited application in Venezuela and very recently has been undertaken in Colombia. In Guatemala, 0·51 per cent of the total number of farms control 41 per cent of the agricultural land; in Ecuador, 0·17 per cent of the farm units own 37 per cent of the land. In Venezuela, until 1959, 1·69 per cent of the agricultural properties held 74 per cent of the farm land. In Brazil, 1·6 per cent of the land-holders control one-third of the agricultural area. In Bolivia, before 1953, 6 per cent of the agricultural properties held 92 per cent of the land. In Cuba, before the agrarian reform, 0·5 per cent of the agricultural units controlled 36 per cent of the area, according to 1946 figures, and sugar plantations, which owned half of the country's arable land, controlled an additional 25 per cent through rental arrangements. In Chile, 1·5 per cent of the agricultural properties

[1] Thomas F. Carroll, The land reform issue in 'Latin America', *Latin American Issues: Essays and Comments*, p. 165.

control 75 per cent of the farm area.[1] Similarly extreme situations still exist in Peru.[2] El Salvador and other countries.

From an economic standpoint, such heavy concentrations of agrarian property have the following consequences: enormous expanses of land are not available for cultivation; the introduction of modern techniques is delayed; the purchasing power of the peasants remains low; desirable relocations of rural population are prevented; and, in general, agricultural production lacks flexibility. From a social and political standpoint, agrarian reform is now so obviously a necessity that there are few places in the world where it is still questioned. Recently, a greater awareness of its economic advantages has developed in Latin America, and several countries have undertaken programmes to reform landholding systems and abolish latifundia. But until more vigorous measures are adopted, in combination with co-operative or community organisations for production, economic development will not receive the support it needs from the agricultural sector.

The issue presented here is more general in character. Because of the scarcity of resources in Latin America, the unrestrained exercise of the right to accumulate private property cannot lead to optimal results: the use made of this property – if any use is made – may interefere with the needs of development. Sooner or later, the concept of property will have to be revised, not only with respect to land tenure and to restrictions imposed in the public interest in urban zones, but more generally.

An attempt may now be made to draw some tentative conclusions. The economist is able to isolate certain problems or important social obstacles to economic development, but he is not qualified to make specific recommendations to remedy these matters. On the other hand, the specialists who approach the social problems in Latin America should familiarise themselves with the problems of economic development, because social measures may solve or alleviate social problems only to the extent that they contribute to economic development. Conversely, it is now evident that economic development is only viable if substantial resources are allocated to relieving social tensions. The real cost of improving social conditions may be

---

[1] Daniel Bitrán, 'Rasgos estructurales de la economía chilena y su desarrollo reciente', *Ciencias Políticas y Sociales* (México), VI 19 (Jan–Mar 1960) 81.

[2] Edmundo Flores, 'El problema agrario del Peru', *El Trimestre Económico* (México), XVII 3 (July–Sep 1950).

disproportionately high, as in agrarian reform of housing programmes. Therefore, in countries where the standard of living and economic capacity are barely average, sociologists and other specialists will be obliged to give any social programme they formulate a well-defined, functional character. The social aspects of economic development and the economic aspects of social development must blend together into a single drive towards progress.

6 The Take-off into Self-sustained Growth

W. W. ROSTOW

I

THE purpose of this article is to explore the following hypothesis: that the process of economic growth can usefully be regarded as centring on a relatively brief time interval of two or three decades when the economy and the society of which it is a part transform themselves in such ways that economic growth is, subsequently, more or less automatic. This decisive transformation is here called the take-off.[1]

The take-off is defined as the interval during which the rate of investment increases in such a way that real output per capita rises and this initial increase carries with it radical changes in production techniques and the disposition of income flows which perpetuate the new scale of investment and perpetuate thereby the rising trend in per capita output. Initial changes in method require that some group in the society have the will and the authority to install and diffuse new production techniques;[2] and a perpetuation of the growth process requires that such a leading group expand in authority and that the

[1] This argument is a development from the line of thought presented in *The Process of Economic Growth* (New York, 1952) chap. 4, esp. pp. 102–5. The concept of three stages in the growth process centring on the take-off is defined and used for prescriptive purposes in *An American Policy in Asia* (New York, 1955) chap. 7.

[2] We shall set aside in this article the question of how new production techniques are generated from pure science and invention, a procedure which is legitimate, since we are examining the growth process in national (or regional) economies over relatively short periods. We shall largely set aside also the question of population pressure and the size and quality of the working force, again because of the short period under examination; although, evidently, even over short periods, the rate of population increase will help determine the level of investment required to yield rising output per capita (see below, p. 90, note 1). By and large, this article is concerned with capital formation at a particular stage of economic growth; and of the array of propensities defined in *The Process of Economic Growth* it deals only with the propensity to accept innovations and the propensity to seek material advance, the latter in relation to the supply of finance only.

society as a whole respond to the impulses set up by the initial changes, including the potentialities for external economies. Initial changes in the scale and direction of finance flows are likely to imply a command over income flows by new groups or institutions; and a perpetuation of growth requires that a high proportion of the increment to real income during the take-off period be returned to productive investment. The take-off requires, therefore, a society prepared to respond actively to new possibilities for productive enterprise; and it is likely to require political, social and institutional changes which will both perpetuate an initial increase in the scale of investment and result in the regular acceptance and absorption of innovations.

In short, this article is an effort to clarify the economics of industrial revolution when an industrial revolution is conceived of narrowly with respect to time and broadly with respect to changes in production functions.

II. THREE STAGES IN THE GROWTH PROCESS

The historian examining the story of a particular national economy is inevitably impressed by the long-period continuity of events. Like other forms of history, economic history is a seamless web. The cotton-textile developments in Britain of the 1780s and 1790s have a history stretching back for a half century at least; the United States of the 1840s and 1850s had been preparing itself for industrialisation since the 1790s, at the latest; Russia's remarkable development during the two pre-1914 decades goes back to 1861 for its foundadations, if not to the Napoleonic Wars or to Peter the Great; the remarkable economic spurt of Meiji Japan is incomprehensible outside the context of economic developments in the latter half of the Tokugawa era; and so on. It is wholly legitimate that the historian's influence should be to extend the story of the British industrial revolution back into the seventeenth century and forward far into the nineteenth century; and that Heckscher should embrace Sweden's transition in a chapter entitled 'The Great Transformation (1815–1914)'.[1] From the perspective of the economic historian the isolation of a take-off period is, then, a distinctly arbitrary process. It is to be judged, like such other arbitrary exercises as the isolation

[1] E. F. Heckscher, *An Economic History of Sweden*, trans. G. Ohlin (Cambridge, Mass., 1954) chap. 6.

of business cycles and secular trends, on whether it illuminates more of the economic process than it conceals; and it should be used, if accepted, as a way of giving a rough framework of order to the inordinately complicated biological problem of growth rather than as an exact model of reality.

There is difficulty in this set of conceptions for the statistical analyst of economic development as well as for the historian. At first sight the data mobilised, for example, by Clark, Kuznets, Buchanan and Ellis exhibit a continuum of degrees of development both within countries over time and as among countries at a given period of time, with no *prima facie* case for a clearly marked watershed in the growth process.[1] In part this statistical result arises from the fact that historical data on national product and its components are only rarely available for an economy until after it has passed into a stage of more or less regular growth; that is, after the take-off. In part it arises from the fact that, by and large, these authors are more concerned with different levels of per capita output (or welfare) – and the structural characteristics that accompany them – than with the growth process itself. The data they mobilise do not come to grips with the inner determinants of growth. The question raised here is not how or why levels of output per capita have differed but rather how it has come about that particular economies have moved from stagnation – to slow, piecemeal advance – to a situation where growth was the normal economic condition. Our criterion here is not the absolute level of output per capita but its rate of change.

In this argument the sequence of economic development is taken to consist of three periods; a long period (up to a century, or conceivably, more) when the preconditions for take-off are established; the take-off itself, defined within two or three decades; and a long period when growth becomes normal and relatively automatic. These three divisions would, of course, not exclude the possibility of growth giving way to secular stagnation or decline in the long term. It would exclude from the concept of a growing economy, however, one which

[1] Colin Clark, *The Conditions of Economic Progress*, 2nd ed. (London, 1951); Simon Kuznets, 'International Differences in Capital Formation and Financing' (mimeographed; Conference on Capital Formation and Economic Growth, Nov 1953) (National Bureau of Economic Research, New York, 1953); Norman Buchanan and Howard Ellis, *Approaches to Economic Development* (Twentieth Century Fund, New York, 1955). See also the United Nations data presented as a frontispiece to H. F. Williamson and John A. Buttrick, *Economic Development* (New York, 1954).

experiences a brief spurt of expansion which is not subsequently sustained; for example, the United States industrial boom of the war of 1812 or the ill-fated spurts of certain Latin American economies in the early stages of their modern history.

Take-offs have occurred in two quite different types of societies; and, therefore, the process of establishing preconditions for take-off has varied. In the first and most general case the achievement of preconditions for take-off required major change in political and social structure and, even, in effective cultural values. In the vocabulary of *The Process of Economic Growth*, important changes in the propensities preceded the take-off. In the second case take-off was delayed not by political, social and cultural obstacles but by the high (and even expanding) levels of welfare that could be achieved by exploiting land and natural resources. In this second case take-off was initiated by a more narrowly economic process, as, for example, in the northern United States, Australia and, perhaps, Sweden. In the vocabulary of *The Process of Economic Growth*, the take-off was initiated primarily by a change in the yields; although subsequent growth brought with it changes in the propensities as well. As one would expect in the essentially biological field of economic growth, history offers mixed as well as pure cases.

In the first case the process of establishing preconditions for take-off might be generalised in impressionistic terms as follows:

We start with a reasonably stable and traditional society containing an economy mainly agricultural, using more or less unchanging production methods, saving and investing productively little more than is required to meet depreciation. Usually from outside the society, but sometimes out of its own dynamics, comes the idea that economic progress is possible; and this idea spreads within the established elite or, more usually, in some disadvantaged group whose lack of status does not prevent the exercise of some economic initiative. More often than not the economic motives for seeking economic progress converge with some non-economic motive, such as the desire for increased social power and prestige, national pride, political ambition and so on. Education, for some at least, broadens and changes to suit the needs of modern economic activity. New enterprising men come forward willing to mobilise savings and to take risks in pursuit of profit, notably in commerce. The commercial markets for agricultural products, domestic handicrafts and consumption-goods imports widen. Institutions for mobilising capital appear;

or they expand from primitive levels in the scale, surety and time horizon for loans. Basic capital is expanded, notably in transport and communications, often to bring to market raw materials in which other nations have an economic interest, often financed by foreign capital. And, here and there, modern manufacturing enterprise appears, usually in substitution for imports.

Since public-health measures are enormously productive in their early stages of application and, as innovations go, meet relatively low resistance in most cultures, the death rate may fall and the population begin to rise, putting pressure on the food supply and the institutional structure of agriculture, creating thereby an economic depressant or stimulus (or both in turn), depending on the society's response.

The rate of productive investment may rise up to 5 per cent of national income;[1] but this is unlikely to do much more than keep ahead of the population increase. And, in general, all this activity proceeds on a limited basis, within an economy and a society still mainly characterised by traditional low-productivity techniques and by old values and institutions which developed in conjunction with them. The rural proportion of the population is likely to stand at 75 per cent or over.

In the second case, of naturally wealthy nations, with a highly favourable balance between population and natural resources and with a population deriving by emigration from reasonably acquisitive cultures, the story of establishing the preconditions differs mainly in that there is no major problem of overcoming traditional values inappropriate to economic growth and the inert or resistant institutions which incorporate them; there is less difficulty in developing an elite effective in the investment process; and there is no population problem.[2] Technically, much the same slow-moving process of change occurs at high (and, perhaps, even expanding) levels of per

---

[1] The relation of the investment rate to growth depends, of course, on the rate of population rise. With stagnant population or slow rise a per 5 cent investment rate could yield substantial growth in real output per capita, as indeed it did in pre-1914 France. On the other hand, as noted below (p. 100), investment rates much higher than 5 per cent can persist in primitive economies which lack the preconditions for growth, based on capital imports, without initiating sustained growth. For some useful arithmetic on the scale and composition of capital requirements in a growing economy with a 1 per cent population increase, see A. K. Cairncross, *Home and Foreign Investment* (Cambridge, 1953) chap. 1.

[2] Even in these cases there have often been significant political and social restraints which had to be reduced or eliminated before take-off could occur; for example, in Canada, the Argentine and the American South.

capita output, and with an extensive growth of population and output still based on rich land and other natural resources. Take-off fails to occur mainly because the comparative advantage of exploiting productive land and other natural resources delays the time when self-reinforcing industrial growth can profitably get under way.[1]

The beginning of take-off can usually be traced to a particular sharp stimulus. The stimulus may take the form of a political revolution which affects directly the balance of social power and effective values, the character of economic institutions, the distribution of income, the pattern of investment outlays and the proportion of potential innovations actually applied; that is, it operates through the propensities. It may come about through a technological (including transport) innovation, which sets in motion a chain of secondary expansion in modern sectors and has powerful potential external economy effects which the society exploits. It may take the form of a newly favourable international environment, such as the opening of British and French markets to Swedish timber in the 1860s or a sharp relative rise in export prices and/or large new capital imports, as in the case of the United States from the late 1840s, Canada and Russia from the mid-1890s; but it may also come as a challenge posed by an unfavourable shift in the international environment, such as a sharp fall in terms of trade (or a wartime blockage of foreign trade) requiring the rapid development of manufactured import substitutes, as in the case of the Argentine and Australia in the 1930s and during the Second World War.[2] All these latter cases raise sharply the

[1] Theoretically, such fortunate societies could continue to grow in per capita output until diminishing returns damped down their progress. Theoretically, they might even go on as growing non-industrial societies, absorbing agricultural innovations which successfully countered diminishing returns. Something like this process might describe, for example, the rich agricultural regions of the United States. But, in general, it seems to be the case that the conditions required to sustain a progressive increase in agricultural productivity will also lead on to self-reinforcing industrial growth. This result emerges not merely from the fact that many agricultural improvements are labour-saving, and that industrial employment can be stimulated by the availability of surplus labour and is required to draw it off; it also derives from the fact that the production and use of materials and devices which raise agricultural productivity in themselves stimulate the growth of a self-sustaining industrial sector.

[2] Historically, the imposition of tariffs has played an important role in take-offs, e.g. the American tariffs of 1828 (cotton textiles) and 1841–2 (rail iron); the Russian tariffs of the 1890s, etc. Although these actions undoubtedly served to assist take-off in leading sectors, they usually reflected an energy and purpose among key entrepreneurial groups which would, in any case, probably have done the trick.

profitability of certain lines of enterprise and can be regarded as changes in the yields.

What is essential here, however, is not the form of stimulus but the fact that the prior development of the society and its economy results in a positive sustained, and self-reinforcing, response to it: the result is not a once-over change in production functions or in the volume of investment, but a higher proportion of potential innovations accepted in a more or less regular flow, and a higher rate of investment.

In short, the forces which have yielded marginal bursts of activity now expand and become quantitatively significant as rapid-moving trends. New industries expand at high rates, yielding profits which are substantially reinvested in new capacity; and their expansion induces a more general expansion of the modern sectors of the economy where a high rate of plough-back prevails. The institutions for mobilising savings (including the fiscal and sometimes the capital-levy activities of government) increase in scope and efficiency. New techniques spread in agriculture as well as in industry, as increasing numbers of persons are prepared to accept them and the deep changes they bring to ways of life. A new class of businessmen (usually private, sometimes public servants) emerges and acquires control over the key decisions determining the use of savings. New possibilities for export develop and are exploited; new import requirements emerge. The economy exploits hitherto unused backlogs in technique and natural resources. Although there are a few notable exceptions, all this momentum historically attracted substantial foreign capital.

The use of aggregative national-income terms evidently reveals little of the process which is occurring. It is nevertheless useful to regard as a necessary but not sufficient condition for the take-off the fact that the proportion of net investment to national income (or net national product) rises from (say) 5 per cent to over 10 per cent, definitely outstripping the likely population pressure (since under the assumed take-off circumstances the capital–output ratio is low),[1] and yielding a distinct rise in real output per capita. Whether real

---

[1] The author is aware of the substantial ambiguities which overhang the concept of the capital-output ratio and, especially, of the dangers of applying an overall aggregate measure. But since the arithmetic of economic growth requires some such concept, implicitly or explicitly, we had better refine the tool rather than abandon it. In the early stages of economic development two contrary forces operate on the capital–output ratio. On the one hand there is a

consumption per capita rises depends on the pattern of income distribution and population pressure, as well as on the magnitude, character and productivity of investment itself.

As indicated in the table on the next page, I believe it possible to identify at least tentatively such take-off periods for a number of countries which have passed into the stage of growth.

The third stage, is, of course, the long, fluctuating story of sustained economic progress. Overall capital per head increases as the economy matures. The structure of the economy changes increasingly. The initial key industries, which sparked the take-off, decelerate as diminishing returns operate on the original set of industrial tricks and the original band of pioneering entrepreneurs give way to less single-minded industrial leaders in those sectors; but the average rate of growth is maintained by a succession of new, rapidly growing sectors, with a new set of pioneering leaders. The proportion of the population in rural pursuits declines. The economy finds its (changing) place in the international economy. The society makes such terms as it will with the requirements for maximising modern and efficient production, balancing off, as it will, the new values against those retarding values which persist with deeper roots, or adapting the latter in such ways as to support rather than retard the growth process. This sociological calculus interweaves with basic resource endowments to determine the pace of deceleration.

It is with the problems and vicissitudes of such growing economies of the third stage (and especially with cyclical fluctuations and the threat of chronic unemployment) that the bulk of modern theoretical economics is concerned, including much recent work on the formal properties of growth models. The student of history and of

---

vast requirement of basic overhead capital in transport, power, education, etc. Here, due mainly to the long period over which such investment yields its return, the apparent (short-run) capital–output ratio is high. On the other hand, there are generally large unexploited backlogs of known techniques and available natural resources to be put to work; and these backlogs make for a low capital–output ratio. We can assume formally a low capital–output ratio for the take-off period because we are assuming that the preconditions have been created, including a good deal of social overhead capital. In fact, the aggregate marginal capital–output ratio is likely to be kept up during the take-off by the requirement of continuing large outlays for overhead items which yield their return only over long periods. Nevertheless, a ratio of 3:1 or 3·5:1 on average seems realistic as a rough benchmark until we have learned more about capital–output ratios on a sectoral basis.

Some Tentative, Approximate Take-off Dates

Country	Take-off	Country	Take-off
Great Britain	1783–1802	Russia	1890–1914
France	1830–1860	Canada	1896–1914
Belgium	1833–1860	Argentine[3]	1935–
United States[1]	1843–1860	Turkey[4]	1937–
Germany	1850–1873	India[5]	1952–
Sweden	1868–1890	China[5]	1952–
Japan[2]	1878–1900		

contemporary underdeveloped areas[6] is more likely to be concerned with the economics of the first two stages; that is, the economics of the preconditions and the take-off. If we are to have a serious theory of economic growth or (more likely) some useful theories

[1] The American take-off is here viewed as the upshot of two different periods of expansion: the first, that of the 1840s, marked by railway and manufacturing development, mainly confined to the East – this occurred while the West and South digested the extensive agricultural expansion of the previous decade; the second the great railway push into the Middle West during the 1850s marked by a heavy inflow of foreign capital. By the opening of the Civil War the American economy of North and West, with real momentum in its heavy-industry sector, is judged to have taken off.

[2] Lacking adequate data, there is some question about the timing of the Japanese take-off. Some part of the post-1868 period was certainly, by the present set of definitions, devoted to firming up the preconditions for take-off. By 1914 the Japanese economy had certainly taken off. The question is whether the period from about 1878 to the Sino-Japanese War in the mid-1890s is to be regarded as the completion of the preconditions or as take-off. On present evidence, I incline to the latter view.

[3] In one sense the Argentine economy began its take-off during the First World War. But by and large, down to the pit of the post-1929 depression, the growth of its modern sector, stimulated during the war, tended to slacken; and, like a good part of the Western world, the Argentine sought during the 1920s to return to a pre-1914 normalcy. It was not until the mid-1930s that a sustained take-off was inaugurated, which by and large can now be judged to have been successful despite the structural vicissitudes of that economy.

[4] Against the background of industrialisation measures inaugurated in the mid-1930s the Turkish economy has exhibited remarkable momentum in the past five years founded in the increase in agricultural income and productivity. It still remains to be seen whether these two surges, conducted under quite different national policies, will constitute a transition to self-sustaining growth, and whether Turkey can overcome its current structural problems.

[5] It is still too soon (for quite different reasons) to judge either the Indian or Chinese Communist take-off efforts successful.

[6] A number of so-called underdeveloped areas may have, in fact, either passed through the take-off process or are in the midst of it, e.g. Mexico, Brazil, Turkey, the Argentine and India. I would commend for consideration – certainly no more until the concept of take-off is disproved or verified – the

about economic growth, they must obviously seek to embrace these two early stages – and notably the economics of the take-off. The balance of this article is designed to mobilise tentatively and in a preliminary way what an economic historian can contribute to the economics of take-off.

III. THE TAKE-OFF DEFINED AND ISOLATED

There are several problems of choice involved in defining the take-off with precision. We might begin with one arbitrary definition and consider briefly the two major alternatives.

For the present purposes the take-off is defined as requiring all three of the following related conditions:

(a) a rise in the rate of productive investment from (say) 5 per cent or less to over 10 per cent of national income (or net national product);

(b) the development of one or more substantial manufacturing[1] sectors, with a high rate of growth;

(c) the existence or quick emergence of a political, social and institutional framework which exploits the impulses to expansion in the modern sector and the potential external economy effects of the take-off and gives to growth an on-going character.

---

dropping of the concept of 'underdeveloped areas' and the substitution for it of a quadripartite distinction among economies: traditional; pre-take-off; take-off; and growing. Against the background of this set of distinctions we might then consider systematically two separable questions now often confused. First, the stage of growth, as among growing economies. It is legitimate to regard Mexico and the United States, Great Britain and Australia, France and Japan, as growing economies, although they stand at very different points along their national growth curves, where the degree of progress might be measured by some kind of index of output (or capital) per head. Second, the foreseeable long-run potential of growing economies. Over the long pull, even after they are 'fully developed', the per capita output levels that different economies are likely to achieve will undoubtedly vary greatly, depending notably on resource endowments in relation to population. The arraying of levels of output per capita for different economies, now conventional, fails to distinguish these three elements; that is, the current rate of growth; the stage of growth; and the foreseeable horizon for growth.

[1] In this context 'manufacturing' is taken to include the processing of agricultural products or raw materials by modern methods; e.g. timber in Sweden; meat in Australia; dairy products in Denmark. The dual requirement of a 'manufacturing' sector is that its processes set in motion a chain of further modern sector requirements and that its expansion provides the potentiality of external economy effects.

The third condition implies a considerable capability to mobilise capital from domestic sources. Some take-offs have occurred with virtually no capital imports, e.g. Britain and Japan. Some take-offs have had a high component of foreign capital, e.g. the United States, Russia and Canada. But some countries have imported large quantities of foreign capital for long periods, which undoubtedly contributed to creating the preconditions for take-off, without actually initiating take-off, e.g. the Argentine before 1914, Venezuela down to recent years, the Belgian Congo currently. In short, whatever the role of capital imports, the preconditions for take-off include an initial ability to mobilise domestic savings productively, as well as a structure which subsequently permits a high marginal rate of savings.

This definition is designed to isolate the early stage when industrialisation takes hold rather than the later stage when industrialisation becomes a more massive and statistically more impressive phenomenon. In Britain, for example, there is no doubt that it was between 1815 and 1850 that industrialisation fully took hold. If the criterion chosen for take-off was the period of most rapid overall industrial growth, or the period when large-scale industry matured, all our take-off dates would have to be set forward; Britain, for example, to 1819–48; the United States to 1868–93; Sweden to 1890–1920; Japan to 1900–20; Russia to 1928–40. The earlier dating is chosen here because it is believed, on present (often inadequate) evidence, that the decisive transformations (including a decisive shift in the investment rate) occur in the first industrial phases; and later industrial maturity can be directly traced back to foundations laid in these first phases.

This definition is also designed to rule out from the take-off the quite substantial economic progress which can occur in an economy before a truly self-reinforcing growth process gets under way. British economic expansion between (say) 1750 and 1783, Russian economic expansion between (say) 1861 and 1890, Canadian economic expansion between 1867 and the mid-1890s – such periods – for which there is an equivalent in the economic history of almost every growing economy – were marked by extremely important, even decisive, developments. The transport network expanded, and with it both internal and external commerce; new institutions for mobilising savings were developed; a class of commercial and even industrial entrepreneurs began to emerge; industrial enterprise on a limited scale (or in limited sectors) grew. And yet, however essential these pre-take-off periods were for later development, their scale and momentum were insufficient to transform the economy radically or, in some cases, to outstrip population growth and to yield an increase in per capita output.

With a sense of the considerable violence done to economic history, I am here seeking to isolate a period when the scale of productive economic activity reaches a critical level and produces changes which lead to a massive and progressive structural transformation in economies and the societies of which they are a part, better viewed as changes in kind than merely in degree.

IV. EVIDENCE ON INVESTMENT RATES IN THE TAKE-OFF

The case for the concept of take-off hinges, in part, on quantitative evidence on the scale and productivity of investment in relation to population growth. Here, as noted earlier, we face a difficult problem; investment data are not now available historically for early stages in economic history. Following is such case as there is for regarding the shift from a productive investment rate of about 5 per cent of N.N.P. to 10 per cent or more as central to the process.[1]

1. *A prima facie case*

If we take the aggregate marginal capital–output ratio for an economy in its early stage of economic development at $3\cdot5:1$, and if we assume, as is not abnormal, a population rise of $1–1\cdot5$ per cent per annum, it is clear that something between $3\cdot5$ and $5\cdot25$ per cent of

---

[1] In his important article, 'Economic development with unlimited supplies of labour', *Manchester School* (May 1954), W. Arthur Lewis indicates a similar spread as defining the transition to economic growth:

'The central problem in the theory of economic development is to understand the process by which a community which was previously saving and investing 4 or 5 per cent of its national income or less, converts itself into an economy where voluntary saving is running at about 12–15 per cent of national income or more. This is the central problem because the central fact of economic development is rapid capital accumulation (including knowledge and skills with capital). We cannot explain any 'industrial' revolution (as the economic historians pretend to do) until we can explain why saving increased relatively to national income.'

Presumably Mr Lewis based this range on empirical observation of contemporary 'underdeveloped' areas on which some data are presented below. As in note 1, p. 90 above, it should be emphasised that the choice of investment proportions to symbolise the transition to growth hinges on the assumptions made about the rate of population increase.

N.N.P. must be regularly invested if N.N.P. per capita is to be sustained. An increase of 2 per cent per annum in N.N.P. per capita requires, under these assumptions, that something between 10·5 and 12·5 per cent of N.N.P. be regularly invested. By definition and assumption, then, a transition from relatively stagnant to substantial, regular rise in N.N.P. per capita, under typical population conditions, requires that the proportion of national product productively invested move from somewhere in the vicinity of 5 per cent to something in the vicinity of 10 per cent.

2. *The Swedish case*

In the appendix to his paper on international differences in capital formation, cited above, Kuznets gives gross and net capital formation figures in relation to gross and net national product for a substantial group of countries where reasonably good statistical data exist. Excepting Sweden, these data do not go back clearly to pre-take-off stages.[1] The Swedish data begin in the decade 1861–70; and the Swedish take-off is to be dated from the latter years of the decade. Kuznets' table of calculations for Sweden follows:

Decade	Domestic G.C.F. G.N.P. (%)	Domestic N.C.F. N.N.P. (%)	Depreciation to D.G.C.F. (%)
1. 1861–70	5·8	13·5–	(42)
2. 1871–80	8·8	5·3	(42)
3. 1881–90	10·8	6·6	(42)
4. 1891–1900	13·7	8·1	43·9
5. 1901–10	18·0	11·6	40·0
6. 1911–20	20·2	13·5	38·3
7. 1921–30	19·0	11·4	45·2

Note (Kuznets): Based on estimates in Eric Lindahl, Einan Dahlgren and Karin Kock, *National Income of Sweden, 1861–1930* (London: P. J. Kingston, 1937), Parts One and Two, particularly the details in Part Two.

These underlying totals of capital formation exclude changes in inventories.

While gross totals are directly from the volumes referred to above, depreciation for the first three decades was not given. We assumed that it formed 42 per cent of gross domestic capital formation.

[1] The Danish data are on the margin. They begin with the decade 1870–9, probably the first decade of take-off itself. They show net and gross domestic capital formation rates well over 10 per cent. In view of the sketch of the Danish economy presented in Kjeld Bjerke's 'Preliminary Estimates of the Danish National Product from 1870–1950' (Preliminary paper mimeographed for 1953 Conference of the International Association for Research on Income

3. *The Canadian case*

The data developed by O. J. Firestone[1] for Canada indicate a similar transition for net capital formation in its take-off (say, 1896–1914); but the gross investment proportion in the period from Confederation to the mid-nineties was higher than appears to have marked other periods when the preconditions were established, possibly due to investment in the railway net, abnormally large for a nation of Canada's population, and to relatively heavy foreign investment, even before the great capital import boom of the pre-1914 decade:

Canada: Gross and Net Investment in Durable Physical Assets
as Percentage of Gross and Net National Expenditure
(for Selected Years)

	$\dfrac{\text{G.C.F.}}{\text{G.N.P.}}$	$\dfrac{\text{N.C.F.}}{\text{N.N.P.}}$	Capital consumption as percentage of gross investment
1870	15·0	7·1	56·2
1900	13·1	4·0	72·5
1920	16·6	10·6	41·3
1929	23·0	12·1	53·3
1952	16·8	9·3	49·7

and Wealth), pp. 32–4, it seems likely that further research would identify the years 1830–70 as a period when the preconditions were actively established, 1870–1900 as a period of take-off. This view is supported by scattered and highly approximate estimates of Danish National Wealth which exhibit a remarkable surge in capital formation between 1864 and 1884.

Estimates of National Wealth in Denmark

	1,000 millions of kroner	Source
1864	3·5	Falbe-Hansen, *Danmarks statistik*, 1885.
1884	6·5	Falbe-Hansen, *Danmarks statistik*, 1885.
1899	7·2	Tax-commission of 1903.
1909	10·0	Jens Warming, *Danmarks statistik*, 1913.
1927	24·0	Jens Warming, *Danmarks erhvervs- or samfundsliv*, 1930.
1939	28·8	Economic expert committee of 1943, *Økonomiske efterkrigsproblemer*, 1945.
1950	54·5	N. Banke, N. P. Jacobsen og Vedel-Petersen, *Danske erhvervsliv*, 1951.

(Furnished in correspondence by Einar Cohn and Kjeld Bjerke.) It should again be emphasised, however, that we are dealing with a hypothesis whose empirical foundations are still fragmentary.

[1] O. J. Firestone, 'Canada's Economic Development, 1867–1952, with Special Reference to Changes in the Country's National Product and National Wealth', paper prepared for the International Association for Research in Income and Wealth, 1953, to which Mr Firestone has kindly furnished me certain revisions, shortly to be published. By 1900 Canada already had about 18,000 miles of

4. *The pattern of contemporary evidence in general*[1]

In the years after 1945 the number of countries for which reasonably respectable national income (or product) data exist has grown; and with such data there have developed some tolerable savings and investment estimates for countries at different stages of the growth process. Within the category of nations usually grouped as 'under-developed' one can distinguish four types.[2]

(*a*) *Pre-take-off economies*, where the apparent savings and invest-ment rates, including limited net capital imports, probably come to under 5 per cent of net national product. In general, data for such countries are not satisfactory, and one's judgment that capital formation is low must rest on fragmentary data and partially subjective judgment. Examples are Ethiopia, Kenya, Thailand, Cambodia, Afghanistan and perhaps Indonesia.[3]

(*b*) *Economies attempting take-off*, where the apparent savings and investment rates, including limited net capital imports, have risen over 5 per cent of net national product.[4] For example, Mexico (1950)

---

railway line; but the territory served had been developed to a limited degree only. By 1900 Canada already had a net balance of foreign indebtedness over $1 billion. Although this figure was almost quadrupled in the next two decades, capital imports represented an important increment to domestic capital sources from the period of Confederation down to the pre-1914 Canadian boom, which begins in the mid-1890s.

[1] I am indebted to Mr Everett Hagen for mobilising the statistical data in this section, except where otherwise indicated.

[2] The percentages given are of net capital formation to net domestic product. The latter is the product net of depreciation of the geographic area. It includes the value of output produced in the area, regardless of whether the income flows abroad. Since indirect business taxes are not deducted, it tends to be larger than national income; hence the percentages are lower than if national income was used as the denominator in computing them.

[3] The Office of Intelligence Research of the Department of State, Washington, D.C., gives the following estimated ratios of investment (presumably gross) to G.N.P. in its Report No. 6672 of 25 Aug 1954, p. 3, based on latest data available to that point, for countries which would probably fall in the pre-take-off category:

	%		%
Afghanistan	5	Pakistan	6
Ceylon	5	Indonesia	5

[4] The Department of State estimates (ibid.) for economies which are either attempting take-off or which have, perhaps, passed into a stage of regular growth include:

	%		%
The Argentine	13	Colombia	14
Brazil	14	Philippines	8
Chile	11	Venezuela	23

Venezuela has been for some time an 'enclave economy', with a high investment

N.C.F./N.D.P. 7·2 per cent; Chile (1950) N.C.F./N.D.P. 9·5 per cent; Panama (1950) N.C.F./N.D.P. 7·5 per cent; Philippines (1952) N.C.F./N.D.P. 6·4 per cent; Puerto Rico (1952) N.C.F. (Private)/ N.D.P. 7·6 per cent; India (1953) N.C.F./N.D.P., perhaps about 7 per cent. Whether the take-off period will, in fact, be successful remains in most of these cases still to be seen.

(c) *Growing economies*, where the apparent savings and investment rates, including limited net capital imports, have reached 10 per cent or over; for example, Colombia (1950) N.C.F./N.D.P. 16·3 per cent.

(d) *Enclave economies.* (1) Cases where the apparent savings and investment rates, including substantial net capital imports, have reached 10 per cent or over, but the domestic preconditions for sustained growth have not been achieved. These economies, associated with major export industries, lack the third condition for take-off suggested above (p. 95). They include the Belgian Congo (1951) N.C.F./N.D.P. 21·7 per cent; Southern Rhodesia (1950) G.C.F./ G.D.P. 45·5 per cent, (1952) G.C.F./G.D.P. 45·4 per cent. (2) Cases where net capital exports are large. For example, Burma (1938) N.C.F./N.D.P. 7·1 per cent; net capital exports/N.D.P., 11·5 per cent; Nigeria (1950–1) N.C.F./N.D.P. 5·1 per cent; net capital exports/N.D.P., 5·6 per cent.

What we can say is that *prima facie* thought and a scattering of historical and contemporary evidence suggests that it is not unreasonable to consider the take-off as including as a necessary but not sufficient condition a quantitative transition in the proportion of income productively invested of the kind indicated here.

V. THE INNER STRUCTURE OF THE TAKE-OFF

Whatever the importance and virtue of viewing the take-off in aggregative terms – embracing national output, the proportion of output invested, and an aggregate marginal capital–output ratio – that approach tells us relatively little of what actually happens and of the causal processes at work in a take-off; nor is the investment-rate criterion conclusive.

---

rate concentrated in a modern export sector whose growth did not generate general economic momentum in the Venezuelan economy; but in the past few years Venezuela may have moved over into the category of economies experiencing an authentic take-off.

Following the definition of take-off (pp. 95–6 above), we must consider not merely how a rise in the investment rate is brought about, from both supply and demand perspectives, but how rapidly growing manufacturing sectors emerged and imparted their primary and secondary growth impulses to the economy.

Perhaps the most important thing to be said about the behaviour of these variables in historical cases of take-off is that they have assumed many different forms. There is no single pattern. The rate and productivity of investment can rise, and the consequences of this rise can be diffused into a self-reinforcing general growth process by many different technical and economic routes, under the aegis of many different political, social and cultural settings, driven along by a wide variety of human motivations.

The purpose of the following paragraphs is to suggest briefly, and by way of illustration only, certain elements of both uniformity and variety in the variables whose movement has determined the inner structure of the take-off.

1. *The supply of loanable funds*

By and large, the loanable funds required to finance the take-off have come from two types of sources: from shifts in the control over income flows, including income-distribution changes and capital imports;[1] and from the plough-back of profits in rapidly expanding particular sectors.

The notion of economic development occurring as the result of income shifts from those who will spend (hoard[2] or lend) less productively to those who will spend (or lend) more productively is one of the oldest and most fundamental notions in economics. It is basic to the *Wealth of Nations*,[3] and it is applied by W. Arthur

[1] Mr Everett Hagen has pointed out that the increase in savings may well arise from a shift in the propensity to save, as new and exciting horizons open up, rather than merely from a shift of income to groups with a higher (but static) propensity to save. He may well be right. This is, evidently, a matter for further investigation.

[2] Hoarding can, of course, be helpful to the growth process by depressing consumption and freeing resources for investment if, in fact, non-hoarding persons or institutions acquire the resources and possess the will to expand productive investment. A direct transfer of income is, evidently, not required.

[3] See, especially, Smith's observations on the 'perversion' of wealth by 'prodigality' – that is, unproductive consumption expenditures – and on the virtues of 'parsimony' which transfers income to those who will increase 'the fund which is destined for the maintenance of productive hands' (Routledge edition, London, 1890, pp. 259–60).

Lewis in his recent elaboration of the classical model.[1] Lewis builds his model in part on an expansion of the capitalist sector, with the bulk of additional savings arising from an enlarging pool of capitalist profits.

Historically, income shifts conducive to economic development have assumed many forms. In Meiji Japan and also in Czarist Russia the substitution of government bonds for the great landholders' claim on the flow of rent payments lead to a highly Smithian redistribution of income into the hands of those with higher propensities to seek material advance and to accept innovations. In both cases the real value of the government bonds exchanged for land depreciated; and, in general, the feudal landlords emerged with a less attractive arrangement than had first appeared to be offered. Aside from the confiscation effect, two positive impulses arose from land reform: the state itself used the flow of payments from peasants, now diverted from landlords' hands, for activity which encouraged economic development; and a certain number of the more enterprising former landlords directly invested in commerce and industry. In contemporary India and China we can observe quite different degrees of income transfer by this route. India is relying to only a very limited extent on the elimination of large incomes unproductively spent by large landlords, although this element figures in a small way in its programme. Communist China has systematically transferred all non-governmental pools of capital into the hands of the state, in a series of undisguised or barely disguised capital levies; and it is drawing heavily for capital resources on the mass of middle and poor peasants who remain.[2]

In addition to confiscatory and taxation devices, which can operate effectively when the state is spending more productively than the taxed individuals, inflation has been important to several take-offs. In Britain of the late 1790s, the United States of the 1850s, Japan of the 1870s there is no doubt that capital formation was aided by price inflation, which shifted resources away from consumption to profits.

The shift of income flows into more productive hands has, of course, been aided historically not only by governmental fiscal measures but also by banks and capital markets. Virtually without exception, the take-off periods have been marked by the extension of

---

[1] Op. cit., especially pp. 156–9.
[2] W. W. Rostow and Alexander Eckstein, *The Prospects for Communist China* (New York and London, 1954) Part 4.

banking institutions which expanded the supply of working capital; and in most cases also by an expansion in the range of long-range financing done by a central, formally organised, capital market.

Although these familiar capital-supply functions of the state and private institutions have been important to the take-off, it is likely to prove the case, on close examination, that a necessary condition for take-off was the existence of one or more rapidly growing sectors whose entrepreneurs (private or public) ploughed back into new capacity a very high proportion of profits. Put another way, the demand side of the investment process, rather than the supply of loanable funds, may be the decisive element in the take-off, as opposed to the period of creating the preconditions, or of sustaining growth once it is under way. The distinction is, historically, sometimes difficult to make, notably when the state simultaneously acts both to mobilise supplies of finance and to undertake major entrepreneurial acts. There are, nevertheless, periods in economic history when quite substantial improvements in the machinery of capital supply do not, in themselves, initiate a take-off, but fall within the period when the preconditions are created, e.g. British banking developments in the century before 1783; Russian banking developments before 1890, etc.

One extremeley important version of the plough-back process has taken place through foreign trade. Developing economies have created from their natural resources major export industries; and the rapid expansion in exports has been used to finance the import of capital equipment and to service the foreign debt during the take-off. United States, Russian and Canadian grain fulfilled this function, Swedish timber and pulp, Japanese silk, etc. Currently Chinese exports to the Communist bloc, wrung at great administrative and human cost from the agricultural sector, play this decisive role. It should be noted that the development of such export sectors has not in itself guaranteed accelerated capital formation. Enlarged foreign-exchange proceeds have been used in many familiar cases to finance hoards (as in the famous case of Indian bullion imports) or unproductive consumption outlays.

It should be noted that one possible mechanism for inducing a high rate of plough-back into productive investment is a rapid expansion in the effective demand for domestically manufactured consumers' goods, which would direct into the hands of vigorous entrepreneurs an increasing proportion of income flows under circumstances which would lead them to expand their own capacity and to increase their requirements for industrial raw materials, semi-manufactured products and manufactured components.

A final element in the supply of loanable funds is, of course, capital imports. Foreign capital has played a major role in the take-off stage of many economies, e.g. the United States, Russia, Sweden, Canada. The cases of Britain and Japan indicate, however, that it cannot be regarded as an essential condition. Foreign capital was notably useful when the construction of railways or other large overhead capital items with a long period of gestation played an important role in the take-off. After all, whatever its strategic role, the proportion of investment required for growth which goes into industry is relatively small compared to that required for utilities, transport and the housing of enlarged urban populations. And foreign capital can be mightily useful in helping carry the burden of these overhead items either directly or indirectly.

What can we say, in general, then, about the supply of finance during the take-off period? First, as a precondition, it appears necessary that the community's surplus above the mass-consumption level does not flow into the hands of those who will sterilise it by hoarding, luxury consumption or low-productivity investment outlays. Second, as a precondition, it appears necessary that institutions be developed which provide cheap and adequate working capital. Third, as a necessary condition, it appears that one or more sectors of the economy must grow rapidly, inducing a more general industrialisation process; and that the entrepreneurs in such sectors plough back a substantial proportion of their profits in further productive investment, one possible and recurrent version of the plough-back process being the investment of proceeds from a rapidly growing export sector.

The devices, confiscatory and fiscal, for ensuring the first and second preconditions have been historically various. And, as indicated below, the types of leading manufacturing sectors which have served to initiate the take-off have varied greatly. Finally, foreign capital flows have, in significant cases, proved extremely important to the take-off, notably when lumpy overhead capital construction of long gestation period was required; but take-offs have also occurred based almost wholly on domestic sources of finance.

2. *The sources of entrepreneurship*
It is evident that the take-off requires the existence and the successful activity of some group in the society which accepts borrowers' risk,

when such risk is so defined as to include the propensity to accept innovations. As noted above, the problem of entrepreneurship in the take-off has not been profound in a limited group of wealthy agricultural nations whose populations derived by emigration mainly from north-western Europe. There the problem of take-off was primarily economic; and when economic incentives for industrialisation emerged, commercial and banking groups moved over easily into industrial entrepreneurship. In many other countries, however, the development of adequate entrepreneurship was a more searching social process.

Under some human motivation or other, a group must come to perceive it to be both possible and good to undertake acts of capital investment; and, for their efforts to be tolerably successful, they must act with approximate rationality in selecting the directions towards which their enterprise is directed. They must not only produce growth but tolerably balanced growth. We cannot quite say that it is necessary for them to act as if they were trying to maximise profit; for the criteria for private profit maximisation do not necessarily converge with the criteria for an optimum rate and pattern of growth in various sectors.[1] But in a growing economy, over periods longer than the business cycle, economic history is reasonably tolerant of deviations from rationality, in the sense that excess capacity is finally put to productive use. Leaving aside the question of ultimate human motivation, and assuming that the major overhead items are generated, if necessary, by some form of state initiative (including subsidy), we can say as a first approximation that some group must successfully emerge which behaves as if it were moved by the profit motive, in a dynamic economy with changing production functions; although, risk being the slippery variable, it is under such assumptions that Keynes' dictum should be borne in mind: 'If human nature felt no temptation to take a chance, no satisfaction (profit apart) in constructing a factory, a railway, a mine or a farm, there might not be much investment merely as a result of cold calculation.'[2]

---

[1] For a brief discussion of this point see the author's 'Trends in the allocation of resources in secular growth', chap. 15, *Economic Progress*, ed. Leon H. Dupriez, with the assistance of Douglas C. Hague (Louvain, 1955) pp. 378–9. For a more complete discussion see W. Fellner, 'Individual investment projects in growing economies' (mimeographed), paper presented to the Center for International Studies Social Science Research Council Conference on Economic Growth, October 1954, Cambridge, Mass.

[2] *General Theory*, p. 150.

In this connection it is increasingly conventional for economists to pay their respects to the Protestant ethic.[1] The historian should not be ungrateful for this light on the grey horizon of formal growth models. But the known cases of economic growth which theory must seek to explain take us beyond the orbit of Protestantism. In a world where Samurai, Parsees, Jews, North Italians, Turkish, Russian and Chinese civil servants (as well as Huguenots, Scotsmen and British North-countrymen) have played the role of a leading elite in economic growth, John Calvin should not be made to bear quite this weight. More fundamentally, allusion to a positive scale of religious or other values conducive to profit-maximising activities is an insufficient sociological basis for this important phenomenon. What appears to be required for the emergence of such elites is not merely an appropriate value system but two further conditions: first, the new elite must feel itself denied the conventional routes to prestige and power by the traditional less acquisitive society of which it is a part; second, the traditional society must be sufficiently flexible (or weak) to permit its members to seek material advance (or political power) as a route upwards alternative to conformity.

Although an elite entrepreneurial class appears to be required for take-off, with significant power over aggregate income flows and industrial investment decisions, most take-offs have been preceded or accompanied by radical change in agricultural techniques and market organisation. By and large the agricultural entrepreneur has been the individual land-owning farmer. A requirement for take-off is, therefore, a class of farmers willing and able to respond to the possibilities opened up for them by new techniques, landholding arrangements, transport facilities, and forms of market and credit organisation. A small purposeful elite can go a long way in initiating economic growth; but, especially in agriculture (and to some extent in the industrial working force), a wider-based revolution in outlook must come about.[2]

[1] See, for example, N. Kaldor, 'Economic growth and cyclical fluctuations', *Economic Journal* (Mar 1954) p. 67.

[2] Like the population question, agriculture is mainly excluded from this analysis, which considers the take-off rather than the whole development process. Nevertheless, it should be noted that, as a matter of history, agricultural revolutions have generally preceded or accompanied the take-off. In theory we can envisage a take-off which did not require a radical improvement in agricultural productivity: if, for example, the growth and productivity of the industrial sector permitted a withering away of traditional agriculture and a substitution for it of imports. In fact, agricultural revolutions have been required

Whatever further empirical research may reveal about the motives which have led men to undertake the constructive entrepreneurial acts of the take-off period, this much appears sure: these motives have varied greatly, from one society to another; and they have rarely, if ever, been motives of an unmixed material character.

3. *Leading sectors in the take-off*

The author has presented elsewhere the notion that the overall rate of growth of an economy must be regarded in the first instance as the consequence of differing growth rates in particular sectors of the economy, such sectoral growth rates being in part derived from certain overall demand parameters (e.g. population, consumers' income, tastes, etc.), in part from the primary and secondary effects of changing supply factors, when these are effectively exploited.[1]

On this view the sectors of an economy may be grouped in three categories:

(*a*) *Primary growth sectors*, where possibilities for innovation or for the exploitation of newly profitable or hitherto unexplored resources yield a high growth rate and set in motion expansionary forces elsewhere in the economy.

(*b*) *Supplementary growth sectors*, where rapid advance occurs in direct response to – or as a requirement of – advance in the primary growth sectors; e.g. coal, iron and engineering in relation to railroads. These sectors may have to be tracked many stages back into the economy, as the Leontief input–output models would suggest.

(*c*) *Derived growth sectors*, where advance occurs in some fairly steady relation to the growth of total real income, population, industrial production or some other overall, modestly increasing parameter. Food output in relation to population, housing in relation to family formation are classic derived relations of this order.

Very roughly speaking, primary and supplementary growth sectors derive their high momentum essentially from the introduction and

---

to permit rapidly growing (and urbanising) populations to be fed without exhausting foreign exchange resources in food imports or creating excessive hunger in the rural sector; and as noted at several points in this argument, agricultural revolutions have in fact played an essential and positive role, not merely by both releasing workers to the cities, and feeding them, but also by earning foreign exchange for general capital-formation purposes.

[1] *Process of Economic Growth*, chap. 4, esp. pp. 97–102; and, in greater detail, 'Trends in the allocation of resources in secular growth' (see above, p. 106, n. 1).

diffusion of changes in the cost–supply environment (in turn, of course, partially influenced by demand changes); while the derived-growth sectors are linked essentially to changes in demand (while subject also to continuing changes in production functions of a less dramatic character).

At any period of time it appears to be true even in a mature and growing economy that forward momentum is maintained as the result of rapid expansion in a limited number of primary sectors, whose expansion has significant external economy and other secondary effects. From this perspective the behaviour of sectors during the take-off is merely a special version of the growth process in general; or, put another way, growth proceeds by repeating endlessly, in different patterns, with different leading sectors, the experience of the take-off. Like the take-off, long-term growth requires that the society not only generates vast quantities of capital for depreciation and maintenance, for housing and for a balanced complement of utilities and other overheads, but also a sequence of highly productive primary sectors, growing rapidly, based on new production functions. Only thus has the aggregate marginal capital–output ratio been kept low.

Once again history is full of variety: a considerable array of sectors appears to have played this key role in the take-off process.

The development of a cotton-textile industry sufficient to meet domestic requirements has not generally imparted a sufficient impulse in itself to launch a self-sustaining growth process. The development of modern cotton-textile industries in substitution for imports has, more typically, marked the pre-take-off period, as for example in India, China and Mexico.

There is, however, the famous exception of Britain's industrial revolution. Baines' table (see next page) on raw-cotton imports and his comment on it are worth quoting, covering as they do the original leading sector in the first take-off.[1]

Why did the development of a modern factory system in cotton textiles lead on in Britain to a self-sustaining growth process, whereas it failed to do so in other cases? Part of the answer lies in the fact that, by the late eighteenth century, the preconditions for take-off in Britain were very fully developed. Progress in textiles, coal, iron and even steam power had been considerable through the eighteenth century; and the social and institutional environment was propitious.

[1] E. Baines, *History of the Cotton Manufacture* (London, 1835) p. 348.

But two further technical elements helped determine the upshot. First, the British cotton-textile industry was large in relation to the total size of the economy. From its modern beginnings, but notably from the 1780s forward, a very high proportion of total cotton-textile output was directed abroad, reaching 60 per cent by the 1820s.[1] The evolution of this industry was a more massive fact, with wider secondary repercussions, than if it were simply supplying the domestic market. Industrial enterprise on this scale had secondary reactions on the development of urban areas, the demand for coal, iron and machinery, the demand for working capital and ultimately the demand for cheap transport, which powerfully stimulated industrial development in other directions.[2]

Rate of Increase in the Import of Cotton-wool, in Periods of
Ten Years from 1741 to 1831

	%		%
1741–51	81	1791–1801	67½
1751–61	21½	1801–11	39½
1761–71	25½	1811–21	93
1771–81	75¾	1821–31	85
1781–91	319½		

From 1697 to 1741, the increase was trifling: between 1741 and 1751 the manufacture, though still insignificant in extent, made a considerable spring: during the next twenty years, the increase was moderate: from 1771 to 1781, owing to the invention of the jenny and the water-frame, a rapid increase took place: in the ten years from 1781 to 1791, being those which immediately followed the invention of the mule and the expiration of Arkwright's patent, the rate of advancement was prodigiously accelerated, being nearly 320 per cent; and from that time to the present, and especially since the close of the war, the increase, though considerably moderated, has been rapid and steady far beyond all precedent in any other manufacture.

Second, a source of effective demand for rapid expansion in British cotton textiles was supplied, in the first instance, by the sharp reduction in real costs and prices which accompanied the technological developments in manufacture and the cheapening real cost of raw

[1] The volume (official value) of British cotton goods exports rose from £355,060 in 1780 to £7,624,505 in 1802 (ibid., p. 350). See also the calculation of R. C. O. Matthews, *A Study in Trade Cycle History* (Cambridge, 1954) pp. 127–9.
[2] If we are prepared to treat New England of the first half of the nineteenth century as a separable economy, its take-off into sustained growth can be allocated to the period, roughly 1820–50, and, again, a disproportionately large cotton-textile industry based substantially on exports (that is, from New England to the rest of the United States) is the regional foundation for sustained growth.

cotton induced by the cotton gin. In this Britain had an advantage not enjoyed by those who came later; for they merely substituted domestic for foreign-manufactured cotton textiles. The substitution undoubtedly had important secondary effects by introducing a modern industrial sector and releasing in net a pool of foreign exchange for other purposes; but there was no sharp fall in the real cost of acquiring cotton textiles and no equivalent lift in real income.

The introduction of the railroad has been historically the most powerful single initiator of take-offs.[1] It was decisive in the United States, Germany and Russia; it has played an extremely important part in the Swedish, Japanese and other cases. The railroad has had three major kinds of impact on economic growth during the take-off period. First, it has lowered internal transport costs, brought new areas and products into commercial markets and, in general, performed the Smithian function of widening the market. Second, it has been a prerequisite in many cases to the development of a major new and rapidly enlarging export sector which, in turn, has served to generate capital for internal development, as, for example, the American railroads of the 1850s, the Russian and Canadian railways before 1914. Third, and perhaps most important for the take-off itself, the development of railways has led on to the development of modern coal, iron and engineering industries. In many countries the growth of modern basic industrial sectors can be traced in the most direct way to the requirements for building and, especially, for maintaining substantial railway systems. When a society has developed deeper institutional, social and political prerequisites for take-off, the rapid growth of a railway system with these powerful triple effects has often served to lift it into self-sustaining growth. Where the prerequisities have not existed, however, very substantial railway building has failed to initiate a take-off, as, for example, in India, China, pre-1895 Canada, pre-1914 Argentine, etc.

It is clear that an enlargement and modernisation of armed forces could play the role of a leading sector in take-off. It was a factor in the Russian, Japanese and German take-offs; and it figures heavily in current Chinese Communist plans. But historically the role of modern armaments has been ancillary rather than central to the take-off.

---

[1] For a detailed analysis of the routes of impact of the railroad on economic development, see Paul H. Cootner, 'Transport Innovation and Economic Development: The Case of the U.S. Steam Railroads', 1953, unpublished doctoral thesis, M.I.T.

Quite aside from their role in supplying foreign exchange for general capital-formation purposes, raw materials and foodstuffs can play the role of leading sectors in the take-off if they involve the application of modern processing techniques. The timber industry, built on the steam saw, fulfilled this function in the first phase of Sweden's take-off, to be followed shortly by the pulp industry. Similarly, the shift of Denmark to meat and dairy products, after 1873, appears to have reinforced the development of a manufacturing sector in the economy, as well as providing a major source of foreign exchange.

The role of leading sector has been assumed, finally, by the accelerated development of domestic manufacture of consumption goods over a wide range in substitution for imports, as, for example, in Australia, the Argentine and perhaps in contemporary Turkey.

What can we say, then, in general about these leading sectors? Historically, they have ranged from cotton textiles, through heavy-industry complexes based on railroads and military end products, to timber, pulp, dairy products and finally a wide variety of consumers' goods. There is, clearly, no one sectoral sequence for take-off, no single sector which constitutes the magic key. There is no need for a growing society to recapitulate the structural sequence and pattern of Britain, the United States or Russia. Four basic factors must be present:

1. There must be enlarged effective demand for the product or products of sectors which yield a foundation for a rapid rate of growth in output. Historically this has been brought about initially by the transfer of income from consumption or hoarding to productive investment; by capital imports; by a sharp increase in the productivity of current investment inputs, yielding an increase in consumers' real income expended on domestic manufactures; or by a combination of these routes.

2. There must be an introduction into these sectors of new production functions as well as an expansion of capacity.

3. The society must be capable of generating capital initially required to detonate the take-off in these key sectors; and especially, there must be a high rate of plough-back by the (private or state) entrepreneurs controlling capacity and technique in these sectors and in the supplementary growth sectors they stimulated to expand.

4. Finally, the leading sector or sectors must be such that their expansion and technical transformation induce a chain of Leontief input–output requirements for increased capacity and the potentiality for new production functions in other sectors, to which the society, in fact, progressively responds.

VI. CONCLUSION

This hypothesis is, then, a return to a rather old-fashioned way of looking at economic development. The take-off is defined as an industrial revolution, tied directly to radical changes in methods of production, having their decisive consequence over a relatively short period of time.

This view would not deny the role of longer, slower changes in the whole process of economic growth. On the contrary, take-off requires a massive set of preconditions going to the heart of a society's economic organisation and its effective scale of values. Moreover, for the take-off to be successful, it must lead on progressively to sustained growth; and this implies further deep and often slow-moving changes in the economy and the society as a whole.

What this argument does assert is that the rapid growth of one or more new manufacturing sectors is a powerful and essential engine of economic transformation. Its power derives from the multiplicity of its forms of impact, when a society is prepared to respond positively to this impact. Growth in such sectors, with new production functions of high productivity, in itself tends to raise output per head; it places incomes in the hands of men who will not merely save a high proportion of an expanding income but who will plough it into highly productive investment; it sets up a chain of effective demand for other manufactured products; it sets up a requirement for enlarged urban areas, whose capital costs may be high, but whose population and market organisation help to make industrialisation an on-going process; and, finally, it opens up a range of external economy effects which, in the end, help to produce new leading sectors when the initial impulse of the take-off's leading sectors begins to wane.

We can observe in history and in the contemporary world important changes in production functions in non-manufacturing sectors which have powerful effects on whole societies. If natural resources are rich enough or the new agricultural tricks are productive enough, such changes can even outstrip population growth and yield a rise in real output per head. Moreover, they may be a necessary prior condition for take-off or a necessary concomitant for take-off. Nothing in this analysis should be read as deprecating the importance of productivity changes in agriculture to the whole process of economic growth. But in the end take-off requires that a society find a way to apply effectively to its own peculiar resources what D. H. Robertson once called the tricks of manufacture; and continued growth requires that it so organise itself as to continue to apply them in an unending flow, of changing composition. Only thus, as we have all been correctly taught, can that old demon, diminishing returns, be held at bay.

7 The Theory of Development and the Idea of Balanced Growth

R. NURKSE

THE VICIOUS CIRCLE OF POVERTY

IN discussions of the problem of economic development, a phrase that crops up frequently is 'the vicious circle of poverty'. It is generally treated as something obvious, too obvious to be worth examining. I hope I may be forgiven if I begin by taking a look at this obvious concept.

It implies a circular constellation of forces tending to act and react upon one another in such a way as to keep a poor country in a state of poverty. Particular instances of such circular constellations are not difficult to imagine. For example, a poor man may not have enough to eat; being underfed, his health may be weak; being physically weak, his working capacity is low, which means that he is poor, which in turn means that he will not have enough to eat; and so on. A situation of this sort, relating to a country as a whole, can be summed up in the trite proposition: 'a country is poor because it is poor'.

Perhaps the most important circular relationships of this kind are those that afflict the accumulation of capital in economically backward countries. The supply of capital is governed by the ability and willingness to save; the demand for capital is governed by the incentives to invest. A circular relationship exists on both sides of the problem of capital formation in the poverty-ridden areas of the world.

On the supply side, there is the small capacity to save, resulting from the low level of real income. The low real income is a reflection of low productivity, which in its turn is due largely to the lack of capital. The lack of capital is a result of the small capacity to save, and so the circle is complete.

On the demand side, the inducement to invest may be low because of the small buying power of the people, which is due to their small real income, which again is due to low productivity. The low level of productivity, however, is a result of the small amount of capital used in production, which in its turn may be caused at least partly by the small inducement to invest.

The low level of real income, reflecting low productivity, is a point that is common to both circles. Usually the trouble on the supply side receives all the emphasis. The trouble there is certainly obvious and serious, and some aspects of it will be thoroughly gone into later. But the possible block on the demand side, once one becomes aware of it, is also fairly obvious, though it may not be so serious, or so difficult to remove, as the supply deficiency.

Besides, let us remember that capital is not everything. In addition to the circular relationships that plague the capital problem, there are, of course, matters of unilaterlal causation that can keep a country poor; for instance, lack of mineral resources, insufficient water or barren soil. Some of the poorer countries in the world today are poor partly for such reasons. But in all of them their poverty is also attributable to some extent to the lack of adequate capital equipment, which can be due to the small inducement to invest as well as to the small capacity to save.

WEAKNESS OF INVESTMENT INCENTIVES

It may at first be surprising to hear that there can be anything wrong on the demand side of the problem of capital formation in under-developed countries. Can there be any deficiency in the demand for capital? Are not the backward areas, almost by definition, greatly in need of capital for the efficient use of their labour and for the exploitation of their natural resources? Is not the demand for capital in these areas tremendous? It may well be; and yet in terms of private incentives to adopt capitalistic methods in the productive process there is the difficulty that stems from the limited size of the domestic market in the early stages of a country's economic development.

The inducement to invest is limited by the size of the market
This proposition is, in effect, a modern variant of Adam Smith's famous thesis that 'the division of labour is limited by the extent of the market'.[1] The point is simple and has long been familiar to the

[1] It was Allyn A. Young who suggested this reinterpretation in his well-known essay, 'Increasing returns and economic progress', *Economic Journal*, Dec 1928 (now reprinted in *Readings in Economic Analysis*, ed. R. V. Clemence (Cambridge, Mass., 1950) vol. I. It is easy to see, and Adam Smith recognised it himself, that the division of labour is closely connected with the use of capital in production.

business world. It is a matter of common observation that in the poorer countries the use of capital equipment in the production of goods and services for the domestic market is inhibited by the small size of that market, by the lack of domestic purchasing power, not in monetary but in real terms, in a sense to be presently defined. If it were merely a deficiency of monetary demand, it could easily be remedied through monetary expansion; but the trouble lies deeper. Monetary expansion alone does not remove it, but produces merely an inflation of prices.

This simple point, that the incentive to apply capital is limited by the size of the market, has a certain validity not only in the exchange economy of the real world, but even in the economy of an isolated individual like Robinson Crusoe, well known to our forefathers from elementary textbooks. Suppose that Robinson Crusoe had two or three hundred nails (which he got, let us say, from a wooden box washed ashore on his island) and wanted to drive them into some trees in order to hang up his fishing nets or personal effects. It would pay him first to sit down and make a simple hammer with which to drive these nails into his trees. His total effort would be reduced; he would do the job more quickly. But if he had only two or three nails it would not be worth his while to make a hammer. He would pick up and use a stone of suitable size. It would be a slow and inconvenient method; but it would be uneconomic to produce capital equipment in the shape of a hammer just for driving in two or three nails.

In the exchange economy of the real world, it is not difficult to find illustrations of the way in which the small size of a country's market can discourage, or even prohibit, the profitable application of modern capital equipment by an individual entrepreneur in any particular industry. In a country, for instance, where the great majority of people are too poor to wear leather shoes, setting up a modern shoe factory may be a doubtful business proposition; the market for shoes is too small. Many articles that are in common use in the United States can be sold in a low-income country in quantities so limited that a machine working only a few days or weeks can produce enough for a whole year's consumption, and would have to stand idle the rest of the time.

These examples may exaggerate the difficult, but I do believe that, to some extent, the difficulty is real. To produce with more capital per unit of output means generally, though not invariably, producing on a larger scale, in the sense of a larger output per plant. This is what matters in the present context, though it may be noted that in a given line of production any increase in output, even when it maintains the old degree of capital-intensity, will be discouraged by the smallness of the market.

The economic incentive to install capital equipment for the production of a certain commodity or service always depends in some measure on the amount of work to be done with this equipment. Naturally the individual businessman must take the amount of work to be done – the size of the market for his commodity or service – more or less as he finds it. He may hope to be able to deflect some of the present volume of consumers' demand in his own favour; but where real income is close to the subsistence level, there is little or no scope for such deflection. The limited size of the domestic market in a low-income country can thus constitute an obstacle to the application of capital by any individual firm or industry working for that market. In this sense the small domestic market is an obstacle to development generally.

How can this obstacle be removed? What is it that determines the size of the market? Some people may think, in this connection, of monetary expansion as a remedy, others of high-powered methods of salesmanship and advertising. Some may think of the size of a country's population as determining the size of the market; others, again, may have in mind the physical extent of the country's territory. All these factors are of secondary importance, if not irrelevant. A popular prescription is that small adjacent countries should abolish restrictions on trade with each other. But the smallness of a country is not the basic difficulty. The difficulty can exist even in very large countries such as China and India.

The crucial determinant of the size of the market is productivity. In an all-inclusive view, the size of the market is not only determined, but actually defined, by the volume of production. In the economy as a whole, the flow of goods and services produced and consumed is not a fixed magnitude. With a given population, it is a variable depending on people's productive efficiency. It is sometimes said that, if only prices could be reduced (money incomes remaining the same), the market could be enlarged. That is true, but if this were to happen it would imply an increase in productivity and real income. The market would be similarly enlarged if people's money incomes could be increased while prices remained constant. Again, this would be possible only with an advance in productive efficiency, implying an increase in real income. We are here in the classical world of Say's Law. In underdeveloped areas there is generally no 'deflationary gap' through excessive savings. Production creates its own demand, and the size of the market depends on the volume of production. In the last analysis, the market can be enlarged only through an all-round increase in productivity. Capacity to buy means capacity to produce.

Now productivity – or output per man-hour – depends largely, though by no means entirely, on the degree to which capital is employed in production. It is largely a matter of using machinery and other equipment. It is a function, in technical terms, of the capital-intensity of production. But, for any individual entrepreneur, the use of capital is inhibited, to start with, by the small size of the market.

Where is the way out of this circle? How can the market be enlarged? Even though in economically backward areas Say's Law may be valid in the sense that there is no deflationary gap, it never is valid in the sense that the output of any single industry, newly set up with capital equipment, can create its own demand. Human wants being diverse, the people engaged in the new industry will not wish to spend all their income on their own products.[1] Suppose it is a shoe industry. The shoe producers cannot live on shoes alone and must depend on the exchange of shoes for the other things they need. If in the rest of the economy nothing happens to increase productivity and hence buying power, the market for the new shoe output is likely to prove deficient. People outside the new industry will not give up other things in order to buy, say, a pair of shoes every year if they do not have enough food, clothing and shelter. They cannot let go the little they have of these elementary necessities. If they *were* willing to renounce some of their present consumption in exchange for an annual pair of new shoes, these things would become available for the shoe workers to make up the balance in their consumption needs. As it is, the new industry is likely to be a failure.

The trouble is due by no means solely to discontinuities in the technical forms of capital equipment, though these will accentuate it. It is due above all to the inevitable inelasticity of demands at low real-income levels. It is in this way that poverty cramps the inducement to invest and discourages the application of capital to any single line of production. The enlargement of the market through the rise in

---

[1] See Paul N. Rosenstein-Rodan, 'Problems of industrialisation of eastern and south-eastern Europe', *Economic Journal*, June–Sep 1943, p. 205.

productivity that would result from increased capital-intensity of production is inhibited by the initial smallness of the market.

The problem of technical discontinuities, in turn, is due not merely to the fact that equipment produced in advanced countries is adapted to domestic mass markets there and is not, as a rule, best suited to conditions in the poorer countries. Even if equipment were devised particularly for the latter, discontinuities would still remain. Additions to capital equipment in any case are apt to come in relatively big units, and there is especially a characteristic lumpiness in the process of investment in overhead capital facilities such as railways, power plants and waterworks.

While thus the technical discontinuities may call for sizeable forward 'jumps' in the rate of output, the small and inelastic demand in a low-income country tends to make such jumps risky if not altogether unpromising in any given branch of business considered by itself. If, in the past, attempts at jumping forward in particular branches have for these reasons come to grief, individual enterprise is likely to take a dim view of future investment prospects; the demand for capital will be depressed.[1]

We recognise, in one of its aspects, the vicious circle of poverty. We perceive a constellation of circumstances tending to preserve any backward economy in a stationary condition, in a state of 'underdevelopment equilibrium' somewhat analogous, perhaps, to the 'underemployment equilibrium', the possibility of which, in advanced industrial countries, was impressed on us by Keynes. Economic progress is not a spontaneous or automatic affair. On the contrary, it is evident that there are automatic forces within the system tending to keep it moored to a given level.

All this, however, is only part of the story. The circular constellation of the stationary system is real enough, but fortunately the circle is not unbreakable. And once it is broken at any point, the very fact that the relation is circular tends to make for cumulative advance. We should perhaps hesitate to call the circle vicious; it can become beneficent.

---

[1] All this is superimposed on the fact that in communities afflicted with mass poverty the qualities of enterprise and initiative are usually in short supply to start with, and that the demand for capital tends to be sluggish for this reason alone. I am grateful to Mr Robert G. Link for a detailed comment setting forth with more precision the possible ways in which the three factors – inelastic consumer demand, technical discontinuities and lack of enterprise – can keep down the demand for capital in low-income countries.

THE THEORY OF DEVELOPMENT AND THE IDEA OF
BALANCED GROWTH

What is it that breaks the deadlock? The nations concerned need not and will not accept the state of underdevelopment equilibrium as an inexorable decree of fate. Besides, we know that in some parts of the world economic development has actually occurred; something must have happened there to break the circle. So the theory of stagnation must be succeeded by a theory of development explaining the forces that are required, or that were observed in the past, to lift the economy out of the stationary state in which it would otherwise tend to settle. As we shall see, it is scarcely possible to consider this subject without finding one's mind turning to Schumpeter's great work.

For the moment, however, let us revert to the market problem which we have just examined. The difficulty caused by the small size of the market relates to individual investment incentives in any single line of production taken by itself. At least in principle, the difficulty vanishes in the case of a more or less synchronised application of capital to a wide range of different industries. Here is an escape from the deadlock; there the result is an overall enlargement of the market. People working with more and better tools in a number of complementary projects become each other's customers. Most industries catering for mass consumption are complementary in the sense that they provide a market for, and thus support, each other. This basic complementarity stems, in the last analysis, from the diversity of human wants. The case for 'balanced growth' rests on the need for a 'balanced diet'.

The notion of balance is inherent in the classical Law of Markets which generally passes under the name of Say's Law. Take John Stuart Mill's formulation of it: 'Every increase of production, if distributed without miscalculation among all kinds of produce in the proportion which private interest would dictate, creates, or rather constitutes, its own demand.'[1] Here, in a nutshell, is the case for balanced growth. An increase in the production of shoes alone does not create its own demand. An increase in production over a wide range of consumables, so proportioned as to correspond with the pattern of consumers' preferences, does create its own demand. It goes without saying that, with a given labour force and with given

[1] J. S. Mill, *Essays on Some Unsettled Questions of Political Economy* (London School of Economics reprint, 1948) p. 73.

techniques and natural resources, it is only through the use of more capital that such an increase in production can be obtained.

Balanced growth may be a good thing for its own sake, but here it interests us mainly for the sake of its effects on the demand for capital. It appears in the present context as an essential means of enlarging the size of the market and of creating inducements to invest.

But how do we get balanced growth? Ordinary price incentives may bring it about by small degrees, though here the technical discontinuities can be a serious hindrance; besides, slow growth is just not good enough where population pressure exists. In the evolution of Western capitalism, according to Schumpeter's well-known theory, rapid growth was achieved through the action of individual entrepreneurs, producing recurrent waves of industrial progress. Schumpeter's *Theory of Economic Development* has commonly been treated by economists in the advanced industrial countries as a theory of business cycles. In the advanced countries there has been a tendency to take economic development for granted, as something like a natural process that takes care of itself, and to concentrate on the short-run oscillations of the economy. Schumpeter's work, properly understood, is just what its title says it is: a theory of economic development. Business cycles appear in it only as the form in which economic progress takes place.

Schumpeter's theory seems to me to provide the mould which we must use, although we may use it with slightly different ingredients. As everyone knows, this theory assigns a central role to the creative entrepreneur, or rather to the action of considerable numbers of such entrepreneurs and their imitators, carrying out innovations, putting out new commodities, and devising new combinations of productive factors. Even if an innovation tends each time to originate in one particular industry, the monetary effects of the initial investment – and other circumstances as well – are such as to promote a wave of new applications of capital over a range of different industries. These waves result, in Schumpeter's own words, 'each time ... in an avalanche of consumers' goods that permanently deepens and widens the stream of real income although in the first instance they spell disturbance, losses and unemployment'.[1]

While the money-income effect of investment accounts, at least in part, for the bunching of investment activities in the course of the

[1] *Capitalism, Socialism and Democracy*, 3rd ed. (New York, 1950) p. 68.

cycle, it is the effect of the investments on the general level of productivity that increases the flow of consumable goods and services. This real-income effect, although it may have depressive monetary repercussions in the short run, is indeed the sum and substance of long-run economic progress – provided of course that the composition of the increased consumable output corresponds, by and large, to the pattern of consumers' demands.

In our present context it seems to me that the main point is to recognise how a frontal attack of this sort – a wave of capital investments in a number of different industries – can economically succeed while any substantial application of capital by an individual entrepreneur in any particular industry may be blocked or discouraged by the limitations of the pre-existing market. Where any single enterprise might appear quite inauspicious and impracticable, a wide range of projects in different industries may succeed because they will all support each other, in the sense that the people engaged in each project, now working with more real capital per head and with greater efficiency in terms of output per man-hour, will provide an enlarged market for the products of the new enterprises in the other industries. In this way the market difficulty, and the drag it imposes on individual incentives to invest, is removed or at any rate alleviated by means of a dynamic expansion of the market through investment carried out in a number of different industries. The rate at which any one industry can grow is inevitably conditioned by the rate at which other industries grow, although naturally some industries will grow faster than others since demand and supply elasticities will vary for different products. Through the application of capital over a wide range of activities, the general level of economic efficiency is raised and the size of the market enlarged.

The technical contribution which capital can bring about in backward countries is not in dispute. The possible increase in physical output with modern machinery, plus efficient management, may be tremendous. But this, after all, is merely the engineering side of the matter. The economic side is concerned, not simply with physical productivity, but with value productivity, and this is limited for any individual business by the poverty of potential consumers. When we think of the primitive methods of production that prevail in most countries and contrast them mentally with the physical productivity of a modern mechanised plant, we readily jump to the conclusion that the marginal productivity of capital in the economically backward areas must be enormous. The case is not so simple. The technical opportunities may be great; the physical increase in output may be spectacular compared with existing output, but value productivity is limited by the low purchasing power of the people. The technical physical productivity of capital can be realised in economic terms only through balanced growth, enlarging the aggregate size of the market and increasing individual investment incentives all round, while on any single investment project, if it were considered in isolation, the prospective return might be quite discouraging or at all events not sufficiently attractive to make the installation of more and better equipment worth while.

The notion of 'external economies' seems applicable here, though not quite in the sense in which Marshall commonly used it. Each of a wide range of projects, by contributing to an enlargement of the total size of the market, can be said to create economies external to the individual firm. Indeed, it may be that the most important external economies leading to the phenomenon of increasing returns in the course of economic progress are those that take the form of increases in the size of the market, rather than those which economists, following Marshall, have usually had in mind (improvements in productive facilities such as transport, communications, trade journals, labour skills and techniques available to a certain industry and dependent on the size of that industry).

The external economies in the market sense, just like those of the more conventional type, can create a discrepancy between the private and the social marginal productivity of capital. The private inducement to invest in any single project may be quite inadequate because of the market difficulty, even where the marginal productivity of capital applied over a range of complementary industries, in the sense just indicated, is very considerable. This is why a wave of new investments in different branches of production can economically succeed, enlarge the total market and so break the bonds of the stationary equilibrium of underdevelopment. In the early dawn of industrial development, it takes the eye of faith to see the potential markets. Schumpeter's creative entrepreneurs seem to have what it takes, and as they move forward on a broad front, their act of faith is crowned with commercial success.

Whether the forces of economic progress are to be deliberately organised or left to the action of private enterprise – in short, whether balanced growth is enforced by planning boards or achieved spontaneously by creative entrepreneurs – is, of course, a weighty and much debated issue. But from our present viewpoint it is essentially a question of method. I feel no need to enter into it at length. We are here concerned with the economic nature of the solution, not with the administrative form of it. Whichever method is adopted, the nature of the solution aimed at may be the same. And the 'miscalculation' Mill warned against (in the passage quoted earlier) seems hard to avoid in either case. Experience has certainly shown that large-scale public investment plans, in their practical execution, if not in their conception, often have a tendency to develop a marked lack of balance. But disproportionalities of one kind or another have also been a feature of the cyclical booms through which economic progress was achieved by private enterprise.

The nature of the solution is what I have tried to indicate. The question of method must be decided on the ground of broader considerations; on the ground, especially, of the human qualities and motive forces existing in any particular society. The economist, as an economist, has no categorical imperatives to issue on this subject. One of the founding fathers of nineteenth-century liberalism, Jeremy Bentham himself, maintained an attitude of relativity in this regard. 'Whether government should intervene, says Bentham, should depend on the extent of the power, intelligence, and inclination, and therefore the spontaneous initiative, possessed by the public, and this will vary as between countries.'[1] For various reasons, some of which could probably be fairly clearly defined, the American economy has been abundantly supplied with the human qualities of enterprise and initiative; but we cannot take it for granted that they are present in the same degree elsewhere. In the industrial development of Western Europe the main source of these qualities was the middle class. In the United States this label, if applicable at all, might be said to cover the great bulk of the people, while in many of the backward countries today the middle class is virtually non-existent.

BALANCED GROWTH AND INTERNATIONAL SPECIALISATION

The limited size of the market in economically backward areas has important effects on the volume of international trade, on the

[1] Jacob Viner, 'Bentham and J. S. Mill: the Utilitarian background', *American Economic Review*, Mar 1949, p. 371. Bentham adds this illustration: 'In Russia, under Peter the Great, the list of *sponte acta* being a blank, that of *agenda* was proportionally abundant' (Viner, ibid.).

pattern of foreign investment, and on the use of domestic savings. Each of these topics calls for some comment.

The size of the market is a basic determinant, not only of the incentives for the employment of capital, but also of the volume of international trade. Because of their low level of productivity and hence of real purchasing power, the backward agricultural countries play, as is well known, a minor part in world trade; by and large, the advanced industrial countries are each other's best customers.[1] The main influence of Keynesian economies on the theory of international trade was to stress the fact that the volume of trade among the industrial countries is closely dependent on the state of employment and effective demand in these countries, and that one cannot expect foreign trade to be active if the domestic economies are depressed. This was a good point to stress, but it is not the most fundamental. A more important determinant of the volume of international trade in the long run is the 'size of the market' and the level of productivity. Balanced growth, as a means of enlarging the market and stimulating the incentives for higher productivity through capital investment, is an essential basis for expanding trade.

Yet the case which the poor countries advance in favour of the 'balanced growth' and 'diversification' of their domestic economies is not always well received. Does it not mean turning away from the principle of comparative advantage? Why do these countries not push their exports of primary products according to the rules of international specialisation, and import the goods they need for a 'balanced diet'? Very briefly, the answer is: because the notion of balance applies on the global scale as well. For fairly obvious reasons, expansion of primary production for export is apt to encounter adverse price conditions on the world market, unless the industrial countries' demand is steadily expanding, as it was in the nineteenth century when both population and productivity in Western Europe were growing rapidly, when synthetic substitutes for crude materials had not yet been discovered, and when Great Britain decided to abolish tariff protection and thus to surrender some of her own agriculture in the interests of international specialisation. In the present century conditions have changed. There has been some sluggishness in the industrial countries' demand for primary products,

---

[1] See Folke Hilgerdt's illuminating study, *Industrialization and Foreign Trade* (League of Nations, 1945).

and despite the recent raw-material boom there is no certainty that this sluggishness is gone for good.

To push exports of primary commodities in the face of an inelastic and more or less stationary demand would not be a promising line of long-run development. If it is plausible to assume a generally less than unitary price elasticity of demand for crude foodstuffs and materials, it seems reasonable also to conclude that, under the conditions indicated, economic growth in underdeveloped countries must largely take the form of increased production for domestic markets. (Whether these conditions will prevail in the future is a question of forecasting, into which we need not enter). Under these conditions, if there is to be any development at all, it must concentrate at least initially on production for local requirements; and so long as this development increases the level of productivity and hence of real purchasing power, it will tend in the long run to help rather than hinder the growth of international trade.

These are some of the considerations that explain the widespread desire for 'balanced growth' and provide some economic justification for it. They do not constitute a case for autarky. The scale of comparative advantage is subject to change. Rash conclusions are sometimes drawn from static analysis. Undeveloped countries endeavouring to build up industries producing for their own market are often regarded as moving towards a state of self-sufficiency. But the size of the market is not fixed. When, for example, a country that consumes annually a certain number of shoes (our favourite commodity), all of which it imports, decides now to set up a domestic shoe industry producing just that number a year, it seems natural to conclude that it is making itself self-sufficient in shoes. But if the new shoe industry is part of an overall process of growth, the market for shoes in that country may increase tenfold, so that its shoe imports are increased instead of cut down to nothing. In Canada, for example, textile manufacturing was one of the first industries to develop, with the aid of tariff protection from 1879 on; yet Canada today is one of the world's biggest importers of textile manufactures.

As productivity increases and the domestic market expands, while the composition of imports and exports is naturally bound to change, the total volume of external trade is more likely to grow than to shrink. But even if it remains the same there is not necessarily any harm in 'balanced growth' on the domestic front. Take a country like Venezuela; petroleum accounts for 90 per cent of its exports, but employs only about 2 per cent of its labour force; the majority of the people work in the interior for a precarious subsistence in agriculture. If, through the introduction of capital and increased productivity the domestic economy were to expand so that people working formerly on the land alone would now supply each other with clothing, footwear, houses and house-furnishings as well as food products, while all the time petroleum exports remained the same and imports likewise constant in total volume, nothing but gain would result to the inhabitants without any loss to the outside world. No doubt there would be a fall in the proportion of foreign trade to national income. But could it not be that this proportion, in the many 'peripheral' countries of this type, has been kept unduly high in the past, simply by the poverty of the domestic economy?

The characteristically important role which international trade played in the world economy of the nineteenth century was partly due to the fact that there *was* a periphery – and a vacuum beyond. The trade pattern of the nineteenth century was not merely a device for the optimum allocation of a given volume of resources; it was, as D. H. Robertson put it, 'above all an engine of growth',[1] but of growth originating in and radiating from the early industrial centres. Even in the United States we have been so accustomed to regard the early nineteenth-century pattern as normal that we seldom stop to notice that the economic development of the United States itself has been a spectacular departure from it.

With the spread of industrialisation we have, however, noticed that the major currents of international trade pass by the economically backward areas and flow rather among the advanced industrial countries. 'Balanced growth' is a good foundation for international trade, as well as a way of filling the vacuum at the periphery.

[1] 'The future of international trade', *Economic Journal*, Mar 1938, p. 5 (now reprinted in *Readings in the Theory of International Trade*, ed. H. S. Ellis and L. A. Metzler (Philadelphia, 1949)).

8 Unbalanced Growth: An Espousal

A. O. HIRSCHMAN

IS BALANCE IN SUPPLY REQUIRED?

WE have criticised the idea that development must take place simultaneously in many activities to provide the element of 'mutual support' that alone will make it possible to clear the market of the newly produced goods. Having discarded this 'pure' theory of balanced growth we must still consider a far less rigorous version, one that insists that if growth is not to be stunted the various sectors of an economy will have to grow jointly in some (not necessarily identical) proportion; no sector should get too far out of line, not because of demand but because of supply or 'structural' considerations. For instance, if secondary industry grows, the food and raw material input needed by the workers and the machines will go up; if some of these requirements are imported, then an increase in exports is necessary, etc.

In this form, the balanced growth theory is essentially an exercise in retrospective comparative statics. If we look at an economy that has experienced growth at two different points in time, we will of course find that a great many parts of it have pushed ahead: industry and agriculture, capital-goods and consumer-goods industries, cars on the road and highway mileage – each at its own average annual rate of increase. But surely the individual components of the economy will not actually have grown at these rates throughout the period under review. Just as on the demand side the market can absorb 'unbalanced' advances in output because of cost-reducing innovations, new products and import substitution, so we can have isolated forward thrusts on the supply side as inputs are redistributed among users through price changes, and at the cost of some temporary shortages and disequilibria in the balance of payments or elsewhere. In fact, development has of course proceeded in this way, with growth being communicated from the leading sectors of the economy to the followers, from one industry to another, from one firm to another. In other words, the balanced growth that is revealed by the two still photographs taken at two different points in time is the end result of a series of uneven advances of one sector followed by the catching-up of other sectors. If the catching-up overreaches its goal, as it often does, then the stage is set for further advances elsewhere. The advantage of this kind of seesaw advance over 'balanced growth', where every activity expands perfectly in step with every other, is that it leaves considerable scope to *induced* investment decisions and therefore economises our principal scarce resource, namely, genuine decision-making.

Classical economics, while not taking so positive a view of the imbalances of the growth process, at least was never particularly concerned about them because it relied on prices to signal, and on the profit motive to eliminate rapidly and reliably, any structural disequilibria that might arise in the course of growth. The critics of classical economics, on the other hand, have always pointed to cases in which these 'market forces' would not act with adequate strength and speed. Having thus convinced themselves that the adjustment mechanism is beset with virtually insuperable obstacles, some of the critics naturally enough took the defeatist view that growth has to be balanced from the start or cannot take place at all.

This counsel of perfection is not only impracticable but also uneconomical. We need not sacrifice the valuable development mechanisms brought into play by unbalanced growth, especially if we go beyond the overly narrow view of the adjustment process that has long dominated economic literature.

Tradition seems to require that economists argue for ever about the question whether, in any disequilibrium situation, *market forces acting alone* are likely to restore equilibrium. Now this is certainly an interesting question. But as social scientists we surely must address ourselves also to the broader question: is the disequilibrium situation likely to be corrected at all, by market or non-market forces, or by both acting jointly? *It is our contention that non-market forces are not necessarily less 'automatic' than market forces.* Certainly the almost monotonous regularity with which interventionist economists have come forward – and with which authorities have acted – when the market forces did not adequately perform their task testifies to the fact that we do not have to rely exclusively on price signals and profit-maximisers to save us from trouble.[1]

[1] Some traditional equilibrium mechanisms were unable to dispense entirely with help from agents outside the market. Thus, the restoration of balance-of-payments equilibrium and the damping of the business cycle was, for a long time,

The case of unbalanced growth provides a good illustration. When supply difficulties arise in the course of uneven progress in sectors – such as education and public utilities – where private enterprise is not operating, strong pressures are felt by public authorities to 'do something'; and since the desire for political survival is at least as strong a motive force as the desire to realise a profit, we may ordinarily expect some corrective action to be taken.[1]

There is no implication here that any disequilibrium whatsoever will be resolved by some combination of market and non-market forces. But if a community cannot generate the 'induced' decisions and actions needed to deal with the supply disequilibria that arise in the course of uneven growth, then I can see little reason for believing that it will be able to take the set of 'autonomous' decisions required by balanced growth. In other words, if the adjustment mechanism breaks down altogether, this is a sign that the community rejects economic growth as an overriding objective.

The inclusion of probable reactions of non-market forces not only serves to make economic analysis more realistic. It also protects us against a fallacious chain of reasoning that is fairly common in development economics and of which the doctrine of balanced growth is itself an excellent illustration. In this reasoning, one first selects some objective of economic policy that seems desirable enough; then one proves that the objective cannot be attained through the operation of market forces; and one concludes that state action surely will bring the objective about. But this conclusion is clearly a *non sequitur*. The fact that private entrepreneurs will be unable or unwilling to do

---

made to depend on correct manipulation by the central bank of the rate of interest, in reaction to developing disequilibria. But this role of the central banker has usually been rationalised as an exception to the rule; and in the minds of many economists the central banker became a sort of honorary member of the market forces.

[1] Sectoral imbalances have of course been a conspicuous feature of Russian economic development. The resulting difficulties have been described in Soviet literature as 'non-antagonistic contradictions' which are not only admitted to exist but apparently considered to perform a useful signalling and corrective function: 'The characteristic trait of our difficulties and contradictions consists precisely in that they themselves indicate to us the basis and the means for their solution' (V. Kozlovskii, *Antagonisticheskie i neantagonisticheskie protivorechiia* (Moscow, Moskovskii Rabochii, 1954) p. 70). These 'non-antagonistic' contradictions which are successfully overcome by administrative action of the Communist Party and the government are then opposed to the 'antagonistic' contradictions which are said to afflict capitalism and which can be resolved only by revolution.

certain jobs which we would like to see done does not in itself ensure that the government can handle them. We must examine whether these jobs are likely to be performed satisfactorily by public authorities, which function after all in the same society as the entrepreneurs.[1]

DEVELOPMENT AS A CHAIN OF DISEQUILIBRIA

As has been shown, the balanced growth theory results from comparing the initial point of underdevelopment equilibrium with another point at which development will practically have been accomplished. A certain impatience with the process that lies between these two points – i.e. for the process of development – is shown by the following quotation from a well-known article by Scitovsky:

> Profits are a sign of disequilibrium, and the magnitude of profits under free competition may be regarded as a rough index of the degree of disequilibrium. Profits in a freely competitive industry lead to investment in that industry; and the investment in turn tends to eliminate the profits that have called it forth. Thus far, then, investment tends to bring equilibrium nearer. The same investment, however, may raise ... profits in other industries; and to this extent it leads away from equilibrium. ... The profits of industry B created by the lower price for factor A, call for investment and expansion in industry B one result of which will be an increase in industry B's demand for industry A's product. This in turn will give rise to profits and call for further investment and expansion in A; and equilibrium is reached only when successive doses of investment and expansion in the two industries have led to the simultaneous elimination of investment in both. It is only at this stage that ... the amount of investment profitable in industry A is also the socially desirable amount. The amount is clearly greater than that which is profitable at the first stage before industry B has made its adjustment. We can conclude, therefore, that when an investment gives rise to pecuniary external economies, its private profitability understates its social desirability.[2]

To my mind, the first part of this passage is a most pertinent portrayal of how development is set and kept in motion, but Scitovsky,

---

[1] Much the same point is made forcefully by Bauer and Yamey with respect to governmental promotion of industrial enterprise: 'A general lack of enterprise in a country does not in itself set up a presumption of such initiative in the public sector' (*Underdeveloped Countries*, p. 161). However, I do not follow the authors in the conclusions which they draw for the role of governments in economic development.

[2] 'Two concepts of external economies', pp. 148–9.

considering the proceedings he describes unnecessarily laborious, proposes to short-circuit them and to reach in a single jump a new point of equilibrium where the 'elimination of investment' has been accomplished. But, actually, development is a lengthy process during which interaction of the kind described by Scitovsky takes place not only between two industries, but up and down and across the whole of an economy's input–output matrix, and for many decades. What point in such a virtually infinite sequence of repercussions are we supposed to shoot at? Which intermediate expansion stages ought we to skip, and which ordinarily successive stages ought we to combine? Some skipping or combining may be possible, but with no more than the modest objective of speeding up development here and there. In general, development policy must concern itself with the judicious setting-up of the kind of sequences and repercussions so well described by Scitovsky, rather than with any attempt to suppress them. In other words, our aim must be to *keep alive* rather than to eliminate the disequilibria of which profits and losses are symptoms in a competitive economy. If the economy is to be kept moving ahead, the task of development policy is to maintain tensions, disproportions and disequilibria. That nightmare of equilibrium economics, the endlessly spinning cobweb, is the *kind* of mechanism we must assiduously look for as an invaluable help in the development process.

Therefore, the sequence that 'leads away from equilibrium' is precisely an ideal pattern of development from our point of view: for each move in the sequence is induced by a previous disequilibrium and in turn creates a new disequilibrium that requires a further move. This is achieved by the fact that the expansion of industry A leads to economies external to A but appropriable by B, while the consequent expansion of B brings with it economies external to B but subsequently internal to A (or C for that matter), and so on. At each step, an industry takes advantage of external economies created by previous expansion, and at the same time creates new external economies to be exploited by other operators.[1]

In Scitovsky's example, these external economies are essentially caused by production complementarities of one type or another, and we are thus returning to the complementarity effect of investment

---

[1] Note that the private profitability falls short of the social desirability of any venture only when its 'output' of external economies exceeds its 'input' derived from other ventures.

which was already invoked in Chapter 2 as a mechanism that would make investment decisions particularly easy or compelling. We were then speaking of the investment-promoting character of investment, not indirectly through additional savings out of the incomes created by investment, but through direct contact or 'contagion'.

Technical complementarity in the strict sense is usually defined as a situation where an increase in the output of commodity A lowers the marginal costs of producing commodity B. This will happen typically as a result of the following situations:

(a) because A is an input of B and is produced under conditions of decreasing costs;

(b) because B is an input of A and is itself produced under conditions of decreasing costs;

(c) because A and B are joint products (or because B is a by-product of A) and are produced under decreasing costs.

Because situations such as these have long been familiar to economists, complementarity is usually associated with economies of scale.[1] But there is no need for so restrictive an interpretation. We can define complementarity as any situation where an increase in the demand for commodity A and the consequent increase in its output call forth an increased demand for commodity B at its existing price. This happens not only when the connection between the two commodities is via the production process. The connection between A and B may also arise because the increased *use* of A leads to greater demand for B. We are not thinking here of situations where A and B *must* be employed jointly in fixed proportions. In this case it would not make much sense to say that demand for A and the subsequent increase in its output provide an incentive for the production of B, as it is rather the demand for the good or service into which A and B enter jointly which explains the demand for both products. This is the familiar case of derived demand. But there are many situations in the course of economic development where the increased availability of one commodity does not *compel* a *simultaneous* increase in supply of another commodity, but *induces slowly*, through a loose kind of complementarity in use, an upward shift in its demand schedule. The pheonmenon has been described under the apt

---

[1] W. Fellner, *Trends and Cycles in Economic Activity* (New York, 1956) pp. 199–200; N. S. Buchanan and H. S. Ellis, *Approaches to Economic Development* (New York, 1955) pp. 279–80.

heading 'entrained want';[1] Veblen observed it long ago and effectively summed it up when he said that 'invention is the mother of necessity' rather than vice versa.

An example of the rigid type of complementarity in use (best treated as derived demand) is cement and reinforcing steel rods in the construction, say, of downtown office buildings. Examples of the looser, 'developmental' type of complementarity (entrained want) can be found in the way in which the existence of the new office buildings strengthens demand for a great variety of goods and services: from modern office furniture and equipment (still fairly rigid), to parking and restaurant facilities, stylish secretaries, and eventually perhaps to more office buildings as the demonstration effect goes to work on the tenants of the older buildings. Here again, failure to arrange for all of these complementary items from the start could be denounced as 'poor planning' which ought to be avoided by centralised decision-making. But, just as in the case quoted by Scitovsky, an attempt to telescope the whole process would be futile because of the virtually infinite number of complementarity repercussions, and because of the uncertainty about a good many of them; moreover, such an attempt would miss the point that the profitable opportunities that arise as a result of the initial development move constitute powerful and valuable levers for subsequent development which are to be carefully nursed, maintained at some optimum level, and if necessary created consciously rather than eliminated.[2]

The common feature of the various complementarity situations is that, as a result of the increase in the output of A, the profitability

---

[1] The term is used by H. G. Barnett in *Innovation: The Basis of Cultural Change* (New York, McGraw-Hill, 1953) pp. 148–51, with the exact meaning we have in mind here: 'The fulfilment of one need establishes conditions out of which others emerge. . . . In most instances it is impossible for people to foresee [these emergent wants] even if they try. . . . Entrained wants are a consistent feature of motivational stresses for cultural change' (p. 148).

[2] This does not mean that when new buildings are put up one should refrain from planning for new parking facilities. Development itself constantly extends the range of complementarities that are rigidly compelled and necessarily simultaneous: the optional equipment of one period becomes the standard equipment of the next, as a result of social and cultural pressures and needs rather than because of purely technological factors. The process of turning loose complementarities into rigid ones is often called 'integrated planning', which is then opposed to 'improvisation'. These terms, particularly dear to city planners, are quite misleading in their antagonism. 'Integrated planning' takes care of *a few* of the *known* repercussions of a development move rather than letting them take care of themselves as best they can independently of that move. But it certainly can never hope to comprehend them all.

of the production of *B* is being increased because *B*'s marginal costs drop, or because its demand schedule shifts upward, or because both forces act jointly.

Put even more generally, complementarity means that increased production of *A* will lead to *pressure* for increasing the available supply of *B*. When *B* is a privately produced good or service, this pressure will lead to imports or larger domestic production of *B* because it will be in the *interest* of traders and producers of *B* to respond to the pressure. When *B* is not privately produced, the pressure does not transmute itself into pecuniary self-interest, and will take the form of political pressure for the provision of *B*. This is the case for such public services as law and order, education, satisfactory monetary and banking arrangements, highways, water, electric power, etc. Complementarity then manifests itself in the form of complaints about shortages, bottlenecks and obstacles to development. Action in this case does not take place through the operation of the profit motive, but through group pressures on public authorities and agencies.

A DEFINITION OF INDUCED INVESTMENT

The complementarity effect provides us with a new concept of *induced* investment which is more meaningful for underdeveloped economies than the conventional one, i.e. investment that is directly related to past increases in output. For this conventional concept of induced investment has validity mainly for countries with a fully built-up industrial and agricultural structure where increases in demand lead to increases in capacity designed to keep marginal costs from entering the area in which they would begin to rise steeply. The required adjustments may cover many industries, but are ordinarily small in any one year in relation to existing capacity. The big dynamic changes in developed economies are expected to originate in 'autonomous' investment.

This is not a realistic picture of the growth process in underdeveloped economies. Here an increase in the demand for beer, for example, may lead not only to the expansion of existing brewing capacity but, at a certain point, to the *start* of domestic production of bottles, of barley cultivation, and to a whole chain of similar repercussions. In other words, the investment that is induced by complementarity effects may help to bring about a real transformation of an underdeveloped economy.

One of the difficulties of the concept of induced investment in its traditional meaning is its precise delimitation. The reason for which investment is undertaken is not that demand has increased in the past, but that the experience of the past is taken as a guide to the future. In other words, investment is undertaken because for one reason or another the ensuing output is expected to find a market. But looked at in this way, all investment is obviously induced and the distinction between induced and autonomous investment becomes untenable or arbitrary.[1]

At first blush, it might seem that the same flaw, in an even more pronounced form, affects the distinction we have drawn. Is not every investment 'induced' in the sense that it complements some other existing investment? With the generously wide definition of complementarity which we have given, cannot every step in the development of a country be considered as called forth by the preceding steps in a never-ending series of 'inducements'? Have we then perhaps explained too much?

At this point we may, however, revert to our earlier discussion of external economies: it was then shown that new projects often appropriate external economies created by preceding ventures and create external economies that may be utilised by subsequent ones. Some projects create more external economies than they appropriate and therefore their private profitability falls short of their social desirability. It is therefore to be expected that the opposite situation can also be encountered – namely, ventures that have a large 'input' of external economies and a much smaller 'output'. The projects thus favoured represent the class of 'easy-to-exploit' investment opportunities which always abound in newly developing economies.

We can then define our concept of induced investment by the provision that the projects that fall into this category must be *net beneficiaries* of external economies.

This definition makes induced investment look very much like the multiplier: each investment is conceived as inducing a series of subsequent investments and there is an element of convergence as the 'output' of external economies diminishes at each step. This, however, does not necessarily mean that the investments themselves converge; there is no rigid connection between the size of an investment and its net 'input' of external economies, although some association between these two magnitudes may be expected to exist.

[1] Fellner, *Trends*, p. 319.

Theoretically, our definition of induced investment is, I believe, more satisfactory than the conventional one and it is far more relevant in the context of development problems. Nevertheless it is extremely difficult to give empirical content to the concept and we shall therefore not attempt to give our reasoning more rigour than it possesses; we shall continue to speak of investment inducing other investments and shall simply be aware that there are widely varying degrees of 'inducements'.

An ideal situation obtains when, as was pointed out in the last section, one disequilibrium calls forth a development move which in turn leads to a similar disequilibrium and so on *ad infinitum*. If such a chain of unbalanced growth sequences could be set up, the economic policy-makers could just watch the proceedings from the sidelines. It may be noticed that in this situation private profitability and social desirability are likely to coincide, not because of the absence of external economies, but because 'input' and 'output' of external economies are the same for each successive venture.

In practice, growth sequences are likely to exhibit tendencies towards convergence or potentialities of divergence, and development policy is largely concerned with the prevention of too rapid convergence and with the promotion of the possibilities of divergence.

One more point. The induced investment defined thus far is a gross quantity. In the previous chapter, we made much of the point that development brings with it external diseconomies as well as economies. The external diseconomies brought into the world by new investments refer primarily to the damage done to existing industrial or handicraft establishments by the introduction of modern methods and products. It must be granted, therefore, that new investments will hold back reinvestment in these establishments while leading to complementary capital formation elsewhere in the economy. The effect is, however, quite asymmetrical, as the greatest damage that new investment will cause to pre-existing equipment consists in failure to maintain and replace that equipment. Thus, in as much as the external diseconomies of new investments result in negative investment, this destructive effect is likely to be spread over several years; whereas the positive effect of the external economies leads at once to a demand for the total capital requirements of whatever ventures are going to be 'induced'. Because of this asymmetry, the investment-reducing effect of new investments resulting from competition and substitution effects seems unlikely to match the investment-creating effects of complementarity except where competitive industries are strong and complementarity effects rather weak. This latter situation may be characteristic of the textile industry and may account for the fact that in several underdeveloped countries the setting-up of this industry has failed to provide the necessary spark for further development.

SOME RELATED POINTS OF VIEW

The way in which investment leads to other investment through complementarities and external economies is an invaluable 'aid' to development that must be consciously utilised in the course of the development process. It puts special pressure behind a whole group of investment decisions and augments thereby that scarce and non-economisable resource of underdeveloped countries, the ability to make new investment decisions.

The manner in which an investment project affects the availability of this resource is for us the principal measure of its contribution to further development. A development strategy that stems from this approach is outlined in the next chapters. Before closing the present one, we shall refer briefly to some development theories that are related to the point of view presented here.

One of the principal characteristics of our approach has been the direct connection we have established between the investment of one period and that of the next. The complementarity effect 'calls forth' new investment; to the extent that savings are determined by this process, they play a perfectly passive role. This situation is very similar to the one recently described by Domar in his analysis of a growth model elaborated thirty years ago by the Russian economist Feldman. The essence of this model is the division of total investment into investment designed to expand the output of consumers' goods on the one hand, and of producers' goods on the other. Domar shows that once this division is made, 'the propensity to save has no life of its own so to speak and is completely determined by the relative productive capacities of the two categories'.[1] The limit to investment in the Feldman model as interpreted by Domar is not the ability or propensity to save, but the productive capacity of the investment-goods sector. Although the model is admittedly unrealistic, especially for an open economy, it is interesting as an attempt to build a sequence

[1] *Essays*, p. 236.

where investment of one period is directly related to the investment of prior periods without the intermediary of the savings ratio.

The rather tormented discussion around an article on investment criteria by Galenson and Leibenstein has yielded a similar line of thought: namely, that savings and reinvestment may depend not only on the productivity of capital but on various other characteristics of the projects in which capital is invested.[1] Although savings out of income are here an important intermediate link in the causal sequence, it is the specific nature of the investment, rather than merely the resulting income flow, that is seen as determining subsequent capital formation.

These are attempts to build generalisations about the required kind and composition of investment into development theory and to establish a closer-than-usual connection between investments of successive periods. However, these results are reached through the use of assumptions that, to my mind, are unnecessarily restrictive. Three other studies come even closer to our viewpoint. First, there is Perroux's concept of the 'growth poles' and his incisive description of the growth process as something that is called forth by these poles.[2] Second, mention must be made of the introductory remarks in Svennilson's work on the *Growth and Stagnation of the European Economy*, which come very close to our point of view. Here Svennilson mentions the importance of complementary developments and describes his work as an attempt to overcome the 'unhappy division between the cost and price theory on the one hand and the theory of growth and employment on the other.'[3] Unfortunately the subsequent analysis, while often ingenious and always interesting, does not entirely fulfil these promises.

Finally, the importance of inter-industry interactions because of external economies, economies of scale and complementarities has been fully recognised by Fellner. He states that these phenomena can

---

[1] See O. Eckstein, 'Investment criteria for economic development and the theory of intertemporal welfare economics', *Quarterly Journal of Economics*, LXXI (Feb 1957) 66. This article sets up a model where the income streams resulting from different investment projects are affected by *project-specific* savings propensities. Cf. W. Galenson and H. Leibenstein, 'Investment criteria, productivity and economic development', ibid., LXIX (Aug 1955) 343–70, and discussions in the Nov 1956, Feb and Aug 1957, and Aug 1958 issues of the *Journal*.

[2] François Perroux, 'Note sur la notion de "pôle de croissance"', *Économie appliquée*, VIII (Jan–June 1953) 307–20.

[3] U.N. Economic Commission for Europe (Geneva, 1954) p. 8.

account for a rise in the yield of capital even when the latter is growing at a faster rate than other factors of production and in the absence of technological improvements.[1] But Fellner relegates the action of these forces to the almost prehistoric phase during which 'primitive economies' accumulate the 'initial capital stock' required for growth. From then on, the only offsets to diminishing returns to capital that are admitted are organisational and technological improvements. I believe that the concept of initial capital stock, like that of 'prerequisites', is not a particularly useful one, and that complementarity effects are extremely important in offsetting diminishing returns from capital during a protracted period. Perhaps an economy is never quite through creating its 'indivisibilities', i.e. its complex of complementary economic activities!

[1] *Trends*, pp. 200, 341 ff.

9 Balanced v. Unbalanced Growth: A Reconciliatory View

ASHOK MATHUR

I. INTRODUCTORY

THE choice between 'balanced' and 'unbalanced' growth is one of the topics in the theory of economic development of underdeveloped countries which has evoked a vast amount of controversy. If one glances through the literature on the subject, one comes across a diversity in the interpretation, definitions and the framework of approach.[1] As one would expect, there is some substance in the points made by writers on both sides of the debate. In some of the recent writings one does find at least implicit suggestions that the two patterns of growth need not be mutually exclusive.[2] As a general rule, however, the authors advocate either a balanced or an unbalanced pattern of growth and the two continue to be viewed as mutually exclusive and polar paths of growth. This paper, on the other hand, presents the point of view that balanced and unbalanced growth need not be mutually conflicting and that an optimum strategy of development should combine some element of balance as well as imbalance.

[1] For example, Hans Singer in 'The concept of balanced growth in economic development: theory and practice', *Malayan Economic Review*, Oct 1958, distinguishes between the non-technical, a general technical, and a specific technical usage of the concept of balanced growth.

[2] Cf. J. M. Dagnino Pastore, 'Balanced growth: an interpretation', *Oxford Economic Papers*, July 1963, where he says, '... As a consequence, "balanced growth" does not exclude "growing points"'; G. O. Bierwag, 'Balanced growth and technological progress', *Oxford Economic Papers*, Mar 1964, similarly writes, 'Balanced and unbalanced models would appear to be complementary and not substitutable approaches'; S. K. Nath, 'The theory of balanced growth', *Oxford Economic Papers*, July 1962, where he says, 'Indeed, in spite of Hirschman's loud and bitter denunciation of balanced growth, it is difficult to see if he has any quarrel with the concept ... none of these considerations is incompatible with balanced growth – in fact they are all included among the considerations cited or implied by Rosenstein-Rodan and Lewis.' A. K. Sen, in his review of Hirschman's *The Strategy of Development*, in the *Economic Journal*, Sep 1960, also expresses a similar view. For example, he writes, 'In sorting out the issues involved in this debate, two considerations strike me as important. First, the balanced and unbalanced growth doctrines have a considerable amount of common ground. ...'

The diversity in the interpretation of the doctrines of balanced and unbalanced growth has been the cause of some of the arguments on both the sides going at cross-purposes and of a certain degree of confusion as regards the objective in view. For example, when Nurkse coined the term 'balanced growth', the objective he had in view was to demonstrate the necessity of balanced growth for creating market inducements to invest, which are essential for generating growth under a free-market mechanism.[1] Balanced growth has also been treated as a means of achieving greater diversification in the under-developed countries, which is considered to be essential in view of the growing barriers to international trade and particularly the resistance encountered by the exports of the developing countries.[2] Other writers use the balanced-growth doctrine to show that some sort of centralised planning is needed for removing divergences between social marginal productivity and private marginal productivity, which is necessary to achieve the potentially possible rate of growth.[3] Lately, consensus seems to be veering in favour of regarding balanced growth as the ultimate objective and of treating unbalanced growth as the means of achieving it[4] – which is, in fact, a step towards the recon-ciliatory view suggested here. In this paper, in order to remove any

[1] Although the notion of balanced growth, in some form or other, has been traced to earlier writers, this particular term first seems to have been used by Ragnar Nurkse in his *Capital Formation in Underdeveloped Countries* (Basil Blackwell, 1953).

Regarding Nurkse's free-market enterprise assumption, see his essay 'Balanced growth and specialisation', printed in his *Equilibrium and Growth in the World Economy* (Harvard University Press, 1961), where he says, 'As a means of creating inducements to invest, balanced growth can be said to be relevant primarily to a private-enterprise system' (p. 249).

[2] Cf. T. Scitovsky, 'Growth: balanced or unbalanced', published in Abramovitz (ed.), *The Allocation of Resources* (Stanford University Press, 1959), where he writes, '. . . political uncertainty, balance of payments difficulties and high competition in world markets have rendered export markets very precarious . . . today we take it for granted that a fair degree of self-sufficiency is desirable and base the arguments for balanced growth on the recognition of economic interdependence.'

[3] This was, for example, the view of one of the original formulators of the doctrine, Paul Rosenstein-Rodan, as presented in his 'Problems of industrialis-ation of eastern and south-eastern Europe', *Economic Journal*, June–Sep 1943.

[4] For example, Albert Hirschman, *The Strategy of Development* (Yale University Press, 1958); also Nurkse's 'Notes on unbalanced growth', published in his *Equilibrium and Growth in the World Economy* (Harvard University Press, 1961), where he writes, 'it might be well to distinguish between balanced growth as a method and balanced growth as an outcome or objective. Even zig-zag growth must have balance as its ultimate aim.'

source of vagueness, we specify the ultimate objective to be the achievement of the maximum possible rate of growth.

First of all we shall spell out a basic framework of approach with reference to which balanced and unbalanced growth paths will be analysed. Since there is no unanimously accepted definition of balanced growth, we shall state what we consider to be the essential content of the doctrine of balanced growth in the form of three propositions: the first one dealing with the requirements for initiation of the process of development, the second with the subsequent pattern of expansion, and the third with the implications of the existence of external economies. These propositions should not be taken to reflect the writings of any particular author, but they bring together the main points made by writers on the doctrine of balanced growth. In what follows we shall analyse the nature of balanced and unbalanced growth with reference to these propositions.

II. THE ESSENTIAL CONTENT OF THE DOCTRINE OF BALANCED GROWTH

The first proposition pertains to horizontal interdependence in consumption demand – an aspect which has received considerable attention from Nurkse and Rosenstein-Rodan. According to this proposition, in order to break through the stagnant levels of income and productivity in the underdeveloped countries, investment must be undertaken simultaneously in a number of projects so that the incomes generated by them could provide demand for one another's output and thus create inducement for further investment. Any isolated act of investment, especially when the investment required is of a lumpy character, would not succeed by itself, for it may not be profitable under the existing demand conditions. This aspect of the doctrine of balanced growth lays emphasis primarily upon horizontal interdependence of demand in the final stages of production, that is, among consumer-goods industries, and has a family resemblance to the Say's Law of markets. However, it has to be borne in mind that '"supply creates its own demand", but, provided that supply is properly distributed among different commodities in accordance with consumers' wants'.[1] The main conclusion which can be derived from this proposition, therefore, is that for successful initiation of the development process it is essential to start with at least a certain

[1] Nurkse, 'Balanced growth and specialisation', op. cit.

minimum size of investment spread over a number of diverse types of mutually supporting enterprise.[1]

The second proposition, which is perhaps more fundamental to our discussion, brings into prominence the supply factors and the vertical structure of production. It postulates that expansion in each line of production should take place in keeping with the national income elasticity of demand for that product.[2] The basic idea underlying this proposition is that the supply of all outputs, at the final as well as the intermediate stages of production, must expand at the same rate as the demand for them, so that bottlenecks may not hold back the rate of growth. Prospective demand for goods at the final stages of production, that is, for consumer goods, can generally be ascertained with reference to income elasticity of demand for them. But in the case of goods in the intermediate stages of production, there may be no strong and direct correlation between growth in demand for them and growth of the aggregate national income. Requirements of outputs in the intermediate stages of production have to be ascertained more specifically with reference to expansion in the scale of operation of the processes in which they serve as inputs. In the case of goods in the intermediate stages of production, the prescription of growth according to income elasticity of demand has, therefore, to be interpreted as implying that the supply of each intermediate output should grow according to expansion in the aggregate of envisaged demand for that output in all sectors of the economy, as determined from the input–output matrix of the economy.[3]

Our third proposition is concerned with the existence of complementarities and the related external economies, both pecuniary and non-pecuniary, as Scitovsky has called them. These imply that the free-market mechanism in the developing economies is not a reliable and quickly responding guide to the socially desirable extent and direction of investment. Investment decisions of private entre-

---

[1] The fact that some authors consider this to be the basic and perhaps the only content of the doctrine of balanced growth may be seen from the fact that Goran Ohlin in his article 'Balanced growth in history', *American Economic Review*, 1959, while trying to test the balanced-growth hypothesis historically, attempts primarily to discover how far there was simultaneity and suddenness in the expansion of a number of consumer-goods industries.

[2] Nurkse, 'Balanced growth and specialisation', op. cit.

[3] Cf. W. W. Rostow, 'Trends in the allocation of economic resources in secular growth', published in Leon H. Dupriez (ed.), *Economic Progress*, proceedings of the International Economic Association's annual conference, 1954.

preneurs are very largely influenced by the past price-trends and profit margins, which do not adequately reflect the potential profitability once investments in certain other lines of production start materialising. A private entrepreneur cannot visualise the full extent to which an investment decision by him, say, in the line of manufacture X, may confer a benefit upon another entrepreneur in line Y, production by whom, in turn, may raise the profitability of investing in the line X. Consequently, private investors may be deterred from venturing into the field of investment X. This, in turn, may hold back investment in other related channels Y, Z, etc., which could have been profitable only if investment in X had been undertaken. Therefore, it is chiefly considerations arising out of the divergence between inducement to invest as reflected by its current profitability and the social desirability of investment, as well as the need to time the production of different inputs appropriately, which make it imperative that there should be some sort of central co-ordination of investment decisions. When investments in a number of related lines are planned together, the overall profitability and desirability of these investments would appear to be higher than the sum total of profitability of individual investments considered separately. Thus the case for some sort of co-ordinated planning of investments is generally derived as one of the corollaries of the doctrine of balanced growth.[1]

III. THE NATURE OF UNBALANCED GROWTH

We have seen that one of the basic characteristics of balanced growth is that depicted by our second proposition, viz., that output of each item should so expand that its supply matches the envisaged demand for it, or what is broadly termed the rule of expansion according to the sectoral income elasticities of demand. This does not, of course imply that with balanced growth all outputs would grow at the same rate. The rate of growth of each output would depend upon the rate of growth of demand for it, with the result that some sectors could grow at a faster rate than the others. This feature, however, makes the task of defining and identifying its supposed antithesis, the unbalanced growth, somewhat difficult. In a broad sense unbalanced growth is generally taken to mean a pattern of growth where some sectors take the lead and advance ahead of others. But, strictly

[1] Rosenstein-Roden, loc. cit.

speaking, the mere fact that some sectors or industries have grown or are growing faster than the others is not sufficient to distinguish it from balanced growth, for, as we have just pointed out, such sectoral differentials in the rate of growth are possible even under balanced growth.

It would therefore appear that the distinctive feature of unbalanced growth is not so much that under it some sectors take the lead over the others, but that this rapid advance of certain sectors should be accompanied by imbalances in the form of emergence of excess capacity in some sectors, probably the ones that lead ahead, and shortages in certain other lines of production, probably those that lag behind. That shortages are considered to be an important characteristic of unbalanced growth can be seen from the very important role assigned to shortages in promoting induced investment and economic development by some of the chief protagonists of unbalanced growth.[1]

On the other hand, the basic feature associated with unbalanced growth or the 'growing points' thesis may be said to be the concentration of resources in a few selected directions – the focal points of development.[2] We shall take this to be the chief distinctive feature of unbalanced growth as a strategy of development, that is, application of resources and energies to the chosen set of interrelated industries.[3] This need not necessarily imply that output in sectors on which the resources are focused would be the most prominent one to start with, for that would also depend upon the capital–output ratio in those sectors. Similarly, such concentration need not mean inevitable emergence of shortages or surpluses. The emergence of shortages or surpluses, as we shall discuss later, is primarily a function of how well the production is planned and organised.

The main arguments for adopting unbalanced growth, that is, concentrating resources at the focal growth points, have been classified by Scitovsky into two categories, viz., the traditional and the modern argument. The traditional argument refers to the benefits derived from concentrating resources and energies on those lines of production which may be particularly suited for development in view

[1] Cf. Hirschman, *The Strategy of Development*, chap. 4; Streeten, 'Unbalanced growth', *Oxford Economic Papers*, 1959; Scitovsky, 'Growth: balanced or unbalanced', op. cit.

[2] Cf. Scitovsky, op. cit.

[3] This, for example, is clearly the view of unbalanced growth taken by Rostow, 'Trends in the allocation of resources in secular growth', op. cit.

of the availability of certain favourable resource combinations, of some specialised skills, raw materials, climatic advantages, or some newly discovered productivity-raising techniques, etc. This argument has a resemblance to the law of comparative advantage. The modern arguments in favour of unbalanced growth, on the other hand, focus our attention upon the advantages of large-scale production associated with concentration of resources, or in other words, economies of scale arising out of growth by large steps. Both these arguments are not contradictory, and the traditional as well as the modern one appear to us to have some validity.[1]

IV. PROPOSITION I

The theory of the 'big push' and the two doctrines

Having briefly analysed the nature and arguments in favour of unbalanced growth, we shall now see whether these are in conflict with the three propositions of the doctrine of balanced growth outlined above. We shall also see whether we can devise a strategy of development which draws upon the arguments advanced in favour of balanced as well as those in favour of unbalanced growth.

The basic point of what we have discussed as our first proposition is that it is necessary to have a certain minimum size of investment spread over a number of industries in order to initiate the process of development. This proposition is akin to what Leibenstein has called 'the critical minimum effort thesis', or what has come to be known as 'the theory of the big push'.[2] The theory of the 'big push' is generally associated with the doctrine of balanced growth, so much so that by some writers it has been taken to be the main characteristic of this doctrine.[3] But the idea that a 'big push' is needed to get the process of economic development moving need not be taken to be specific only to a balanced pattern of growth. Even an unbalanced pattern of growth would be facilitated by the momentum imparted by a reasonably high minimum scale of investment along the lines selected for advance. The idea of the need for an adequate minimum scale of investment is in fact common both to the balanced and unbalanced

---

[1] So also is the view of Scitovsky, op. cit.

[2] Harvey Leibenstein, *Economic Backwardness and Economic Growth* (New York, 1957) chap iv; Rosenstein-Rodan, 'Notes on the theory of the big push', published in *Economic Development for Latin America*, ed. H. D. Ellis and H. C. Wallich (Macmillan, 1962).

[3] Cf. Ohlin, 'Balanced growth in history', loc. cit.

patterns of growth, though the reason for this is different in case of the two doctrines. Whereas the doctrine of balanced growth arrives at the necessity of a 'big push' primarily in terms of the need to create a sufficient amount of mutually self-supporting market demand, in the case of unbalanced growth the case for a 'big push' would rely upon considerations of economies of scale and the indivisibilities of investment. But the role of high initial doses of investment in imparting momentum to the process of development would be true whatever the pattern of growth adopted.

There may be some difference between the two doctrines in respect of the size and coverage of the 'big push'. The extent of this difference would, however, depend upon how the two doctrines are interpreted. But the difference need not be wide. If the doctrine of balanced growth is taken to mean that investment should be undertaken in all those industries which could be established in an economy to meet each other's and other final demands, then certainly coverage in the two cases would be widely different and the size of initial impetus needed under balanced growth would be really vast. But it is not a very meaningful interpretation to conceive the doctrine of balanced growth as implying that an attack has to be made on all the possible industries which might be envisaged to come up ultimately once the economy has reached a fully developed stage. In fact, it is this sort of interpretation which makes the doctrine of balanced growth look impracticable and has evoked the criticism that it is most unrealistic to expect that a completely new and vigorous modern industrial sector can be implanted over a backward and stagnant economy.[1]

The essentials of the doctrine of balanced growth do not exclude the possibility of a start being made with a much smaller nucleus of 'mutually supporting' industries than is often envisaged. For example, to start with, it is not necessary to embark upon production of half a dozen types of shoes, a score of shades of clothing materials, several types of cars, etc., to satisfy consumers' wants, or to jump ahead with the electronics industry and the manufacture of heavy electrical gadgets.[2] The criterion of 'mutual support', which is the essential aspect of the first proposition of balanced growth, can hold true even for a limited number of selected industries serving the basic

[1] Cf. Hirschman, *The Strategy of Development*.
[2] Cf. W. B. Reddaway, *The Development of the Indian Economy* (Allen & Unwin, 1962).

requirements. With the passage of time, as economic development picks up pace, the small 'mutually supporting' nucleus can become extended, horizontally as well as vertically, and grow into a much bigger 'mutually supporting' industrial conglomeration. What is basically implied by the doctrine of balanced growth is that to get economic development going there must be a minimum number of industries meeting the necessary requirements, which lend each other support, both in the demand and in the supply aspects. But to start with, the diversity of these industries may be much less than what is potentially possible.[1] Moreover, the possibility of importing the requisite items through the medium of foreign trade can considerably reduce the range of industries with which the start need be made initially.[2]

Viewed in this light, the area of difference between the two doctrines in respect of the size and coverage of the 'big push' may be much narrower than apparent. Unbalanced growth would perhaps indicate a greater degree of selective emphasis within the small nucleus of industries with which the start is made, but in respect of the main substance of the first proposition, viz. the need for a 'big push', there appears to be no conflict between the two doctrines.[3]

V. PROPOSITION II

Some analytical issues

We now come to an analysis of the second proposition, which we consider to be fundamental to the doctrine of balanced growth, that is, that there should be a continuous equilibrium between supply and demand for each output, so that bottlenecks and shortages may be avoided. In this context two issues deserve our attention. First, whether avoidance of shortages is desirable or otherwise for achievement of the maximum possible rate of development, which is the objective we have in view. This question is of some importance in view of the central role assigned to shortages and the pressures induced by them, in the process of growth, by the protagonists of unbalanced growth. Secondly, if the verdict is in the affirmative, that is, that there is nothing in the nature of shortages which makes them inevitably

---

[1] This sort of reasoning was also implicit in Nurkse's 'Balanced growth and specialisation', op. cit.

[2] Cf. Rosenstein-Rodan, 'The theory of the big push', op. cit.

[3] An identical view has been presented by Robert B. Sutcliffe, 'Balanced and unbalanced growth', *Quarterly Journal of Economics*, Nov 1964.

growth-promoting, does it mean a victory for the doctrine of balanced growth and that the strategy of unbalanced growth should be discarded?

Let us take up the former issue first. On *a priori* grounds one would say that the emergence of shortages and bottlenecks would retard the pace of growth, for the simple reason that in the face of shortages, output of final goods cannot expand as fast as it could have if the supply of all requisite inputs were readily available. Unbalanced growth theorists, however, consider the emergence of bottlenecks as beneficial on the ground that shortages evoke maximum reliance upon the inducement mechanism and minimise the use of that 'scarce factor, the decision-taking ability'.[1] The argument runs this way: if shortage in the supply of a certain commodity appears in the market, it would raise its price and hence profitability of investment in that line of production. This would automatically attract some entrepreneur to the manufacture of the commodity which is in short supply. While it is not denied that the inducement mechanism may work in this manner – we shall shortly point out the situations where it may not – it should not be difficult to see that the expansion of output would have been faster if the output of the commodity in short supply had been increased in anticipation of the demand for it. This would have avoided the delays involved in reliance upon emergence of short-term profit signals as a guide to embarkation upon production plans, which are inherent in the market inducement mechanism. The longer the fruition period in production of the bottleneck commodity, the longer the delay involved in reliance upon the inducement mechanism. The conclusion, therefore, is inevitable that although shortages may help to sharpen the inducement mechanism, they do not serve the ends of our objective, that is, achievement of the maximum possible rate of growth. As to how far it is essential to sharpen the inducement mechanism in this manner, even if it be at the cost of a slower rate of growth, is a point to which we shall refer shortly.

This conclusion is not likely to go unchallenged, for reference is often made to formidable historical evidence, most generally the history of the textile industry, to show how shortages can be the mainspring of innovations and thus of rapid growth. The history of the British textile industry vividly illustrates how the shortages of

---

[1] Cf. Hirschman, *The Strategy of Development*, chaps 1 and 4; also see Streeten, loc. cit.

yarn and of the weaving capacity led to a chain sequence of innovations which revolutionised textile manufacture and multiplied manifoldly the output of textiles. It is not intended to dispute this historical evidence and the conclusions which may be drawn from it, but the flaw lies in generalising these conclusions indiscriminately to each and every type of shortage. The nature of shortages can vary and it is imperative to make a distinction between the different types of shortages.

The nature of shortages

The main distinction which we have in mind here is that between the type of shortages which the case of the textile industry exemplifies and the shortages arising on account of failure to plan and time the production in such a manner that the requisite inputs are forthcoming when they are needed for production of further outputs. The former type of shortages arises because in spite of full utilisation of available inputs and factors of production, with the known techniques, output of the required commodity which is in short supply cannot be increased. In such a case increase in output of the needed commodity has to await invention and the discovery of new techniques. For example, in the history of the British textile industry, Hargreaves's spinning jenny, Arkwright's water-frame, Crompton's mule, etc., were all inventions aimed at overcoming the shortage of yarn, whose production could not be increased with the available spinning techniques and resources. On the other hand, Kay's flying shuttle, Cartwright's water-frame, etc., were aimed at raising productive capacity in the weaving section to enable fuller utilisation of the considerably increased supply of yarn made available as a result of the above-mentioned inventions in spinning. The inducement to innovation which results from such shortages is all to be desired, for it leads to discovery of new methods of production for raising productive capacity and output of the commodity in short supply, and to alternative techniques requiring minimum use of scarce commodities, etc. Such shortages and the inducements generated by them can certainly be claimed to be growth-promoting.

But these shortages need to be distinguished from the second type of shortages, which are not due to inability to increase output with the available techniques but are the result of inadequate foresight and phasing of the production of different items. In their case, what is needed is not a spur to discover new methods of production but a better-organised production plan. Reliance upon the inducement mechanism to bring about co-ordination between different production activities and to eliminate shortages in an unnecessarily long-drawn-out and time-consuming process.

Moreover, even within the second of the above-mentioned categories of shortages, a further subdivision needs to be made – between those which we can hope to get eliminated ultimately through the inducement mechanism and those where the whole inducement mechanism may succumb under the pressure of shortages. The distinction can best be illustrated with the help of examples of each type. An example of the former would be a shortage of pneumatic tyres for the manufacture of finished automobiles or of dyes for the textile-finishing industry. Here the inducement for the setting-up of another pneumatic tyre or dye-making factory would be quite strong and, therefore, these projects may be undertaken directly by the entrepreneurs. In contrast, if shortage of steel is felt by the cycle-making industry, here this shortage is not likely to induce a direct expansion in the capacity of the steel industry. On the other hand, it may check any further expansion of the cycle and other allied industries.

In both these types of shortages, the ultimate output targets would have been attained more quickly if shortages had not occurred. But assuming that the shortages do occur, the former example represents what may be called 'semi-growth-promoting shortages' because the targets are ultimately reached, though perhaps after time-lags. The latter type may be called 'growth-thwarting shortages', because here the whole engine of expansion gets choked. The 'real growth-promoting shortages', which positively aid the growth process, would be those which lead to innovations of the type referred to while discussing the case of the textile industry. The failure on the part of the unbalanced growth theorists to make any distinction between different types of shortages has been the cause of some vagueness and confusion and that is why we have devoted some time to the question whether shortages are growth promoting or otherwise.

Before going over to the next point, we may refer to another aspect of the distinction between different types of shortages that we have made above. Long-term growth requires an economising of scarce resources (e.g. labour in the U.S.A. in the nineteenth century) and a substitution for them of resources in relatively plentiful supply. Where

the temporary shortages are of a type which provide an advance
warning of longer-term shortages, they induce the right sort of adaptation and innovation. This type of shortage would conform to what
we have called the 'real growth-promoting shortages'. On the other
hand, those temporary shortages or over-supply which do not in any
way reflect the longer-run position, may not only reduce growth in
the short run but may also provide incentives for an incorrect pattern
of longer-run adaptation. This type of shortage would be similar to
the category of 'growth-thwarting shortages' outlined above, which
generally arise on account of defective phasing of a production plan.
Thus the long-run effects of shortages can be beneficial as well as
harmful, depending upon the nature of shortage involved.

Public overhead investment

The 'semi-growth-promoting' type of shortages is likely to be
prominent where direct and specific ancillary or complementary
relationships exist and the scale of investment required is not very
substantial; for example, in the case of the pneumatic tyre industry,
where the bulk of such tyres would be consumed by the automobile
industry. On the other hand, wherever the output of any industry
has highly diversified uses and the scale of investment required in it is
large, a shortage in its supply is likely to be of the 'growth-thwarting'
type. The more diversified the uses to which the output of a particular industry is put, the less the possibility of shortage in one particular
use being able to induce investment in the industry supplying that
output. We have already indicated the steel industry to be an example
of this type. Electricity generation, facilities for technical education,
and in fact all the overhead facilities as well as the basic heavy
industries fall into this category. Thus, in the case of these more than
in any other industry, it is essential to ensure as far as possible that
the requisite volume of supplies from these be forthcoming when the
demand for them arises. This is particularly important in the case of
overhead facilities like electric power, transportation, etc., because,
unlike other outputs and services, these cannot be imported. These
industries generally yield significant economies of scale. The magnitude of investment required in them is therefore large, and considerable resources have to be concentrated on them in the initial
stages of development. Minimum economic size of production units
in this sphere being substantial, ensuring ready availability of supplies from these industries, therefore, requires creation of surplus

capacity. Moreover, surplus capacity is also justified on the ground that this type of imbalance in the case of overheads offers incentives and aids expansion of other economic activities.

On these considerations, therefore, an unbalanced pattern of growth in the form of surplus capacity is indicated in the case of overhead and basic industries. This does not, however, conflict with the doctrine of balanced growth. It is so in the first place because, as we have seen, this pattern of expansion helps in satisfying one of the basic postulates of the balanced-growth doctrine as given in our proposition II, viz. adequate supply should be forthcoming to match demand so as to avoid bottlenecks. Secondly, the need for surplus capacity is confined primarily to overhead investment and does not exist in the case of the other industries where the normal course of expansion may be followed. The fact that an uneven advance in case of overhead facilities is not denied by the doctrine of balanced growth was conceded even by Nurkse, one of the chief formulators of the doctrine of balanced growth. In fact, in the case of overhead investment, the prescription of the balanced-growth doctrine, even according to Nurkse, is that supply should not only keep in step with demand, but proceed ahead of it[1] – a conclusion which is identical to that derived by Streeten.

The strategy of balance within imbalance

We thus see that with regard to overhead investment, the conclusions of both the doctrines are the same. We now come to the second issue posed for discussion by us, that is, how far the need to avoid shortages, as required by the principle of balanced growth, contradicts or can be reconciled with the unbalanced pattern of growth, when we turn to direct investment in various sectors of the economy. We shall first discuss the problem in relation to the vertical structure of production and then its horizontal aspect.

The basic contention of the doctrine of balanced growth, that the supply of each output should grow in balance with the ex-ante demand for it, in order to avoid the growth-retarding influence of bottlenecks, does not in any way clash with the principle of unbalanced growth. The basic point of unbalanced growth, as outlined above, is that resources should be concentrated along a few strategic

---

[1] See Nurkse, 'Some reflections on the international financing of public overhead investments', and 'Notes on unbalanced growth', both published in his *Equilibrium and Growth in the World Economy*.

growth points of an economy in some order of priority. In fact, both these principles are mutually supporting ones, instead of being contradictory, and adherence to both of them would increase the potential rate of growth above what would otherwise have been possible. In the evolution of the mature Western economies, it was the sectors in which some path-breaking technical discoveries were made that usually emerged as what Rostow has called the leading sectors of growth. The position in the case of the late-coming underdeveloped countries differs from that of the Western countries in the course of their evolution, for in their case even within the existing framework of technical knowledge, technical possibilities can be exploited in a number of sectors. But in view of the limited availability of the complementary resources needed for exploitation, a few points of attack have to be picked out. The selection of industries which are chosen as the focal points of growth and the sequence in which they have to be developed, depends not so much upon the relative pace of technical progress in the different industries, but upon considerations of development strategy based on availability of natural resources, advantageous location in respect of some important items of production, availability of skills, need to fill up certain important gaps in the industrial structure, or the existence of some other favourable factors.[1]

Once the potential areas have been chosen, development of these would create demand for a number of inputs which can be ascertained from the input–output relationships. Now, it would be generally agreed that growth along these lines of advance would be faster if steps were taken to ensure that the supplies of those items which are necessary to support the expanding vertical structure of production were forthcoming in adequate quantities at the appropriate time, that is, when the demand for them arose. We have already emphasised that the shortages which arise on account of inadequate foresight and faulty organisation of the production plan tend to slow down the pace of growth. The optimum strategy of development should, therefore, be that within an unbalanced pattern of growth of the type elaborated above, steps be taken to see that the supply of each input matches the demand for it as it arises. In other words, the fastest possible rate of growth will be attained if one of the basic postulates of balanced growth dealing with the balance between demand and supply is adopted within an overall framework of unbalanced

[1] Cf. Rostow, 'Trends in the allocation of resources', op. cit.

growth. The principles of balance and of selective emphasis are thus complementary.[1]

We shall now analyse how far it is desirable to have balance or imbalance in the horizontal aspect of growth of different sectors and industries. In respect of the vertical expansion of the structure of production we have emphasised above that the supply of each item should expand in keeping with the demand for it. This principle of balance, when applied to the final stages of production, mostly the consumer goods, implies that their output should expand according to the income elasticity of demand for them. Now, whereas this principle of balance may be ideal for outputs in the intermediate stages of production, it has to be modified in at least two important respects when applied horizontally to goods in the final stages. Achievement of the highest possible rate of growth implies that maximum attention should be paid to the expansion of the capital-goods sector and the production of inessential consumer goods should be minimised as far as possible. It is being increasingly recognised that for attainment of self-sustained growth, it is imperative that the underdeveloped countries should build up their own basic capital-goods manufacturing industries.[2] The existing machine-making capacity, capacity for manufacturing a number of intermediate outputs, availability of foreign exchange as well as the supply of some other resources like entrepreneurial ability being limited in the underdeveloped countries, if consumer-goods industries are free to draw upon these without any restrictions, this will naturally bring down the pace at which the capital-goods manufacturing sector can expand. Thus, if all consumer-goods industries are allowed to grow in keeping with the free-market demand, or if these are allowed to be imported freely, this is likely to have adverse repercussions on capital formation and, therefore, the rate of growth of the economy. Growth of inessential and luxury consumer-goods industries which compete with capital-goods industries for scarce inputs like steel, electric power, etc., needs to be curbed to the maximum possible extent and a deliberate imbalance created in favour of the producer-goods industries.[3] For example, even though income elasticity of demand for refrigerators, air-conditioners, limousines, cosmetics, etc., may

[1] Ohlin, in his 'Balanced economic growth in history', loc. cit.

[2] See P. C. Mahalanobis, 'The approach of operational research to planning in India', *Sankhya*, Dec 1955.

[3] See W. G. Hoffman, *The Growth of Industrial Economies*, chap. iv (Oxford University Press, 1958).

be quite high, in the interests of long-term growth their expansion should initially be kept to the minimum possible through licensing procedures, etc. The resources and inputs thus conserved could be diverted towards building up of the capital-goods manufacturing sector. Similarly, although consumer tastes may demand a large variety within each type of consumer good, maximum possible extent of standardisation is needed in the earlier phases of development.[1] With the passage of time, as the capital-goods manufacturing sector goes on expanding, the supply as well as variety of consumer-goods output could, of course, be enlarged. But in the initial stages of development before a successful-take off has been attained, achievement of the objective of rapid growth requires a departure from our second proposition of balanced growth to the extent indicated above.

But this departure from the doctrine of balanced growth is indicated only in the case of inessential industries. When we come to the basic consumer-goods producing sectors, the principle of balance is as essential as in the case of the vertical structure of production. Here we obviously have got in mind the need for balance between industry and agriculture. Whereas the demand for inessential consumer goods can and should be suppressed, the basic requirements of human existence must be provided.[2] Since agriculture is the source of the most important item of consumption, viz. food, a substantial increase in the output of this sector, to meet in full the growing requirements of the population, is one of the chief prerequisites of steady and rapid economic development without inflation. The need for balance between industrial and agricultural growth is being increasingly recognised and hardly needs any further emphasis.

The second qualification to the principle of balance in the final stages of production, in addition to that in respect of the inessential consumer-goods industries which we have just discussed, has been referred to by us already, viz. the desirability of going ahead with the development of those industries which possess substantial potential for expansion. Unbalanced growth in their case, as implicit in our earlier discussion, is not determined by demand considerations but primarily by cost and resource availability considerations. However,

---

[1] Cf. Reddaway, *The Development of the Indian Economy* (see p. 8, n. 2), and P. J. Wiles, 'Choice versus Growth', *Economic Journal*, 1956.

[2] Cf. Reddaway, *The Development of the Indian Economy*, p. 8, n. 2.

though these imbalanced advances may not have been induced by considerations associated with the growth of demand for them, they would create further demand for various other items and thus induce growth in their output. As a general rule, while it may be desirable to have a horizontal balance between growth in broad sectors of the economy like agriculture, industry and other essential productive activities, within subsectors of these broad sectors imbalanced horizontal expansion is permissible.[1] In conclusion, we could say that the main emphasis of the above discussion has been on the desirability of balance between output availabilities and input requirements in the vertical 'pipelines' of production, whereas there could be uneven advances of the 'pipelines' themselves along the horizontal frontier. The pattern of growth suggested here could, therefore, be designated as the strategy of vertical balance within horizontal imbalance.

VI. PROPOSITION III

Planning in relation to balanced and unbalanced growth

Lastly, we now take up the third proposition, that is the role of external economies and the consequent need for planning, in relation to the balanced and unbalanced growth. As pointed out earlier, the need for planning is generally associated with the doctrine of balanced growth, for centralised investment decisions are considered to be necessary to co-ordinate simultaneous expansion of a number of economic activities. This reasoning seems to conceal an implicit conclusion that unbalanced growth does not need any investment planning. This implication is also revealed by the fact that historically development followed the path of unbalanced growth in the Western countries,[2] and since this unbalanced pattern emerged without any conscious planning, there may naturally be a tendency to conclude that only balanced growth needed planning. However, in the light in which we have visualised balanced and unbalanced growth, that is, as alternative strategies of development, growth along either pattern would be faster with some sort of planned central co-ordination than without any.

---

[1] A somewhat similar view is presented by O. G. de Bulhoes in 'Agriculture and economic development', published in W. W. Rostow (ed.), *Take-off into Self-sustained Growth* (Macmillan, 1963).

[2] Cf. Scitovsky, op cit.

The case for planning, as discussed earlier, rests primarily upon two arguments: first, the divergence between private profitability and social desirability may withold investment from certain essential spheres of economic activity; and secondly, reliance upon operation of the price and profit signals may be too sluggish in evoking investment in the desired channels, resulting in avoidable bottlenecks and consequent waste. These justifications for planned investments, however, underlie not only balanced but unbalanced pattern of growth as well. For, left to themselves, those directions of investment in which concentration of resources and the resulting imbalance could be rewarding may not be clear to the private entrepreneurs. Even if one individual entrepreneur could visualise these, there is nothing to ensure that the others would immediately fall into line with him and thus permit a speedy and smooth advance along the potential frontiers of growth. We have already argued that once the 'growth points' have been selected, pace of advance along these would be much faster if bottlenecks and the resulting delays in the expansion of output are avoided. This requires planned co-ordination of investment decisions to ensure that production of the needed items is timed appropriately.[1]

Planning should not be taken to be synonymous with state ownership and control. From the point of view of implementation of either of the strategies considered in this paper, what is essential is that there should be some central agency which is able to co-ordinate and ensure execution of the various investment decisions in keeping with the requirements of the pattern of growth which has been adopted. In so far as the private entrepreneurs can be made to conform to the plan through licensing procedures, directives of the type usually employed by the central banks to control the banking system, a system of controlled grants and subsidies, etc., direct investment by the state is not essential.

The debate about efficiency of operation of industrial enterprises by the state vis-à-vis private enterprise is not directly relevant to the issue under discussion. But the point which needs to be borne in mind is that if private enterprise is not forthcoming in certain directions requiring heavy investments, the obvious example being the overheads, or in the interests of ensuring availability of certain essential outputs, and the state does have to step into such activities, this need not curb private initiative and suppress the inducement

---

[1] Cf. Nath, loc. cit.

mechanism, as is sometimes implied. Given certain objectives and targets, a plan would basically indicate the directions in which investment is needed, determined from the input–output relations. This need not destroy – it would in all probability strengthen – the inducement mechanism for investment in the requisite directions, for the industrial gaps which need to be filled up, or may arise in future, would become clearer once a blueprint has been prepared. Even if the government decides to invest directly in the production of certain key outputs on the basis of the considerations mentioned above, it would strengthen the inducement to invest in the industries ancillary to the parent government-operated unit. Planning, again, does not imply that the government must step into production of all the items. Once it takes the lead in certain projects, the tempo in the related activities can pick up, and should be able to pick up much more easily than if no plan or co-ordination by the state existed. The state should, however, take adequate steps to disseminate information regarding the plans about envisaged lines of production in order to facilitate investment decisions by the private entrepreneurs. There is thus no inherent conflict between making the maximum use of the inducement mechanism and the planning of investments in keeping with a particular pattern of growth. Economic planning in India is also based upon such a model of mixed private and public enterprise economy.

In the above pages we have tried to outline the essential theme of the doctrines of balanced and unbalanced growth. Throughout this discussion our point of view has been that there are some positive points in both the doctrines, from which a development strategy can benefit. A lot, of course, depends upon the interpretation of the two doctrines, especially as no specific and universally accepted definitions of the two doctrines exist in the available literature. We have, however, attempted to show that there is nothing contradictory between the essential content of the two doctrines and that the most suitable strategy should, in fact, draw upon the strong points of both the doctrines. Stray remarks in the recent literature on the subject do show that the realisation about the non-contradictory nature of balanced and unbalanced growth has been growing. This paper is an attempt to formalise this line of thinking.

10 External Capital and Self-help in Developing Countries

W. B. REDDAWAY

IT is misleading to talk about 'the developing countries' as if they were all alike: the problems of India and Sierra Leone – to take two examples with which I have personally had contact – differ widely. Nevertheless, it would be wrong to say that developing countries have nothing in common and that each has to be considered separately as a special case. There are considerable differences in detail among them, but a broad scheme of analysis can be outlined, which can be applied to each country according to its special characteristics.

Analysis of the problems of these countries leads to the conclusion that external aid is desirable, preferably a free grant but, failing that, as a long-term loan or equity capital. The object of this article is not to deny that such external assistance is desirable, but rather to examine whether it is right to place a preponderant importance on it and, in particular, to see whether it should not be thought of as but one factor in a detailed overall plan. Since very few developing countries are likely to receive their full 'requirements' of external aid, it is worth examining methods of making the best possible use of it by the countries themselves.

First, however, let us see just why it is that so much stress is normally laid on the need for external capital. Put crudely, the argument is both simple and appealing. It is a common characteristic of developing countries that the average income of the inhabitants, measured in real terms, is extremely low. This low income enforces a low level of consumption per head and reflects a low level of productivity – i.e. a low level of real output per head of population. The crucial question for those who want to raise living standards is, therefore, what causes this?

There are a number of factors which contribute to the explanation. One might say quite simply that the people in these countries do not usually feel the same urge to work hard or conscientiously in order to earn a substantial income, as do people in the West; rather, they are content to 'sit in the sun' as soon as they have earned enough for their modest tastes, or at least to take their working lives fairly easily. Or it might be said that a substantial proportion of the man-days which the labour force is willing to provide cannot be utilised because of intermittent unemployment – the result of casual daily, even hourly, hirings with little presumption of continuity. Or again it might be put that the average worker, though willing, is inefficient, so that his output is small and much of what he produces unsatisfactory.

These and other factors play some role, varying from country to country. Nevertheless, the traditional analysis generally leads to one thing as being of outstanding importance: what the economist calls 'the lack of co-operating factors'. By this he means that, even though the available workers may not be very efficient or industrious, nevertheless output could be greatly increased if they were provided with a better supply of 'things to work with'. Under this heading predominant importance is normally given to capital, meaning real capital equipment (factories, machinery, tools, etc.). A succinct summary of this view would be simply: 'Very little can be produced with bare hands alone and not much more with the rudimentary equipment available to the average worker in a developing country.' Hence the stress on increasing the amount of capital available, so that output per head can be increased 'out of all recognition' (in the view of the optimists), or at least 'very substantially' (a more realistic appraisal).

This process of raising output her head of population by providing capital equipment for workers to use can be pictured most vividly by imagining that, previously, the would-be workers were un-employed, and then a new factory is opened, in which they can produce a substantial amount per head. But the problem in develop-ing countries is not usually one of 'unemployment' in the sense in which that term is understood in Britain – a state in which people are able and willing to work but cannot find a job. Indeed there are usually not many people who are literally unemployed in the sense of having done no work for the last week; outside a welfare state, unemployment of this kind would imply a large number of beggars or thieves. More typically, in a developing country the would-be worker who cannot find a proper job will turn to some relative who has a small business (commonly in agriculture or distribution) and who will allow him to 'dip into the family rice-bowl'; in return he will do some work in the family business, though this does not imply that its output will be increased since it is usually adequately staffed already. He simply shares in its work, as he shares in the family's meals.

Alternatively, the person who cannot find employment may seek to scrape some sort of a living as a self-employed pedlar of goods obtained on credit, or a purveyor of minor services (shoe-shining, bag-carrying, etc.). These occupations are generally over-manned already, so that the total output of such services may not increase at all, but the newcomer obtains some part of the business which is going and so keeps alive.

In brief, the trouble in the labour market of a developing country is not so much that there are insufficient employment opportunities of some kind, but that the opportunities which are available are of such a poor quality. The increase in the nation's stock of capital may perhaps reduce the number of totally unemployed people a little, but its main function is to increase the number of people in jobs which yield a respectable output per head, at the expense of those where it is very low.

This traditional analysis in terms of the need for more capital obviously contains a good deal of the truth, and it is normally followed by an analysis of the 'vicious circle of poverty'. In a country in which incomes are so low that a visitor from a developed country is always mystified how the inhabitants can stay alive, it is obviously very difficult for those inhabitants to set aside any significant part of their incomes in order to provide the tools with which to earn larger incomes in future years, even though the reward for such saving might be very large in proportion to the amount involved. This leads naturally to the call for capital from developed countries to break the vicious circle and help the virtuous circle of development and expansion to get moving; but any tendency to optimism which may be engendered by references to snowballs growing and so on is liable to be dispelled by a little elementary calculation of the enormous sums of capital which are needed merely to equip the annual addition to the population at the old inadequate standard, when the population of developing countries is increasing by tens of millions of people every year. Extra capital – whether from internal savings or from external aid – is needed for this purpose before one can effectively start on the task of more adequately equipping the existing population. The task is both to deal with the growth in population and to make up the back-log represented by the unemployed and the 'pseudo-employed'.

There is a further powerful argument to support the need for a substantial element of external capital to supplement internal savings in the task of improving the equipment of a developing country. In almost all cases a large part of the machinery which is needed will have to be imported: developing countries seldom have an engineering industry of any size, even if they have one at all. This does not mean that developing countries cannot obtain the machinery through the ordinary process of international trade, if they are prepared to do the necessary saving, but it is extremely common (except for oil-rich countries) to find that an attempt at speedier development rapidly leads to a severe problem of the balance of payments. Consequently, external capital is needed not only to increase the total amount which can be added to the nation's stock of capital equipment each year, but also to enable this to take the desired form – to enable it to include a good deal of machinery, instead of being confined to buildings, roads and the like which might be made with local resources.

One has, therefore, two powerful reasons – one quantitative and one qualitative – for emphasising the importance of a flow of external aid to help in accelerating the development of these countries; but studies undertaken under the auspices of the United Nations and other bodies have shown that the total amount of such aid which would be required each year to secure even a moderate rate of growth in all the developing countries far exceeds the amount which has been made available in the past, and indeed far exceeds what is likely to be made available in the future. Hence the crucial importance of studying other methods of accelerating the development, while recognising that these do not in any way rival the use of external capital but rather complement it. Indeed, the calculations of the amount of external capital 'required' often implicitly assume that action will also be taken under other headings, and the disappointing achievements of many countries reflect the absence of supporting action more than the inadequacy of the aid.

If one wants to carry the analysis of a developing country's problems further, it is in some ways convenient to say that the 'shortage of capital' thesis both exaggerates the problem and at the same time makes it appear too easy.

Let us start with the ways in which the thesis makes the problem appear too easy. Essentially, these can be summed up by saying that it is not sufficient merely to increase the supply of capital and then expect to find the level of output 'automatically' rising in accordance with some magical 'capital–output ratio'. The expansion in the output of any commodity requires all sorts of things besides the necessary capital equipment; and in a developing country it is fatal to take it for granted that supplies of these complementary factors will automatically be available, even though one can assume that there will be an abundance of unskilled labour willing to work in a genuinely productive job for a wage which is both more reliable and higher than their previous precarious income.

To take some leading examples, skilled labour, management, raw materials, components, power and transport are all things which will usually be needed, and which may be even more difficult to supply in the proper quantities and qualities than capital itself. Of course, imports may get over some of the difficulties, particularly on components, provided that the balance of payments will permit adequate purchases. But even if we can stretch the term to cover foreign technicians, imports cannot overcome all the various shortages – notably power, a shortage of which can have a devastating effect on a whole development programme. Consequently, even if imports can be used to avoid some of the worst bottlenecks, nevertheless the introduction of additional capital will not be very fruitful unless complementary action is taken to secure that the new productive units have adequate supplies of the other scarce factors. This in turn means that the development programme must be properly co-ordinated and, far more important, that its execution shall conform sufficiently closely to the programme to avoid hold-ups caused by a lagging performance at some key point. Without this, factories are liable to be working below capacity for lack of a few skilled workers or of key materials, power or imported components.

So far I have been dealing with other difficulties on the supply side beside shortage of capital. An expansion of output is also, however, dependent on the existence of an adequate market. This implies two rather different things: there must be a sufficient general framework of law and order, credit and 'marketing facilities', so that a producer can expect to dispose of this output in an orderly way and to collect payment 'in due course'; and secondly, the goods which he has in fact to offer must be in sufficient demand to justify full working of the factory or other productive unit. This latter point brings us back again to the need for a proper development programme, based on economic considerations and not on false ideas about the 'prestige' attaching to a country's having a steel-works (independently of the market for its products) or about the desirability of expanding an industry to make use of abundant local materials, again without any regard to the market for the product.

In what way, then, does the 'shortage of capital' thesis exaggerate the difficulties of raising the national income of a developing country? Put very briefly, the answer is 'because it ignores the possibility of raising output by making better use of the capital which already exists or of the new capital which is being introduced'.

Presumably nobody would deny the principle that output can be raised by making better use of the available capital; the proponents of the 'scarcity of capital' theory would be likely to assert that they took it for granted that everything possible would be done in this direction, both in respect of existing equipment and on new schemes. What seems to me important is that one should not take this sort of thing for granted. The rest of this article will be largely devoted to illustrations of the sort of improvements which are possible, the need to bring the same urgency to efforts to achieve this as inspire efforts to secure external capital and translate it into new factories or hydro-electric schemes, and to give some plausibility to the idea that the quantitative results from such a campaign can be of really significant importance. (The last point is, of course, one which can only be treated realistically when one is making a proper study of some individual country, and I hope that the illustrative examples of the kind of improvements which are possible will stimulate better-informed people to attempt that exercise.)

Let me start by one important methodological distinction. Although developing countries are frequently, and indeed rightly, said to be short of capital, nevertheless it is commonly found that much of the capital which they do possess is under-utilised for lack of adequate demand. This frequently applies, for example, to textile mills, and the same may be true of some roads, railways, airports and the like, where the amount of facilities which has to be provided for a service to exist at all is capable of carrying a good deal more traffic than at present exists. The same thing may also apply, for rather different reasons, to the capital which is locked up in stocks held by distributors, which would be adequate to serve as a 'reservoir' even if the flow of trade were very much increased.

In this sort of case, the level of utilisation would be raised almost automatically if demand increased; it is one of the benefits which comes with a general expansion and development in an economy that the wastefulness of having facilities which are under-utilised in this way is reduced. Sometimes, of course, the inadequacy of the demand to keep the facilities fully employed reflects the fact that it was unwise to install them – or to install so many textile factories, for example – rather than the fact that there is a good case for having a service – it is, for example, impossible to build a railway with less than one track. Even in these cases, however, a general expansion in the economy may reduce the seriousness of the initial mistake; and – what is the really important point for the present discussion – there is usually nothing which can be done to secure a greater amount of saleable output from the existing capital unless there *is* an increase in demand. This is in direct contrast to the second type of case, with which I am primarily concerned, where the low level of output from a given factory or other productive unit reflects inefficient utilisation, rather than lack of orders, and can be cured if, and only if, better methods of working are introduced.

This last statement needs amplification. Let me start by emphasising that the accusation of 'inefficiency' is, for this purpose, to be considered essentially in terms of the amount of output produced by the factory, rather than in terms of the number of workers required to produce that output. Western economists and businessmen tend to think of 'efficiency' so much in terms of *output per man* that an efficiency drive has come to be associated primarily with the introduction of methods reducing the number of men employed in running the factory. In developing countries, however, it is capital which is the scarce and expensive factor, rather than manpower; consequently, the emphasis in the efficiency drive should be on raising the output from a given amount of capital, rather than on raising the output per man. Of course, the result may be to secure improvement on both counts: if the number of breakages is reduced, or idle time (for men and machines alike) reduced by better co-ordination or quicker repairs, then output rises without any increase in the amount of capital or labour employed. But in some cases the raising of the output of the factory may require an increase in the amount of labour employed proportionate (or even perhaps more than proportionate) to the increase in output.

Where machines are scarce and men are plentiful, it may well be in the national interest to do this. To take a very simple example, the introduction of a second or third shift will raise the daily output from the factory, and this increase is obtained without any additional capital, by making better and fuller use of capital which already exists. By making the plant work for more hours in the day – and the same applies to making it work on more days in the year – the national income will benefit, and this will very probably also be true of the profits of the proprietors, even if output per man-hour is rather lower on the additional shifts. The main counterpart of the increased national income will, of course, be increased payments of wages, reflecting the increased number of people employed – a clear case where efficient utilisation of the plant increases the number of jobs, rather than reducing it. (This would clearly not be the case were capital to be spent making the factory concerned as fully automated as possible: productivity would increase but employment opportunities would contract sharply.) The initial difficulties involved in organising the extra shifts – ranging from the social problems of night-work to the difficulty of securing a supervisor for the extra shift whom the employer can trust and perhaps the installation of artificial lighting – should not be allowed to outweigh the important continuing benefits.

The introduction of multiple shifts is perhaps the easiest and biggest single method of raising output from capital which is already available. Nevertheless, at least as much importance should be attached to the detailed and continuing review of operations to see how a better output can be secured. This may make all the difference to the speed with which a country's economy can be developed, because an increase in output through better utilisation of existing plant may render it unnecessary to devote capital to building more plants in that industry. There may be particularly great scope for this when a virtually new industry is in process of being introduced to a country, especially if it is one which requires a large amount of capital. If an African country, for example, is seeking to build up its own output of cement so as to dispense with imports, the increase in output required in the second five-year plan period will be attained with a much smaller allocation of development funds for building new plants if the plants installed in the first five years can be made to produce at 100 per cent of their rated capacity instead of (say) 75 per cent. This will make it correspondingly easier to achieve other parts of the plan; or it may even be possible (if development funds are available) to embark on a more ambitious plan, reckoned in terms of output and national income. It can never be repeated too frequently that the achievements of a plan should be judged by the outputs secured, and not by the amount of money spent on new plants.

The work of mastering the problems involved in getting the full output from a cement factory which has already been installed will, however, seem much less glamorous than, for example, the decision to build the plant, the announcement of its location, the laying of the foundation stone, and finally the ceremonial opening. Nevertheless, this rather humdrum task is an essential part of the whole process, without which the others cannot yield their fruits, and it should be a prime object of government policy to ensure that it receives at least as much care and attention as the others; moreover the people who successfully achieve it should receive corresponding credit and rewards. The task is not, of course, entirely within the control of the plant manager: success will depend, for example, on timely provision of necessary transport, fuel and power, production and supply of which will normally be the concern of other authorities; other authorities may also be partly responsible for the training of the necessary personnel in advance of the plant being ready. In both these respects one must stress the importance of advance planning and co-ordination. In a developed country, one can frequently take it for granted that there will be supplies of power and skilled labour, but in developing countries the problem must be examined in good time, and someone given the necessary power to take action.

It is perhaps worth emphasising that the principle of more efficient utilisation is very far from being confined to manufacturing industry, since this sector tends to attract such a large share of attention when development plans are considered. One place where most countries would find it desirable to introduce better methods, so as to raise the effective output from existing equipment, is on the railways. Where they are inevitably under-utilised for the sort of reason indicated above, the matter is not perhaps so important to the railways themselves; but, even there, if better working could enable trains to move faster, then the amount of rolling stock needed to convey the traffic would be reduced, because each locomotive or wagon or coach would do more journeys in a year – and this economy would be further increased if delays at marshalling yards, etc., could be shortened. Moreover, the fact that goods spent less time in transit on the railway would reduce the amount of the nation's capital locked up in 'stocks in transit', and the stock which industrialists or traders thought it necessary to hold in reserve in their warehouses would also be reduced.

The really important gains through better working of the railways come, however, when the expansion of a country's economy is increasing the amount of traffic to be carried sufficiently for there to be an apparent need to lay down additional tracks and enlarge facilities generally. If, in such circumstances, better working means more trains moving along a given track in an hour, large amounts of capital needed for expanding the railway system might be saved. In addition, of course, there will be all the economies of rolling stock mentioned earlier, particularly important in helping to obviate large purchases of extra rolling stock.

In most developing countries, however, it is probably true to say that there is more to be gained by the introduction of better methods into agriculture, with the object of raising output, than there is over the whole of the rest of the economy put together. This is a subject on which I am personally not well qualified to write in detail, but I would like to re-emphasise the point that increased efficiency in the agriculture of a developing economy should primarily be judged in terms of output per acre, rather than output per man engaged on the holding, or output per man-hour actually worked. To take a simple example, more intensive cultivation of the land may actually reduce output per man-hour worked, but the extra output is a real gain, especially if the additional hours are provided by members of the cultivator's family who would otherwise be underemployed.

There is, indeed, usually considerable scope for increased efficiency to mean not only increased output but also more employment. Thus the greater use of artificial fertilisers is likely to mean that more employment is provided on each acre of land, firstly because the fertilisers must be spread over the fields and secondly because the resultant larger crops will require and justify more work weeding and harvesting. Similarly, the conservation of water by means of small dams on a cultivator's holding, or the use of small wells, not only requires labour to construct them but also means that more labour will be used irrigating the land, and keeping the channels cleaned, etc. – as well as in weeding and harvesting larger crops. The fundamental objective is to increase output, but incidentally it provides more employment, and this may bring some benefits to the landless labourers.

The introduction of better methods into agriculture is an extremely complex process, which requires a special study of the problems arising in each country and indeed, often, in the various parts of each country. The only contribution which a general economist can make is to emphasise the fact that 'half a loaf is better than no bread at all', so that one should not relapse into fatalistic inaction in the face of a list of the formidable tasks which have to be tackled to ensure a complete solution of the problem. These are likely to range from land reform to better marketing methods (possibly based on a guaranteed minimum price, where uncertainty about prices seriously affects the incentive to the cultivator), and, on the way, one generally meets such 'insoluble' problems as agricultural credit and illiteracy. The problem of introducing better methods to agriculture will continue to be with us until all these lesser problems have been effectively tackled, but some important progress can usually be secured without solving them all. In particular, while it is obviously desirable that agricultural advisory services and all the other improvements should effectively reach all the cultivators, nevertheless a substantial increase in output can be secured with a more limited coverage: in most countries it is a fact (brutal from a sociological point of view but merciful for an output drive) that the greater part of the increase in output is dependent on the response of the relatively small proportion of cultivators who occupy considerably more than the average holding of land. Furthermore, where it is a matter of spreading knowledge rather than (say) land reform, there is the well-known fact, which all commentators can regard as 'merciful', that, if the larger cultivators introduce the new methods and manifestly raise the output from their land, then smaller ones will gradually copy them, so that the process will snowball.

A development plan which stressed the importance of the ideas set out in the last section might seem to be doubly unattractive on political grounds: not only does it emphasise the humdrum business of introducing better methods, rather than the exciting one of launching new enterprises, but it also concentrates attention on agriculture, rather than the more fashionable field of industrialisation. Manifestly, this article does not provide space for a full consideration of the rival merits of different types of development plan, but I would like to conclude by making a few brief observations arising out of this apparent paradox.

Firstly, let me stress the fact that my insistence on the importance of a drive for better methods is not in any way meant to imply that there should be no new projects, let alone no new capital introduced into existing ones. To some extent the introduction of better methods may require small amounts of capital to enable the new technique of working to be introduced, but in the main the approach via new capital and the approach via better methods are independent and additive: the only important resource for which they are in conflict is administrative time and drive. If external or internal capital can be secured, there will in nearly all countries be plenty of good uses to which it can be put; the trouble is that there will not be enough of it to give an adequate increase in output, unless the country also devotes considerable energy to improving the utilisation of available capital.

Secondly, it seems to me manifest that most developing countries should include some amount of industrialisation in their development plan, but again this does not mean that agriculture should not also be developed. The proportions in which additional output should be sought in agriculture or in industry must inevitably vary according to the circumstances of each particular country, and little can be said by way of generalisation. Even in the case of India, however, where the limits to industrialisation set by the size of the internal market are much less than those in other developing countries, the Third Plan is in fact looking for a very substantial part of the additional output in agriculture rather than in industry. In small countries – notably islands such as Mauritius – it is apparent that the limitations of the market make it foolish to introduce many kinds of industry, so that a large range of manufactures will continue to be imported.

Finally, where a country is anxious to diversify its economy rather than rely on the specialised production of, for example, cocoa, for the export market, there will frequently be a strong case for seeking an increase in the production of foodstuffs for internal consumption, rather than devoting all the available capital and administrative energy to introducing new types of manufacture. This will commonly require much less in the way of new capital expenditure for a given addition to the national income than would be the case if the emphasis were put on industrial production, partly because less capital expenditure will be needed for the costly and difficult process of transferring large numbers of people from country districts to the towns. Other arguments in its favour are that developing countries commonly have a rapid rate of population growth, which ensures a market for an increasing output of foodstuffs suitable for local consumption – and indeed requires that the output be increased, if a strain on the balance of payments is to be avoided; that there is often a great need for a qualitative improvement in the country's diet, which will be much more easily secured if the necessary products (e.g. milk) are produced inside the country, rather than being imported; and that the expansion of agricultural production of this kind can be done in relatively small-scale enterprises, which not only reduces the management problem, but also means that the output can be continuously adjusted to the demand, whereas for industry one often finds that the market is not big enough even for one efficient unit.

There is no easy universal remedy for the problems of the developing countries. Capital, the right use of capital and manpower in industry, efficient methods and additional equipment in agriculture are all urgent needs, but the developed world must not imagine that the mere giving of money, capital goods and technical advice will alone suffice.

11 Agriculture and the Development of West Africa

H. ISNARD

THERE are two alternative solutions to the problems of economic development in the countries of West Africa: industrialisation or the modernisation of agriculture.

It may be argued that successful development cannot be brought about by arbitrarily imposing methods from outside, foisting them, as it were, on people ill prepared to assimilate them. So if, on the other hand, success lies in renewing and strengthening traditional forms of activity which are inherent in the psychological and social make-up of these countries, there can be no doubt as to which alternative is to be preferred. Development can only be brought about by modernising agriculture – at least during the early stages when economic development is just getting under way. Progress is, however, slow and painful.

For a start, there are a number of retarding factors which are constantly increasing, so that the civilisation of West Africa almost seems to be essentially static.

One of the most powerful impediments to progress is the paucity of human settlement. The Sahelo-desert zone stretching from Mauritania to Chad has scarcely three inhabitants per square kilometre (7·7 per square mile). This density increases in the south in the humid tropical zone that includes the Atlantic coastal states from Gambia to Gabon, though it does not reach 20 on average (51·2 per square mile). Only Nigeria with 40 inhabitants per square kilometre appears well populated.

Bio-geographical conditions obviously play a large part. In some areas the climate is extremely dry, in others there are dense flourishing forests; elsewhere, barren soil. Everywhere numerous endemic diseases make the region unhealthy. And one can find equally important historical reasons. The black slave traffic wrought havoc on these regions and deprived them of tens of millions of young people. This awful depletion of manpower brought evolution to a halt and forced communities to fall back upon themselves.

West Africa has not yet recovered from this. There is an obvious lack of population. Whereas for the teeming multitudes in Asiatic monsoon lands industrialisation is vitally needed in order to rid agriculture of a paralysing excess of population, in Africa it would lead to a complete decline in agriculture by reducing what is already a barely sufficient labour force.

Also over the centuries, slavery and differences of demographic pressure between regions have set populations in motion across the virtually empty continent. To take but a few examples, there are the incursions by Saharian nomads into the countries of black peasants, the low infiltration by Peul sherpherds who came from the north-east and reached the edges of the humid forest, or the migration of the Bantus fleeing from East Africa. All these population movements only ceased, more or less, at the end of the nineteenth century with the arrival of the Europeans. The consequences are well known. Old races taking refuge in hostile environments such as Pygmies in the forests and Kirdis in the mountains all lead a precarious and isolated existence. As for the invaders, they are even today badly adjusted to their physical environment, and somewhat unstable. They make off at the least sign of danger. Colonial administrators discovered this when they tried to set up their systems of taxation, forced labour or compulsory forms of farming. In speaking of the peasant population of Africa one should not make the mistake of always treating them as rural societies in close touch with their natural environment which, after long years of contact, they have exploited to the full.

Strong political organisation would have been capable of embracing and ultimately integrating these populations, originating as they did from such different backgrounds. In fact the great black empires of Ghana, Mali and Surhai were feebly constructed and their successors, the monarchies and sultanates, simply created hierarchies within the ethnic groups by subordinating conquered to conqueror. Therefore the human societies of West Africa lack cohesion. There is a hotch-potch of individual units, each jealously guarding its own character-istic customs, language, religious beliefs and way of life. They are just so many microcosms, each one indifferent if not hostile towards its neighbour. This explains the instability and internal conflicts within the modern states which are still a good way from becoming nations united in their desire for development.

The ethnic groups that make up this many-sided African society are in themselves firmly integrated social structures. All the constituent elements are solidly linked together and, in economic terms, are based on the specific way of life of the group. Only by practising this does a group show its individuality, using the techniques and tools proper to itself. There is no shortage of examples. Thus, in the valley of the Niger the Somono and Bozo are fishermen.[1] But whereas the first will fish in deep water in the middle of the river, standing on canoes and holding large nets in a group, the others will catch fish in streams or flooded fields, using small nets, traps or harpoons. In the case of the Dogon and the Surhai, both cultivate millet but though the formers' fields are much bigger and better kept up, the latter farm more profitably by being prepared to travel tens of miles to sell their crop. The Marka on the banks of the Niger specialise in irrigated rice growing. All conscious of their ethnic origins, the Bambara will not raise livestock; the Moors and Targui believe they will be ruined if they cultivate the land; the Peul is convinced that his personal prestige and happiness depend on his owning a large herd of oxen.

Ethnic groups and patterns of life are so closely interrelated that one is lost if the other is changed. The Bozo fisherman turned farmer calls himself a Surhai. However, these changes only happen in a few individual cases. Most often it is a case of loyalty to one's group, traditions and techniques. To harm these is to harm the very existence of the group. The result of all this is that the African is generally lacking in enterprise and has none of the initiative required to adopt the innovations that bring about progress.

One must not, however, exaggerate this immobility. On several occasions the black peasant population has shown itself adaptable to revolutionary new ideas. Several hundred years ago it first overcame its taboos over food and learned to incorporate in its farming systems crops brought over from America such as groundnut, maize, manioc, bean and sweet potato. More recently, in imitation of European colonists, it turned to raising cash crops like cotton, coffee and cocoa with the result that it now controls the majority of plantations.

Evolution could come about even more rapidly if the new states make a determined effort in the struggle against illiteracy. I agree completely with J. K. Galbraith, the leading American expert, when

[1] Jean Gallais, 'Signification du groupe ethnique au Mali', *L'Homme*, ii 2 (May–Aug 1962).

he writes: 'Then comes the task of popular enlightenment. This enables the masses of the people to participate in economic activity. And it opens men's minds, as they can be opened in no other way, to new methods and new techniques. Apart from its cultural role, popular literacy is a highly efficient thing. Needless to say, it is also the mainspring of popular inspiration. As such it adds strongly to the desire for development.[1] Only education can open the mind to a knowledge of the outside world and provide a yardstick by which people can become conscious of their state of underdevelopment. Without this there is no desire to change things.

Yet, to achieve this, enormous efforts are needed. In the whole of West Africa less than a third of all children are receiving any schooling. In the Upper Volta and Sudan the proportion falls to 6 per cent. The majority of the adult population is illiterate.

Thus we can see how far the black peasant population still is from creating the socio-cultural conditions necessary to trigger off agricultural development. And all this is further aggravated by the fact that the economic conditions governing the working of the market are unfavourable.

Agriculture in West Africa consists of two sectors serving different markets: the subsistence farming sector and the export sector.

Subsistence farming is organised in such a way as to cater for the needs of rural communities, and basically all produce is for family consumption: grain (millet, sugar cane, bean) in the dry Sahelian zone; root crops or tubers (sweet potato, manoic, yam) in the humid Guinean zone. Practically every region suffers more from malnutrition and vitamin deficiencies than from hunger as such.

This kind of farming can only be expected to develop through the stimulus of financial gain. In other words, there must be a change from consumption of one's own produce to commercial exploitation of crops, a process which presupposes a demand from huge inland markets which must be towns.

The low level of urbanisation in the West African states is well known. On average, 18 per cent of the total population may be regarded as dwelling in towns, and this falls to its lowest point of 4 per cent in Chad or the Sudan. Nevertheless urban growth has given rise to several large agglomerations such as Dakar, Abidjan and

---

[1] J. K. Galbraith, *Economic Development* (Oxford University Press, 1965) p. 47.

Lagos, which have populations of several hundred thousand. This is the result not so much of the lure of more employment as the arrival of country folk hoping for an easier form of existence. In fact many of them remain without regular jobs, forced to live cramped up in wretched homes on the outskirts of town, on the fringes of the economy. Most of them are not consumers. They live, temporarily or voluntarily unemployed, on the produce of little gardens scratched out of waste ground or even on the roadside. The produce of this subsistence farming is also liable to find outlets in bulk in town markets. Nowhere is this 'urban agriculture' more widespread than in Brazzaville, for which it helps provide the food. Some of the produce crossing the Pool each day was even sold in Kinshasa.

At all events, the demand created in towns does not extend to more than twenty or so miles outside because of both the weakness of this demand and the inadequacy of transport. Vegetables, fruit and poultry are carried in lorries or bicycles or just simply on the heads of peasants. The difficulties of providing coastal towns with fresh meat are well known. The herds of livestock in the Sahelo-desert zone journey from north to south over distances of a hundred miles or more, at the end of which the tired and emaciated animals have lost some of their market value. It would have been better to use the cargo plane between Fort-Lamy and Fort-Archambault, where the livestock markets take place, and consumer centres such as Brazzaville, Libreville, Douala and even Angola. But the cost of transporting frozen quarters of meat is very high.

In order to make towns play a decisive part in the development of agriculture, all their citizens must draw from regular and remunerative work the financial resources needed to meet their food requirements. In this way they can become consumer markets, creating that huge, growing demand which is at the heart of the process of modernising rural life. In other words, there must be more jobs in towns.

How can this be achieved without industry, today the largest employer of wage-earning labour? Obviously, there can be no doubt that progress in the sphere of agriculture depends on industrialisation. However, we must avoid the kind of industrialisation artificially grafted on to a country, in which raw materials are imported and finished products exported, leaving nothing behind but wages for a small local labour force. This is what happened in the case of the aluminium factory at Edea in Cameroun, built on the Sanaga Dam which provides low-price electricity. What is needed is a form of industrialisation based on raw materials provided by the mines and agriculture of the country itself. Farming, particularly, can offer a number of products that might profitably be converted on the spot either for home consumption or for export. There are many examples of this process: cotton can be used in a textile industry manufacturing cloth which the peasant population needs; oil-yielding products such as groundnut, together with palm-oil, form the basis of a flourishing fat-producing industry making oils, soaps and vegetable oils; the food industry can use sugar cane in refineries and distilleries, manioc in potato-starch and tapioca works, pineapple for juice and tinned slices; forest timber can undergo the first stages of manufacture in export ports and be made into plywood.

This kind of industrialisation is, as we know, already under way in Senegal, the Ivory Coast and Gabon in particular, but it is not yet carried out systematically, and too much produce is still exported in its raw state and processed in the country that imports it. Nevertheless it must not be forgotten that this industrialisation is the way to initiate a snowball effect that in turn will lead to further development both in plantation farming from which industry draws its raw material and in subsistence farming from which it draws food for its wage-earners.

Thus during the initial, jumping-off stage we see all kinds of activity: subsistence farming, farming for profit, and manufacturing industry. This is not to say that the establishment of large-scale basic industry is to be neglected; merely that this should come after-wards when, after initial momentum has been achieved, it can benefit most from investment and the existing infrastructure and take firm root. For, once again, J. K. Galbraith is correct when he writes: '. . . the ability to use capital in any considerable volume is in itself the result of development'.[1] If capital flows in before conditions exist for utilising it, it will be ineffective and probably wasted. W. W. Rostow confirms this opinion by stating: 'Industry cannot be solidly based without revolutionary changes taking place in two non-industrial sectors; agriculture and the existing infrastructure and especially transport.'[2]

The whole produce of plantation farming cannot be manufactured by local industry. On the other hand practically the only outlets for certain crops like coffee, cocoa and fresh fruit (bananas and

[1] Ibid., p. 54.
[2] W. W. Rostow, *Stages of Economic Growth* (Cambridge U.P., 1960) p. 41.

citrus fruit) lie in outside markets. Thus it is absolutely necessary to export. Besides, exporting makes it possible to obtain the currencies which are indispensable for procuring equipment. However, international trade is subject to the laws of liberal economy and very often acts against the interests of the states of West Africa.

Commercialisation starts with the gathering of produce. In isolated areas this still retains the character of trading. Small travelling traders, either Dioula or Syro-Lebanese, go from village to village selling imported articles at a high price and collecting the harvested crop at the lowest available rate. The merchandise, passing from one person to the next, ends up in the shops of import–export companies.

The latter make substantial profits from their operations. In 1956 (and there is no reason to think that things are any different now), according to the *Economic Statistics for French West Africa*,[1] commercial companies bought for some 40,000 million francs C.F.A. produce sold again for export for some 67,000 million francs C.F.A., gaining thus a profit in terms of prices paid to the African producer of 43 per cent on unroasted coffee, 50 per cent on cocoa, 71 per cent on fruit and 100 per cent on oil-yielding crops. As most of these profits are exported, this kind of commercial parasitism obviously does nothing to facilitate investment in the regions in which it is rife.

A further aggravation stems from the fact that for more than a century, terms of trade have consistently got worse for countries exporting agricultural products and importing industrial products, and tropical countries inevitably suffer from this trend. Let us take the example of Brazilian coffee, which is very much open to world speculation. In 1929 twenty sacks of coffee would have bought you a Ford motor-car; in 1940 you would have needed 200 sacks and in 1962 new fewer than 260 sacks! In other words, development of plantation farming does not benefit the black peasant population. A growing volume of exports does not always cover an increase in imports of equipment.

On the other hand prices for tropical produce, which are extremely dependent on international trends, vary considerably from one year to the next and even from month to month in a given year. During the great crisis in 1929–34, the price of coffee fell by 63 per cent, cotton 67 per cent, rubber 73 per cent, palm-oil 81 per cent. 1958 was a particularly catastrophic year for coffee. Quoted in London at £288 per ton in June, it slumped to £187 at the end of the year. The

[1] Dakar, 1959.

slight recession in the United States in 1957 had the effect of reducing by at least $4,000 million the income that the underdeveloped countries earned from the export of their products the previous year. This figure exceeded the sum total of public aid of all kinds that these countries had received.

How difficult it is then to establish a development programme when the resources reckoned on from exports which are needed to carry it out are subject to such uncertainties and fluctuations!

This is made worse by the fact that former colonial administrations had very often been so foolish as to put all their eggs in one basket. Single-product plantations remain the general rule. In Chad, cotton accounts for 80 per cent of known exports; groundnut 75 per cent in the Niger region; cocoa 60 per cent in Ghana; oil-yielding crops 77 per cent in Dahomey; groundnut and its derivatives 90 per cent in Senegal. Statistics such as these illustrate just how vulnerable the economics of these countries are.

It may be argued that this vulnerability is attenuated for French-speaking African states that market their produce in the franc area at protected prices which are more stable and more favourable than international rates. This is true, but this market is so restricted that plantations cannot be developed to any significant extent without running the risk of saturating it very quickly. And these countries must be able to increase their export produce considerably if they are to be certain of getting sufficient capital for development.

The colonial powers at last became aware of this state of affairs, which did less harm to trade than it did to production. The English authorities set up marketing boards in almost every African territory under their control; the French Government followed this example by organising in its colonies sales co-operatives and compensation funds. All these bodies link the mass of small farmers and the large export companies, and their aims are to standardise trade procedure and to eliminate market fluctuations by buying harvested crops at average prices that are more or less constant from one area to the next. The new African states have retained these bodies, some have even developed and systematised them and added features to make them more effective. Take, for example, the case of Nigeria. In the place of four marketing boards specialising in the commercial exploitation of cocoa, cotton, groundnuts and palm-oil products respectively, four general boards have been set up to acquire in their allotted regions all the so-called 'controlled' produce, namely cocoa, palm-oil, groundnuts, cotton, beni seeds, sesame, soya beans and citrus fruits. Before the start of the buying season they announce the minimum prices they will pay. Transportation by sea and selling abroad are carried out by the Nigerian Produce Marketing Company Ltd, which is under the complete control of the general boards. The company hands over to the boards all sales returns from marketing its products, having first deducted its expenses.

A more radical approach to overcoming the costly hazards of the market is to try to open up trade with countries based on a socialist economy. Several West African states, notably Guinea and Ghana, have attempted this. Trade with the East is based on long-term agreements linked with conditions to allow better terms of trade. The agreements which Ghana has made stipulate that her cocoa exports are to be paid for in sterling (55 per cent) and products and services (45 per cent).[1] In addition there are credit concessions for building projected factories – a metallurgical plant for ferro-manganese, a reinforced concrete works, a tractor assembly plant, a pharmaceutical factory – all of which amounts to some £100 million to be paid back in ten years at an interest rate of 2·5 per cent in Ghananian currency, which virtually means cocoa.

Despite blunders such as the time when a snow-plough was sent to Guinea, agreements like this not only help to increase and stabilise terms of trade[2] but, above all, lessen the dependence of new states on their traditional markets.

Fear breeds wisdom, and Western Europe has fully appreciated the threat to its interests in this reorientation of Africa's trading links. One member of the Common Market Commission declared in 1960: 'To prevent Africa from drifting towards the East and China, one of two solid masses must be fashioned in Africa and a firm bond established between these and Europe. If a European and African community were created with firm economic and commercial conventions binding the partners, we would have a real chance of avoiding subversion in Africa.' Doubtless, in the speaker's mind one of these masses, perhaps the most important one, is constituted by the

[1] W. Schwarz, *Accra Daily Telegraph*, 5 Mar 1962. Quoted by Basil Davidson, *Présence Africaine*, XLV (1963).

[2] 'While world markets are undergoing depression, such agreements, which stipulate in advance a precise volume of trade at fixed prices, have a stabilising influence on the turnover from external trade in countries producing raw material' (*World Economic Survey* (New York, 1959) p. 84).

whole of West Africa. Setting aside any political ulterior motives embodied in this statement, it would seem that access to the large consumer market represented by the six E.E.C. countries would open up hitherto unknown export opportunities for West Africa, particularly as regards timber, cocoa, coffee and oil-yielding crops. Plantation farming would gain considerable stimulus from this.

At the same time, the formation of an inter-African common market could stimulate subsistence farming. The Balkanisation of West Africa into a number of states of different sizes, all independent and belonging to different currency zones, has held back trade between them. The African states formed from the Old French Equatorial Africa and French West Africa conduct barely 10 per cent of their outside trade with other African states, while in Cameroun the figure falls to 7 per cent, in Ghana 4 per cent and in Nigeria 1 per cent. And yet there is considerable potential for internal trade between such complementary geographical zones as the Sahelian zone which is suitable for stockbreeding, the Sudan zone that favours cereal growing, and the Guinean zone that produces rice, kola-nuts, root crops and tubers (potatoes, yams, manioc, taro).

If a powerful and continuous pattern of trade were established between different latitudes, this would enable economic development to spread throughout the whole of West Africa. In fact, there is a serious risk of unequal development that could generate some tension between the coastal and the inland states. The former have abundant resources such as export produce (coffee, cocoa, bananas), dense forests, minerals (bauxite, manganese), hydro-electric power, as well as a communications network of railways, ports and large towns. Thus their growth, relatively speaking, is already at quite an advanced stage. They can represent for the isolated inland states, confined to their agricultural and pastoral produce, consumer markets whose needs will go on increasing alongside their expansion.

Agreements such as the customs union between the former French Equatorial African territories or between Senegal, the Ivory Coast, Mauritania, the Upper Volta, Dahomey and Niger are just a tentative beginning to this policy of division of labour and economic integration without which West Africa would be simply a juxtaposition of weak states.

Thus we can see that the development of West Africa turns into something other than financial and technical aid for building spectacular new factories. It needs both an organised internal market for disposing of food crops and a degree of normalisation if not moral reform of international markets to make for regular commercial exploitation of the produce of plantations. Unfortunately it is easier to send credit and engineers to underdeveloped countries than to control the working of the capitalist system that is holding them to ransom.

12 Land Consolidation in the Kikuyu Areas of Kenya

G. J. W. PEDRAZA

INTRODUCTION: THE OBSTACLES

LAND consolidation, farm planning and resettlement are being carried out in many of the tribal areas of Kenya. There are, however, considerable differences in the methods employed in the various regions, resulting from the various traditional systems of land tenure, the degree of co-operation of the people and from climatic and other conditions. This article sets out to describe the problem only as it affects the three Kikuyu districts in which there is a general similarity of procedure.

Before the advent of the European, and indeed for many years afterwards, there was no pressure on the land generally conceded to be the preserve of the Kikuyu. All land was held communally by ten clans, whose elders had the power of allocation to clan members. Much of the land was under forest, which was, however, steadily destroyed as the people looked for more fertile areas to replace their exhausted patches of cultivation. The problem of an apparent land shortage emerged only with the rapid increase of population, resulting from the cessation of inter-tribal wars and the introduction of medical facilities and famine relief measures.

In the interval between the two world wars, and for some years afterwards, there were three major obstacles to be overcome before any real contribution to the problem could be made. The first, and probably the most difficult, was the suspicion with which the tribe looked upon any move by government affecting land. Land, to the Kikuyu, is a possession transcending in value even that of his wives and children. The process of conditioning the mind of the Kikuyu to the acceptance of better methods of agriculture, in its widest sense, was therefore long and tedious. It was aggravated for many years by opposition to progressive measures which emanated from political agitators and by the shortage of trained staff. All these difficulties have now been overcome to a large extent.

The second major obstacle which had to be overcome was the inborn conservatism of the peasant farmer, who was accustomed to the traditional methods of agriculture which had remained unchanged for many years. This difficulty has almost been overcome and the farmer now accepts the fact that he has much to learn, even though he, or to be more accurate his wives, may not relish the additional work entailed.

The third obstacle to progressive farming has been the system of land tenure and inheritance. It is only in the last few years that the leading Kikuyu farmers have accepted the fact that their customary laws on these questions constitute the most formidable barrier to good farming practices. Intensive propaganda and demonstration, together with the removal of subversive influences during the emergency, have resulted in a widespread realisation that the old customs must give way to modern methods. It is now probably true to say that a majority of the tribe wish to proceed as quickly as possible with land consolidation and to follow the advice which they receive on agricultural improvement.

THE CUSTOMARY SYSTEM OF LAND TENURE

It is perhaps best to look briefly at the customary system of land tenure and inheritance before describing the process of consolidation itself.

As stated above, all clan land is held in trust by the elders of the clan. They have the power to allocate any available land to a member of the clan if he is landless. In practice, however, there is now little land left for allocation. Land may also be inherited once it has been allocated. A third method of acquiring land is by purchase. Until recently, land which had been sold could be redeemed at will by the vendor, on repayment of the purchase price. It was, however, essential to abolish the right of redemption before consolidation could proceed, and this has been done by the African district councils of the three districts, acting on the advice of their respective law panels.

The traditional laws of inheritance lead direct to rapid fragmentation and are primarily responsible for the present condition of agriculture in the reserve. A man may have the right to cultivate 12 acres of land, which, in most areas, would, if properly farmed, be an economic unit capable of supporting a wife and family at a good standard of living. He may well, however, have three wives, to each of whom he allots 4 acres to cultivate on his behalf. Moreover, under customary law the area cultivated by each wife is divided between her sons on the death of the father. The son of the first wife, being an only son, would receive the full 4 acres cultivated by his mother. The three sons of the second wife would receive $1\frac{1}{3}$ acres each. None of these areas are economic units, but they will nevertheless be subdivided again on the death of the sons and as a result it is not uncommon for a man to inherit as little as one-quarter of an acre. Furthermore, as a result of other customary laws of inheritance, or through purchase, a man frequently finds that he has a number of fragments of land, often separated from each other by some miles, so that he cannot farm them properly however much he may wish to do so. Finally, insecurity of tenure, resulting from the great volume of litigation over land which was common before the declaration of the emergency, dissuades the farmer from improving his land. Of what use is it, he thinks, to improve my land when I may well lose it tomorrow before the courts?

The effort on the part of government officers to improve the standard of agriculture in the reserve has been going on for many years and has been attended by considerable success in many areas. It eventually became necessary, however, to attack the problems posed by the basic system of land tenure and inheritance before any further spectacular progress could be achieved. This called for agreement by the people to four major changes in custom. They were, respectively:

(a) the consolidation of widely separated fragments into one holding;

(b) the abolition of boundaries between different clan areas, where the requirements of consolidation make this desirable;

(c) the prohibition of the subdivision of land through inheritance below what is considered to be an economic holding; and

(d) the issue of individual titles, which are necessary to give security from litigation, but which will, in fact, also abolish the authority of the clan elders over land.

These principles have been accepted generally by the leading Kikuyu during the past few years. The majority of the population has also accepted consolidation of the fragments as being desirable, but it is uncertain to what extent the people have appreciated the full implications of land consolidation on their customary systems of tenure and inheritance. It is, however, unlikely that they will sustain any objections which they may have when the great benefits to be derived from the process become apparent.

THE METHOD OF CONSOLIDATION

Consolidation is necessarily a lengthy process. At present no legal sanction exists to authorise either its implementation or its end product. It is based purely on the agreement of the people concerned and is not carried out in any area where there is opposition to its introduction.

Land consolidation teams have been formed in each division of the three Kikuyu districts. Their composition varies between the districts, but basically they consist of a team leader; a number of recorders, or measurers, whose main task is to measure up fragmented holdings and to compute the total acreage held by each individual; and a staff of farm planners, who lay out each consolidated holding on sound agricultural lines. All these are Africans who are specially trained for the work. Apart from their specialised knowledge they must be honest, since the opportunities for corruption are innumerable in an exercise of this kind.

Choice of a consolidation area depends on several factors. While the emergency continues, only those areas which are co-operative are likely to be selected. Subject to this condition, it is essential that the people themselves wish to have their land consolidated, since the whole scheme is based on agreement and consent. It is equally essential that the people are prepared to practise good husbandry after consolidation is completed, in order not to waste the time and effort involved. Amongst other considerations are the acreage of the areas selected and the desirability of building up blocks of sufficient size to justify aerial survey at a later date.

Consolidation is carried out area by area, and these areas may vary in size between 1,000 and 3,000 acres. Before measurement can begin, the team must effect exchanges of land, so that the fragments of each man who is to be settled in the area to be consolidated are concentrated in that area. This involves a long process of negotiation, but it is hoped that the people will eventually themselves carry out these exchanges in advance of the team, as the desire for consolidation increases. The recorders proceed to ascertain and measure the boundaries and extent of each fragment, and the approximate total acreage held by each man is then computed. No attempt is made to carry out an accurate survey, nor is this possible with the staff and the time available. Clan elders and local people are co-opted to assist in determining each man's boundaries, and the team leader is responsible for settlement of the more difficult disputes which arise. Records are kept of the location and measurements of each fragment.

Whilst this work is going on, a staff of plane tablers make a topographical map of the area. This shows sufficient local landmarks to enable individual boundaries, and a soil conservation plan, to be inserted later, and includes contours at 12-ft vertical intervals. Although a certain degree of precision is required in the compilation of this map, there is no attempt at very great accuracy.

On the completion of these two concurrent stages, representatives of the administration, agricultural, health, education, police and of the other departments which have particular interests in the consolidation area, meet together to plan the future layout of the area. These officers are now in possession of a topographical map of the area, a record of the total acreage held by each man, information concerning the location of each of his fragments and the names of the landless persons.

The agricultural officer first draws in on the map the soil conservation plan for the area. This includes provision for the water consumption requirements of humans and stock, in the shape of dams and boreholes. The next phase consists of marking on the map the area to be occupied by the village. Choice of a suitable site depends on the availability of water, health requirements, accessibility and other factors. The size of the village is governed by the acreage required to house those who own 3 acres or less, together with the acreage required for a church, school, shops, recreation area, community hall, cemetery, medical centre and the police post. Further areas are also reserved on the map for tree nurseries, agricultural demonstration plots, coffee and tea factories and any other facilities which are likely to be required by any of the departments concerned. A road plan, designed to open up the area, is then superimposed. Finally, the total acreage required for all these public purposes is computed and is found by making a proportionate deduction from the total acreage held by each individual.

Representatives of the administration and agricultural department, together with the consolidation team and clan elders, are now in a position to put in the new boundaries of consolidated holdings, both on the ground and on the map. At this stage, close supervision is required to ensure that each individual receives land of agricultural value comparable to that which he has vacated. His consolidated holding must also contain a proportion of arable, cash crop and grazing land, to facilitate planning of an economic farm. As a general rule, allotments of under 3 acres are grouped round the village where the owners will have to live, and holdings of 3 to 6 acres are placed beyond these. Holdings of over 6 acres are placed still further away from the village. The object of this grouping is to encourage those with 3 to 6 acres to buy up the adjacent allotments in order to increase their holdings to an economic size. Those who own less than 3 acres contribute one-quarter of an acre to their housing plot in the village, whilst the landless are given a similar plot, for which they will pay rent to the African district council. The landless and the allotment holders will become the village artisans and shopkeepers of the future and will also be available to work as paid labourers on the larger holdings. In this way it is intended to absorb a large proportion of the surplus population in productive labour. When the allocations have been made the new boundaries are then agreed with clan elders and owners and marked in on the topographical map.

During the process of measuring up fragments, the team has already noted down the cash crops and other improvements for which compensation will be payable in the event of the owner being moved elsewhere on consolidation. A scale is laid down for all items which attract compensation. The rates given are not binding, but they nevertheless form a useful guide to all concerned. While they are seldom exceeded, they are frequently reduced, with the consent of the elders and the landowners concerned. Compensation is paid between landowners and the transactions are recorded at a specially convened meeting held after the consolidation has been carried out.

ENCLOSURE AND FARM PLANNING

Consolidation is followed as soon as possible by enclosure. Boundaries are fenced with the most suitable material at hand and, where necessary, are also planted up with seedlings, which will grow into permanent hedges. Immediate enclosure is necessary, both to give the owner an increased pride in his holding and to provide boundary marks which will show up on an air photograph. It is proposed that consolidated holdings should be surveyed by air at a later stage, preparatory to the issue of individual titles to land. Meanwhile, consolidation is followed up by a team who make an accurate survey of new boundaries. This forms the basis on which individual farm plans will be made.

Farm planning by the agricultural department also follows the completion of consolidation. In the early stages this planning consists of treating each feature as a whole. The general plan which has been adopted is that slopes of between 0° and 20° should become arable land; those between 20° and 35° should be bench-terraced and planted with cash crops, and slopes steeper than 35° should be put down to grass. This will suffice as an interim measure to raise agricultural production without delay. As soon afterwards as the staff position permits, individual and detailed farm plans are made in order to show the farmer the best division of his land between the various food and cash crops and grazing; the cycle of rotation for each portion and the ideal layout for the homestead area with adequate paths of access, paddocks and other improvements.

It is at this stage also that an assessment is made of the need of each individual for a loan to assist him in developing his land. Loans of up to £125 may be paid from African district council or government development funds and these are repayable over five years at $4\frac{1}{2}$ per cent interest. The form of loan agreement contains, amongst other conditions, a declaration by the landowner and his heirs that the consolidated holding will not be subdivided below what is considered to be an economic size.

Soil conservation works are carried out as soon as possible after consolidation, since it is essential to follow up this initial work with measures to raise production and to show visible results to the people. Bush and unwanted trees are cleared and bench-terraces, 'cut-off' drains, spillways and narrow-base terraces are constructed, either by the people themselves or by paid gangs. The newly made terraces are then prepared for planting by the application of manure from village cattle sheds and compost which is made on the spot. A proportion of the wages of the paid gangs is paid from development funds and the balance is debited to the loan which the smallholder will receive. This is done in order to extend the life of development funds and of the available loan capital, and also to ensure that the individual makes some contribution towards the work done on his behalf.

It is hoped that it will be possible to arrange for two aerial surveys of the consolidation areas. The first of these would give the consolidation teams a map of the present fragmented holdings, with contours at 12-ft vertical invervals, which would be used for planning purposes. This would replace the production of a topographical map by the ground survey methods which are described above and would thereby release staff and so speed up the issue of detailed farm plans. The second survey would provide a map showing the boundaries of the consolidated holdings and would form the basis for the issue of individual titles to land.

THE SIGNIFICANCE OF CONSOLIDATION

There is no doubt that land consolidation and farm planning is of primary importance and urgency in the post-emergency reconstruction policy. It will, in addition, make a major contribution towards the resettlement of the Kikuyu because it results in the increased capacity of the land to carry the population and provides employment, as farm labourers, for a large number of those with little or no land, on the holdings of their more fortunate neighbours. Consideration is, therefore, being given to the staff and finance required to increase the rate of progress, so that consolidation and farm planning of the three Kikuyu districts may be completed within the next five years. Experiments designed to streamline the methods employed are also under way and these indicate good prospects of success. Additional funds required will probably be found by African district councils. Although the cost will be heavy, it would be inequitable and unwise to increase government contributions to this work without making even greater contributions to the agricultural progress of those other tribes which have remained loyal during the emergency. Financial considerations preclude such a policy. In order to lighten the burden, it has been proposed that fees should be charged for preparation of the farm plan and for registration of individual titles. This has yet to be approved and will require enabling legislation.

Considerable discussion has already taken place on the legislation required to give legal authority to the consolidation of holdings and to cover the issue of individual titles. At present, as has been shown above, the whole process is based only on agreement. Although local customary law gives some protection, through the power of the clan elders to re-allocate land amongst members of the clan, it is un-desirable that this should continue to be the only safeguard. This power does not, for instance, extend to land which has been pur-chased. It would, therefore, be possible for a man whose consolidated holding did not include land which he had previously bought to demand that the latter be restored to him. This would lead to a series of similar demands, which would produce chaos in the entire scheme.

It is clear that some form of interim title will be required to give landowners reasonable security of tenure pending the issue of a valid title. Without such security there will be no incentive to develop holdings during the interval which inevitably intervenes between consolidation and final registration. It is also probable that it will be necessary to limit the period during which the work of the con-solidation teams can be challenged after the new holdings have been demarcated. Legislation will, in addition, be required to prevent subdivision below what is considered to be an economic unit.

Land consolidation constitutes an agricultural revolution in the Kikuyu Land Unit and it will have the most profound effect on the lives of the people. The increased prosperity and purchasing power of the individual will lead to a higher standard of living and to a greater demand for goods of all kinds. The effect of this, and of other similar schemes elsewhere, which are aimed at improving the productive capacity of the land, will, in turn, have a profound effect on the economy of a country the prosperity of which will inevitably be based on agriculture for many years to come.

13 New Railway Construction and the Pattern of Economic Development in East Africa

A. M. O'CONNOR

IT is widely accepted that transport facilities are among the most important factors affecting the distribution of economic activities, and improvements in this field are often recommended as one way of tackling the problems of the 'underdeveloped' countries of the world, and especially that of the uneven spread of development within such countries. This is a serious problem in East Africa, and high hopes have rested on the substantial amount of new railway construction which has taken place since 1950. The new lines and some proposed further extensions are shown on Fig. 13.1.

Lord Lugard was expressing a widely held opinion when he stated in 1922 that 'the material development of Africa may be summed up in one word "transport"'.[1] Today views have been modified, but in 1956 Lord Hailey could still say of transport: 'There seems to be no other type of development which can effect so speedy a change in the economic and social conditions of a backward country.'[2] In recent years roads have come to be regarded as being at least as important as railways in this connection, but within East Africa it is still frequently suggested that railway construction will automatically bring economic development to the surrounding area. Thus a committee appointed to examine the proposal for a western rail extension in Uganda referred to 'the development that must inevitably follow in the wake of a railway',[3] and in the parliaments of the region similar words continue to be uttered from time to time. The proposition rests on the assumption that inadequate transport facilities are one of the main reasons for the underdeveloped nature of these areas. This was clearly expressed in a recent United Nations paper which stated: 'It is obvious that the general inadequacy of the transport

[1] Sir F. D. Lugard, *The Dual Mandate in British Tropical Africa* (1922) p. 5.
[2] Lord Hailey, *An African Survey* (1957) p. 1595.
[3] Uganda Protectorate, *The Way to the West* (1951) p. 15.

system has been one of the principal obstacles to development in practically the whole African region.'[1]

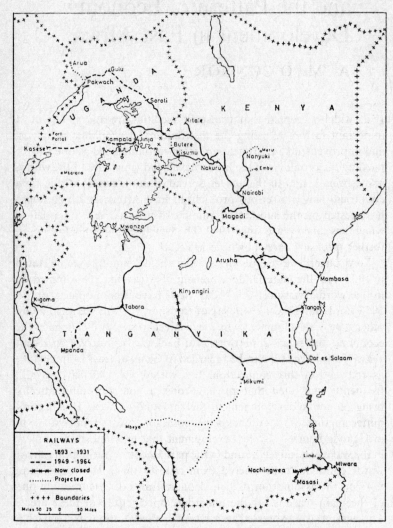

Fig. 13.1   East African Railways: reference map. The place names are generally those referred to in the text, and their inclusion does not necessarily indicate relative importance.

[1] United Nations, *Transport Problems in Relation to Economic Development in West Africa* (1962) 2.

However, very few studies have been made of recent African railway developments in terms of the part they are playing in the economic progress of the areas they serve. This paper examines the effects
of the railways that have recently been built in East Africa upon the
economy of the surrounding country, and indicates certain factors
which appear to limit these effects.

The establishment of the present East African railway network has
taken place in two main phases. The first line, leading inland from
Tanga, was started in 1893, and construction was in progress somewhere in Tanganyika, Kenya or Uganda almost continuously from
then until 1931. The most important lines were the Uganda Railway
from Mombasa to Kisumu, opened in 1902, from which a branch
into Uganda was later built, reaching Kampala in 1931; and the
Tanganyika Central Line built between 1905 and 1914. Little further
development took place until after the Second World War, but since
then railway construction has again proceeded almost without a
break. The main railways laid during the post-war period were the
Southern Province Line and the Mpanda Branch in Tanganyika,
and the Western Uganda Extension. In addition a new link between
the Tanga and Central Lines was opened in 1963. This phase still
continues, for during 1963 and 1964 work was in progress on two
other lines. In Uganda the branch leading north from Tororo to
Soroti has been extended to Gulu and Pakwach, and the Government
is anxious that it should be carried beyond the Nile. In Tanganyika a
branch is being built southward from the Central Line: how far it
is to go has yet to be decided.

THE RAILWAYS BUILT BEFORE 1931

There is no doubt that the earliest lines had a profound impact on the
areas which they served. The railway from Mombasa to Kisumu
played a vital role in the development of a commercial economy in
Uganda, and contributed to the concentration of activity near Lake
Victoria. It also provided a stimulus for European settlement in
Kenya, and guided its areal pattern. The distribution of commercial
agriculture in Kenya still shows a close relationship to the main railway and the branches leading from it. Nairobi, the capital of the
country, began as a railway camp, while the other three largest
towns, Mombasa, Nakuru and Kisumu, all lie along the course of
the original Uganda railway. In Tanganyika also the pattern of

commercial activity is clearly related to the rail facilities provided in the early part of this century.

The striking effects of the early railways are often quoted as evidence that the construction of new lines today will stimulate economic growth in the areas through which they pass. Thus, with reference to a rail extension into southern Tanganyika, the East Africa Royal Commission observed that while it would not prove an economic proposition at first, 'it must be remembered that the same can be said of the Kenya and Uganda railway without which both Kenya and Uganda would today be in an entirely primitive state'.[1] This surely overstates the case, but even if it were entirely acceptable it would be important to consider whether conditions have altered over the past fifty years, and also whether they differ from one area to another.

The existence of such differences is suggested by the fact that the extension of the railway into Uganda had much less effect on that country than had the earlier construction in Kenya. Economic activity is concentrated in the south-eastern part of Uganda, served by the railway, but this pattern became established before the main line reached the country, and at a local level there is no concentration of activity along the railway. The contrast between the two countries is in part related to the circumstances in which each was provided with rail facilities. In Kenya the railway preceded the establishment of a commercial economy, and it was the only means of transport available at that time. In Uganda the service across Lake Victoria to Kisumu had already provided the basis for external trade, while during the 1920s motor transport began to play an important role in the local haulage of goods. Any assessment of the likely impact of a new railway must, therefore, take into account the nature of existing communications.

Both Kenya and Uganda are primarily agricultural countries, but they differ greatly in the extent to which large-scale enterprise enters into agriculture. The establishment of European farms and estates in Kenya involved a conscious choice of location, and any slight advantage to be gained from a site near the railway could influence the choice. Such enterprises depend on a high output at a relatively low profit margin, and are therefore greatly concerned with transport costs. They are also often self-sufficient in respect of marketing, and are thus in a position to benefit directly from proximity to rail

[1] East Africa Royal Commission, 1953–5, *Report* (1955) p. 344.

facilities. In Uganda, where development has been based almost entirely on peasant production, the farmers have not normally selected a particular site for their farm. Their profit margins may be large but their turnover is very small, so that transport costs are of less concern. The main cash crops have to be processed before export, while the farmers are dependent on traders in the towns for marketing other crops and so they are not themselves in a position to use the railway.

It might be noted that the only railway built in Kenya to serve an area of African settlement, that from Kisumu to Butere, has had no greater effect on the distribution of economic activities than those in Uganda. There is no obvious differences between the country beside this line and that thirty or forty miles away. It is also perhaps significant that the emerging pattern of African cash-crop production in Kenya shows little relationship to the railway system. Coffee is the chief crop, and the districts with the largest acreages in 1962 were Meru, Embu and South Nyanza, none of which is served by railways.

Tanganyika will receive more attention later, for it has been the scene of much of the recent construction. It is sufficient here to say that it falls between Kenya and Uganda in many respects. European settlement has been concentrated to some extent in the Southern Highlands despite the fact that these are not served by a railway; but partly for this reason much less settlement has taken place than in Kenya. The two main lines certainly affect the distribution of sisal, the leading export of the country, which is an estate crop. But a later line from Manyoni to Kinyangiri, built to assist peasant agriculture, had almost no impact, and was closed in 1947.

The changes which took place in East Africa as a whole between 1901 and 1931 have been further accentuated in more recent years. In particular, the road network has been greatly improved, so that there are now few areas which are entirely lacking in modern communications. There has also been a substantial rise in the prices of both exports and imports, while transport costs by both rail and road have risen much less. Transport costs are, therefore, a less significant factor in economic activity than in the past. The cost of moving cotton 200 miles by road now represents only 2 per cent of its value. Economic development in all three countries still depends heavily on agriculture, especially in the poorer parts of each country: today this must take the form of peasant production almost everywhere. The emphasis is on crops such as *arabica* coffee and tea, which are of high value, and which bring very nearly the same return to the farmer in areas near to and far from a railway.

These considerations suggest that the example of the railway built across Kenya sixty years ago may not be of great relevance to the question of railway construction in East Africa today. It is perhaps more important to examine the effects of the railways that have been built more recently.

THE TANGANYIKA SOUTHERN PROVINCE RAILWAY

The railway from Nachingwea to Mkwaya in southern Tanganyika was built in 1949, and extended to a new deep-water port at Mtwara in 1954. Its construction was related to the infamous groundnut scheme, but when this was largely abandoned the railway was retained in the hope that it might stimulate other forms of economic development in the area. It was considered that 'in economic potential the Southern railway dominates every other project in Southern Province because of the development which may follow it'.[1] There is undoubtedly scope for much expansion of agriculture in the area, and transport problems have generally been cited as the chief factor hindering this.[2] Yet the railway failed to have any appreciable impact, and while traffic estimates made in 1953 anticipated 121,000 tons of freight in 1956 and 242,000 tons in 1960,[3] the figures for those years were in fact 32,043 tons and 25,056 tons respectively.

Some economic development took place between 1949 and 1957, but at a slower rate than in most other parts of Tanganyika; and since 1958 some ground has been lost. Cashew nuts form the chief cash crop, and production has expanded greatly in the past fifteen years: but the expansion has been no greater in the area near to the railway than elsewhere, and the 7,747 tons railed in 1960 compared with a total export from the Southern Province of 30,000 tons. At first the railway assisted an export of grains, but from 1956 onwards this traffic steadily declined. Sisal is an important export crop from the province, but by 1949 the period of sisal planting was largely over, and the Southern Railway did not stimulate the establishment of new estates beside it. The effects on local trade were equally dis-

---

[1] Tanganyika, *Review of Development Plans in Southern Province* (1953) 41–2.

[2] For example, I. S. Van Dongen, *The British East African Transport Complex* (1954) pp. 71–2.

[3] East African Railways and Harbours files, Nairobi.

appointing, for by 1958 there were still no signs of any development at the Nachingwea railhead. A branch was then laid to Masasi, the chief township of the area: but although this could have provided a nucleus for trade development, none occurred there either.

It has often been said that although the groundnut scheme was a failure, it left Tanganyika with certain assets, among which was the Southern Province Railway.[1] In fact the line was a severe liability. In 1961 the earnings of £45,154 compared with an expenditure of £290,113, and the total losses between 1954 and 1961 amounted to £1·7 million. It was then clear that no dramatic improvement could be expected, and in June 1962 the line was closed. A sad chapter in the story of East African Railways was also closed, but it is important that its lessons should be remembered.

Various factors contributed to the small effect of the railway in an area with a physical environment which compares favourably with that in other more developed parts of the country, and with a density of population well above the average for Tanganyika. The most important were probably the traditional concentration of trade at the port of Lindi, which was not served by the railway, and the improvement of road transport facilities. Having become firmly established at Lindi, merchants were reluctant to move to the new port at Mtwara, while new traders hesitated to come into the area until signs of trade development were apparent. Around 1949 the road from Masasi to the coast was very poor, and passable for only seven months in the year. But the opening of the railway coincided with a period of road improvements: ten years later lorry transport was usually available, and for some commodities the rates charged were no higher than those by rail. As a result many goods were carried along the road running parallel to the railway, and of the 34,000 tons of cargo received at the ports of Lindi and Mtwara in 1960, less than 2,000 tons moved inland by rail.

There is reason to suppose that a more fundamental cause of the lack of development around the railway is the fact that it did not offer any real attraction to agricultural or business enterprise, and that no development was likely unless the government took action to exploit the opportunities it provided. Inadequate transport facilities may not in fact be the main problem in this area, and if this is the case their improvement could not be expected to stimulate new development.

[1] For example, L. D. Stamp, *Africa, a Study in Tropical Development* (1953) p. 424.

THE MPANDA LINE

The Mpanda Branch was built in 1950 primarily to assist the exploitation of a lead deposit. Unfortunately, the deposit proved smaller than originally thought, and the mine had to be closed in 1961. Since lead accounted for over half the total traffic, the line has subsequently been operated at a substantial loss, and its future is in doubt. The volume of traffic handled in 1963 amounted to 9,320 tons, compared with about 28,000 tons in 1960.

For most of its length the line passes through almost uninhabited country, which is infested by tsetse fly, but which has a relatively reliable rainfall of 30 to 40 in. and offers some scope for agriculture. The railway has no impact on this area. There is only one intermediate station, and the freight traffic handled there is under 100 tons a year. There is more settlement around the terminus, but the economy is still predominantly of a subsistence nature. The railway assists some export of maize, and sales from Mpanda rose from 1,200 tons in 1951 to 5,000 tons in 1954; but they have not increased any further. As yet no new crops have been established in the area. Some cattle from Ufipa are now railed to Dar es Salaam, but the trade amounts to only about 2,500 head a year. There was a marked expansion of retail trade in Mpanda after 1950, but this seems to have been related more to the mine than to the railway, for many of the traders have now left.

The railway has not as yet had any lasting effect on the Mpanda district, and if it is not to prove a serious liability and to suffer the same fate as the Southern Province Line, some positive action must be taken to encourage new economic activity in the area. The East Africa Royal Commission observed that 'examples of the stimulus given by railways are to be seen in the Uganda railway, the recently-constructed Southern Province Line in Tanganyika and the branch from the Central Line of that Territory to the Mpanda minefields. In all of these instances railways originally built for purposes other than the stimulation of African peasant farming have, in the event, had this result; and a similar one may confidently be anticipated from the current extension of the Uganda section of the railway to Lake George.'[1] Again, railways of 1902 and 1950 are bracketed together; while the picture presented of the more recent lines is not confirmed by assessment over a longer period.

[1] East Africa Royal Commission, *Report*, p. 260.

THE WESTERN UGANDA EXTENSION

This extension was built primarily to serve the copper mine at Kilembe, in the foothills of the Ruwenzori. It forms a continuation of the main line from the coast to Kampala, and was built between 1951 and 1956. It has been more successful than the lines considered above in terms of both traffic handled and its effect on economic development. It was essential to the development of the Kilembe mine, which is making a valuable contribution to the Uganda economy since copper now ranks third among the country's exports. The line has also shown a small profit in some years in terms of current receipts and expenditure. The long-term prospects are less bright, however, for the known reserves of copper are sufficient to permit mining at the present rate only until 1971, and the copper traffic accounts for half the ton-mileage of freight on the extension. Since the railway represents an investment of over £5 million, its success as an agent encouraging economic activity cannot be accepted solely on the basis of an industry with a life expectancy of only fifteen years.

When approval was given for the construction of the line, the decision was based on the report of an economic survey committee, which forecast a tremendous impact on the whole economy of western Uganda. Since their highly optimistic forecasts were made for the years 1955 and 1960, it is perhaps not too early to make an interim assessment of the line. The committee considered that 'the impact of the line upon south-west Uganda will be immeasurable',[1] and that 'perhaps the greatest contribution of this line to Uganda will be the opening up of spacious tracts of new country'.[2]

These hopes have not so far been fulfilled. In the first sixty miles westward from Kampala the railway passes through fertile and settled country, and it has carried some agricultural traffic: but it has had no significant effect on the area, and no differences have developed between places close to the line and those far from it. The very sparsely populated area farther west suffers from low and unreliable rainfall, and is suited only to grazing. This has been hindered, however, not by transport problems, but by the presence of tsetse fly. For the last sixty miles the extension passes through potentially more productive country, and it is there that it was

[1] *The Way to the West*, p. 15.
[2] Ibid., p. 11.

expected to have most effect by 'opening up' the country. It has become clear, however, that the railway provides little attraction for peasant settlement, since the peasants are dependent on traders for the sale of their produce and for their supplies, and traders show no interest in going to an almost uninhabited area.

Even at the terminus of the line, where plans were drawn up for a town of 15,000 to 20,000 people, little development has taken place. The plans have been scrapped, and some of the rail sidings provided for a large industrial area have been taken up. 'A township at Kasese that may eventually be third only to Kampala and Jinja in size'[1] now seems a very remote prospect. A few small shops have been built at Kasese, together with three warehouses to handle Congo transit traffic, but there are no signs of its even rivalling the small town of Fort Portal as the trade centre of Toro District. The assumption that a railhead function is sufficient to draw trade and industry to a township has proved to be as unjustified in Uganda as in southern Tanganyika. In fact supplies for much of Toro, and in some cases even for Kasese, are brought from Kampala by road.

The railway might have had more effect on the surrounding country if it had been built through the more populated parts of western Uganda: but it was built along a belt of almost uninhabited country, taking the most direct course towards Kilembe, and it passes through none of the towns of the area. This has substantially reduced its significance, since trade is strongly focused on the headquarters of each district, and from each of these towns a long haul is required to reach a station. It was felt that the present alignment offered a positive advantage in that it would encourage the settlement and development of an area where resources were not being tapped. The economic survey committee declared that 'in a very short time new trading centres would undoubtedly spring up around all station sites, and grow rapidly'.[2] Yet by 1964 there was still nothing more than two tiny stores at any of the station sites, apart from the terminus.

The railway was also expected to be of value by carrying more cheaply the traffic already moving to and from western Uganda. However, the level of traffic other than from Kilembe has been far below even the estimates of what it would have been if the line had been in existence in 1950, for little traffic has been transferred to it from the roads. The Congo has been an important source of traffic

---

[1] Ibid., p. 16.   [2] Ibid., p. 16.

as expected, but a large amount of Congo traffic still moves by road
to and from Kampala rather than Kasese.

The disappointing results may be attributed partly to changing
circumstances over the past decade. The main change is exemplified
by the statement that 'the ultimate dependence of Ankole and
Kigezi on this line cannot be overstressed, for there is likely to be
little help from elsewhere in any future which can be foreseen'.[1]
Help has in fact been provided by the expansion of road transport,
with the result that the line has carried no imports to these districts
and hardly any of their export traffic. At the same time adequate
new feeder roads to the railway have not been provided.

Another important factor has been the structure of production
and trade in the area. Cotton, coffee and tea are the chief export
crops, of which the first two are grown by peasant farmers. Cotton
marketing is so organised that transport costs do not affect the
producer, who is paid a uniform price wherever his farm may be
located. There is thus no reason why the provision of rail facilities
should stimulate increased cotton cultivation. The coffee has to be
sent to a curing works before shipment, and it is then bought at a
standard price by the Coffee Marketing Board which pays all transport costs from a central fund. Only in the case of tea are differences
in transport costs felt by the producers. They could be quite significant since most tea is grown on estates, but this crop is of such value
that the saving effected by railing it at Kasese rather than Kampala
amounts to under 0·5 per cent of its value. The import trade of western
Uganda is mainly in the hands of Asian merchants operating on a
very small scale. Most are prepared to use road transport rather
than rail even when higher rates are charged, because of its speed
and flexibility, while many operate their own lorries and are unwilling to patronise the railway at the expense of their own transport
business.

While the assessment of the effects of a railway after only eight
years is open to criticism, it is important to note that the forces
limiting the role of the line show no signs of weakening. Until 1963
coffee produced west of Kampala was exported through stations on
the extension, but now all has to be graded in Kampala and this
traffic has been lost. No improvements to the feeder roads are
planned: the current road developments can only reduce the impact
of the railway, for the tarring of the Kampala–Mbarara road was

[1] Ibid., p. 11.

completed in 1962, and future plans envisage similar improvement westwards from Mbarara and also on the Kampala–Fort Portal road. In view of this it seems particularly important that active steps should be taken to promote development to make use of the railway, if it is not to be a liability when the Kilembe copper resources are exhausted.

CONCLUSIONS

The available evidence suggests that in the three areas examined closely in this paper transport problems have not formed the chief hindrance to economic development. The provision of rail facilities has made little difference to the local economy in each case. The present situation in East Africa is very different from that prevailing sixty years ago: few areas remain to be opened up in the sense in which the phrase was used at that time, since this has generally been done by roads. A new railway will not automatically stimulate development in an area already served by road transport, especially where the local economy is based on peasant agriculture.

It is interesting to note that no great local impact seems to have been anticipated for the new link joining the Tanga and Central Lines, or for the short Jinja–Busembatia cut-off. There was no need to make such claims for these lines since both were fully justified in terms of railway operating alone. The former in fact passes through an area offering considerable scope for agricultural development and very poorly served by roads.

The situation is different in the case of the recent extension into northern Uganda. This line was built primarily to replace an outdated steamer service rather than to provide transport facilities where none had existed before; and a report on the proposal to build this line was much more cautious about its likely impact than that on the western extension.[1] But those who later approved the proposal claimed that 'there is a lot of land there lying idle, requiring development, for the want of the railway'[2] and that the line 'will result in increased production of cotton and other crops'.[3] It is difficult to see why cotton production should increase when all growers receive a standard price, while it is by no means obvious

---

[1] Uganda Protectorate, *Northern Communications* (1956).

[2] Uganda Protectorate, *Report on the Proceedings of Legislative Council* for 30 Jan 1961.

[3] Ibid.

what other crops the railway is likely to handle. The traders of northern Uganda show little interest in the line, and claim that road transport was equally satisfactory for them. This relatively poor part of Uganda would benefit from the establishment of some local industries, but while the railway makes this more feasible it also helps the concerns in the more advanced areas to supply the north more easily.

The writer believes that rail transport is playing a role of very great importance in the economy of East Africa, and that new construction could be of value in the economic development of the less accessible parts of the region through the new opportunities it offers. It is essential, however, that action should be taken to make use of these, and new railways will be of most value if they form part of an integrated development programme in which problems other than bulk transport facilities are tackled at the same time. The provision of local marketing facilities, of local roads to reduce the burden of headloading, and of financial assistance for agricultural settlement are examples.

The main proposal for rail construction in East Africa over the next few years is for an extension into the Kilombero Valley and possibly on to the southern highlands in Tanganyika. Zambia's search for a new outlet to the sea has brought renewed interest in the idea, which was investigated at length some years ago.[1] In Tanganyika it is hoped that such a railway would do much more than provide an outlet for Zambia, for there is abundant scope for the expansion of agricultural production in the areas through which it would pass. There are also local coal and iron deposits which cannot be exploited without bulk transport facilities. It is doubtful whether a railway alone would bring development, but as part of a comprehensive plan it might be of great value.

Various other parts of East Africa, such as the Kisii and Meru Districts of Kenya, could benefit from new railway extensions. Some goods now moving to and from them by road would then move by rail, which is still generally cheaper. Some forms of production, especially of such low-value commodities as maize, might become more attractive. Nevertheless, development is already taking place in areas such as these, and the building of a railway cannot now be expected to make a great difference to them. Except perhaps

[1] Sir Alexander Gibb and Partners, *A Development Survey for the Central African Rail Link* (1952).

at the local level, inadequate transport facilities do not constitute one of the major problems facing the countries of East Africa.

These conclusions relate specifically to East Africa, but it is possible that they may have some relevance to other parts of the continent where new railways are being built. In some projects, such as the extension into Swaziland, there is a substantial mineral deposit which cannot be developed without rail facilities, and which offers assured long-term traffic. In others, such as those in the southern Sudan where major rail extensions are in progress, existing transport facilities are much poorer than in East Africa, all-weather roads being almost non-existent. The railway being built to Maiduguri in north-east Nigeria is perhaps more comparable to those in East Africa. The decision to proceed with it was based partly on the view that 'the soil is ideal for the cultivation of indigenous foodstuffs, groundnuts and cotton, and the lack of a reasonably cheap and organised means of evacuation is the sole factor that has hitherto retarded expansion'.[1]

A geographer would not suggest that an examination of the situation in East Africa provides a basis for judging the likely effects of developments elsewhere. But it would at least seem worth while for the considerations noted here to be studied in other areas. It might then be shown that in different geographical circumstances rail facilities are a more decisive factor in the pattern of economic development than they appear to be in East Africa today.[2]

[1] Nigerian Railway Corporation, *Bauchi–Bornu Railway Extensions, Supplementary Traffic Survey Report* (1956) p. 28.

[2] A detailed study of the situation in Uganda is provided in A. M. O'Connor, *Railways and Development in Uganda* (Nairobi, 1965). The writer thanks the publishers of that study for permission to include some material from it in this paper.

14 The Form of Industrialisation

ALAN B. MOUNTJOY

INDUSTRIAL growth commences in order to supply a growing home demand and begins with simple processing of agricultural and mineral commodities formerly traded in their raw state. Such industries include milling, leather tanning, oilseed pressing, spinning and weaving, brewing and brick-making.

Generally the early processing of agricultural commodities by hand, and later by hand-worked machines, was to remove waste matter, or change the produce into a more edible form, or to one that could be moved or stored more easily. Gradually processing became more complicated and with the development of commerce and communications the handicraft stage began to give way to power-operated machinery. These changes became consolidated with the growth of a money economy and expanding demand which have led to the manufacture of consumer goods both for home and export and finally, in some countries, to industries producing capital equipment.

FACTORS INFLUENCING THE SELECTION OF INDUSTRIES

The nature and scope of various industries and the possibilities of their adoption in underdeveloped countries are influenced by limitations already mentioned: namely lack of skilled labour, lack of capital, lack of market and scarcity of foreign exchange. These impose restraints upon the kind, size and scope of the industrial development, the methods used, and the order of priorities. The dearth of skilled labour is one very serious handicap, imposing limits not simply on types of industrial activity, but also upon methods of working and the kinds of machinery introduced. Machines requiring individual operations of a comparatively simple level of skill are far more suitable than fewer more complicated machines each capable of a complex series of operations. Not only the operating but also the maintenance of the latter type of machine would be beyond the competence of practically all the local skill. The highly skilled engineer is a product of long training and tradition and plays a vital part in a modern factory; it will be a very long time before underdeveloped countries have such personnel in large numbers.

Another limitation is capital: it is both scarce and expensive and must be used to best advantage. The amount of capital investment particular industries require varies enormously. For comparative purposes, it may be expressed in terms of capital required per worker, and in Britain this varies from about £620 in the china and earthenware industry to £13,350 in oil refining. In British West Africa the initial amounts of capital per worker recently needed to establish certain industries included £550 for a canning factory, £3,000 for a vehicle assembly plant, and £13,150 for a cement works.[1] These high costs have to be borne in mind in selecting projects and it does not follow that those projects with highest yield per unit of invested capital are automatically the best. The returns of some projects, notably public utilities, are not to be measured solely in monetary terms, but by the fact that projects such as railways, port facilities and electricity supplies resemble catalysts, reacting upon other industries and making them far more remunerative. Further, some capital-intensive projects produce far greater output than many with a low ratio of capital to labour; thus selection in terms of low capital investment per worker in turn is not necessarily best.

The size of the market limits the division of labour and the inducement to invest and is therefore a further determinant of the character of industrial development. Here we are concerned not merely with numbers but with the size of the subsistence-only element in the economy, of the availability of export markets, and governmental policies regarding competing imports of manufactured goods. It is possible to satisfy the home demand for manufactures of many underdeveloped countries with surprisingly few modern industrial establishments and a smaller industrial labour force than is generally supposed. A single modern factory employing about fifty operatives could manufacture enough biscuits to satisfy the complete Ghanaian and Nigerian demand, and in Nigeria at present a singlet factory employing 150 workers supplies one-fifth of that country's needs. As we have seen, home demand for manufactures may be expanded if productivity in other sectors of the economy is increased, but where

[1] United Africa Co., *Statistical and Economic Review*, no. 23 (1959) p. 6.

large-scale rural underemployment prevails, industrial development needs to be on a very great scale to absorb surplus population, and is only likely to do this by finding export markets to supplement the limited home demand. Countries seeking success in export markets must extract the maximum benefit from low industrial wages, the one great advantage they usually possess. To obtain entry into established markets manufactured exports must be highly competitive in price and quality. Low industrial wages do not necessarily imply low labour costs, for this depends upon the productivity of the labour and the degree of skill. It has been estimated that wages in British West Africa are about one-tenth those of the United Kingdom, while the difference in industrial productivity, given similar equipment, averages one-third to one-half. Where wages are low and skill and productivity high, as in the Hong Kong textile industry, marked success has attended the penetration of export markets.

Problems of foreign exchange also throw emphasis upon production for export, for even if much foreign capital is available as grants or loans, subsequently interest and capital repayments must be made. Foreign exchange shortage means a favouring of activities requiring a minimum of imported machinery and using indigenous rather than imported raw materials; in other words it favours some emphasis upon labour-intensive technology and small rather than large establishments. Such a pattern of development is also favoured where labour costs (based on low wages) are low, for in this kind of operation labour costs forms a major element of total costs.

Theoretically, in examining the character of industrial development in underdeveloped lands, the classical doctrine of comparative advantage might seem to have substantial application, but in practice it may not be so, especially in initial phases. According to the theory a country will gain by specialising in the production of those commodities in which its comparative advantage is greatest, exporting those goods in exchange for ones where its comparative cost advantage is less. The theory underlines optimum use of resources and invokes international levels of cost comparison. However, a substantial body of industry in underdeveloped countries cannot be assessed in this way, for its products really do not enter into world trade (e.g. much food processing, building, electricity generating, and other utilities). Also we must remember that the pattern of comparative costs is not static; if it were so there might be very little industrial development in underdeveloped lands and established advantages of the industrial nations would be omnipotent. The reason why governments are so intimately involved is that they alone have the power to interfere with the play of forces in the market and to alter comparative costs in the home market by supporting and sustaining new industries through their birth-pangs and early years. A brief discussion of the role of governments in this connection follows later.

THE INFLUENCE OF TRANSPORT COSTS

The economic geographer is well aware that the interplay of certain factors such as value and bulk of raw materials in relation to the character of the end product, cost of assembly of raw materials and of distribution of the finished goods, amounts of fuel, power and labour required, all have a bearing upon the locations within a country of particular industrial plants. These factors also carry varying weight in determining the character of industry and the nature of the manufacturing that a newly industrialising country may successfully undertake. One of the most decisive among these factors is transport cost. Cost of transport makes local manufacture advantageous where heavy low-value raw materials are required and are available locally; also it is advantageous to set up local industry either on home or imported raw materials where the finished products are bulkier, and therefore more expensive to transport, than the raw materials. In these categories we may include cement, bricks and tiles, furniture and motor-vehicle assembly. Raw materials that vary little in bulk when manufactured are not much affected by transport costs, nor are those materials of such high value that transport costs form a relatively small proportion of total costs. In these groups we may include cigarettes, clothing, cotton and other textile materials. Transport costs would be similar whether raw materials or finished goods were imported and the high value relative to amount of raw material, bulk and weight makes exports possible.

On the other hand transport costs discourage setting up local industry where raw materials have to be imported and lose weight in processing, for this would incur freight rates being paid on useless waste material (e.g. pulp and paper utilising only two-fifths of the pulp wood, and iron and steel manufacture may be regarded as examples, but it should be remembered in the latter industry where more than one raw material is involved that a country may have some of the raw materials at sufficiently low procurement cost to offset freight rates on the import of the others). Also a country lacking good supplies of various fuels is discouraged from establishing those industries where fuel requirements are heavy owing to the high cost of transporting fuel.

This outline, in many respects oversimplified, should help to explain the general pattern of industrial growth in most under-developed countries, especially those not well endowed with fuel and ore supplies. A range of food-processing industries first becomes established, based upon local agricultural raw materials and proximity to market and freed from external competition by the perishability of the raw material – milk processing, baking, the canning and preserving of fruit and vegetables, and beverage manufacture such as aerated drinks and beer (where water is an important raw material). Then industries based upon wood, such as furniture-making, and those connected with construction and derived from local mineral resources: cement, pre-stressed concrete, bricks and tiles, sanitary ware, glass, pottery, crockery. Assembly industries follow, these being based upon cheaper transport costs of importing component parts assembled locally to make, e.g., bicycles, motor vehicles. These are the customary early industrial activities that arise, for their resource bases are either practically ubiquitous or, as we have seen, they are generally sheltered from competition by transport costs and perishability.

With these industries we find others appearing that have less substantial bases and sometimes more hazardous lives. These produce such consumer goods as textiles, clothing, footwear, soap, cigarettes. Unless there is the advantage of local raw materials these industries gain no advantage from the level of freight rates on raw materials against finished goods and are likely to be exposed to competition of mass-produced goods from abroad (often of higher and more reliable quality). The main offsetting advantage they have is low labour costs, but generally this is insufficient and these industries exist (and at times stagnate) beneath a protective tariff.

The industries listed above are the major ones established during the 'pre-take-off' period, generally restricted in character and scale by limited demand, capital, skill, public utilities, etc. However, these articles, which in many cases can be based upon indigenous raw materials, are those that absorb an increasing proportion of spending power as incomes begin to rise above subsistence level; consequently there is a considerable potential home market for them in all under-developed lands. A disadvantage worth remembering, however, is that for these very reasons every underdeveloped country is able to make these goods for itself. In these goods there is little scope for export, for, as we have seen earlier, world trade in these commodities is scarcely expanding. For countries that possess resources of fuel and ores the industrial path is likely to be somewhat smoother. Metal manufactures form substantial proportions of the imports of underdeveloped countries and command expanding markets in developed lands; consequently world demand for metal goods is increasing and export markets are more readily available. Absence of ores, particularly iron ore, places a curb upon the character and degree of industrial expansion. If fuel is readily available and wages low, some metal manufactures are possible based upon imported ingots, but generally they are limited to such items as nails, nuts and bolts, pots and pans, and simple agricultural implements.

The need for export markets has been stressed as being a key factor in successful industrial development of overpopulated underdeveloped countries, but the range of goods likely to be exported successfully is small, particularly so if ores and fuel are not plentiful. Transport costs now act in reverse and only favour goods made from indigenous raw materials that lose weight in manufacture. It is not feasible to use imported raw materials for export industries unless a great deal of labour and skill lavished upon them will materially raise their value (e.g. watches, instruments, high-quality ceramics), or where the ratio of value to weight is sufficiently high for cost of transport to be a minor element in the final cost (e.g. textile raw materials). Success in these activities depends especially upon low labour costs (generally present) allied with considerable skill and technical knowledge (generally absent); it follows that the training and education of the labour force needs to have a high place. Hong Kong provides an example of success here; her millions are supported by widely disseminated exports of cheap textiles, toys, electronic and transistor devices, etc.

INFRASTRUCTURE NEEDS

Advances in the range of manufactures by means of successful new promotions and the expansion of existing industry from workshop to factory character will depend essentially upon prior or parallel expansion of utilities, education and technical training: the establishment of what is now called the infrastructure. The provision of railways, power stations, harbour installations, schools, hospitals, in themselves large employers of labour, also serves to stimulate local industry, especially the constructional ones such as cement manufacture, manufactures of pre-cast and reinforced concrete, bricks and tiles, metal windows, pipes and tubes.

The considerable capital investment and the lengthy period of fulfilment required in establishing the infrastructure is now an accepted part of planned or systematic development, and reflects changing views during the decade 1950–60 when economic planning with the enhanced role of government became internationally respectable. A widespread experience in many underdeveloped countries was of industries mushrooming during the war and immediate post-war years and failing because their costs were too high and quality too poor or, despite this, surviving at public expense thanks to government support. This has brought home the realisation that industrialisation cannot afford to develop on a patchy and haphazard trial and error basis with misdirected and misused capital investment, but that first a proper infrastructure beneficial to all sectors of the economy is essential. Thus the closing years of the 1950s saw a variety of basic works being put into effect in a considerable number of the world's poorer countries. Afghanistan's first Five-Year Plan (1956–61) concentrated on education, the provision of roads, basic irrigation works and power stations. At the end of the period four hydroelectric stations had been built and three others were under construction, while two cement factories were constructed and coal mining began. Pakistan, under its first Five-Year Plan (1955–60), devoted 31 per cent of the capital expenditure to agriculture, water and power development; while India in her three completed Five-Year Plans allotted to communications and power 40 per cent, 38 per cent and 33 per cent of total allocations.

Among these basic works are iron and steel plants, not in themselves utilities, but nevertheless the foundation of a large sector of the industrial field. Modern civilisation is based on iron and steel and the establishment of iron and steel works is one of the most desired features of planned development, opening the doors to a great range of other industries, particularly those making heavy capital goods. Not every country possesses raw materials, fuel bases and transport facilities for this industry which, owing to very considerable loss of weight on fabrication, cannot be operated economically on imported supplies. A number of post-war examples may be cited where these economic factors have been ignored and iron and steel works erected for prestige or strategic reasons. Hungary's iron and steel town of Sztalinvaros, on the Danube forty miles south of Budapest, is such an example. It is a relic of autarkic policies and up to 1960 the works had cost about £200 million and had an annual capacity of 600,000 tons of pig iron and 350,000 tons of crude steel. Hungary has no iron-ore deposits and the plant obtains its ore from Krivoi Rog in the U.S.S.R. Four-fifths of the coal is Hungarian, but of indifferent coking quality, and is combined with coking coal imported from Poland. The economic soundness of the project is doubtful, but under a Communist regime this is not made public.[1] A project likely to prove more sound is the iron and steel plant being erected at Bône in Algeria. It is expected to cost £58 million and the output to be 500,000 tons of metal per annum. Here the country possesses the fuel and raw material supplies necessary for the industry; she is, in fact, a major exporter of high-quality iron ore. An under-developed country having the resources necessary for an iron and steel industry has much to gain from its establishment. A far wider range of manufactures becomes possible, cost to already established metal-using industries are lowered, foreign exchange will be saved and export possibilities created. It is unlikely that sufficient skill and management ability to run such works will be built up locally for a number of years, but even at very high salaries the hiring of foreign skill and knowledge (provided that these are passed on) is here a good investment. Great prospects for the future are opened up; as time passes and skills develop, engineering, the manufacture of machinery for factories and of other capital goods becomes possible, and also the development of chemical and fertiliser manufacturing industries based upon the by-products of the coking process, of particular value to agrarian countries.

Oil refineries also offer much scope for associated chemical and plastics industries, but these plants are very expensive and need highly skilled staff. There has been a swing away from the earlier location of many refineries at the oil field to sites nearer the larger markets for the refined products and by-products, as in Western Europe. It must be expected that full-scale refineries will not be established easily in underdeveloped countries, even if they them-

[1] *The Times*, 14 Mar 1960.

selves are crude-oil producers, until substantial home markets for their products arise, but basic refineries without cracking and by-product plants are now being built in a number of populous under-developed countries, including Gabon, Tanzania, Malaya and Costa Rica.

THE CHARACTER OF INDUSTRIAL DEVELOPMENT

1. *Labour-intensive policies*

Power plants, iron and steel works and oil refineries require immense investments of capital; they in themselves give relatively little employ-ment (i.e. the capital investment per worker is very high), but the output per worker is high and particularly beneficial to a very wide sector of the developing industrial economy. It is possible, however, that the return per unit of capital invested in such capital-intensive processes will be less initially than if the money had been invested in a greater number of other and more labour-intensive projects. Decisions as to the appropriate capital intensity in the industrialisa-tion of an underdeveloped country are of fundamental importance, since they will have notable effects upon the character and pattern of the industrial development. They will require early examination of the emphasis to be given to 'heavy' as opposed to 'light' industry and thus the tempo of industrialisation itself, for many experts consider there is an implicit correlation between capital per worker and the type of industrial output. In other words, there are not only capital- and labour-intensive *processes* but also capital- and labour-intensive *industries*. Labour-intensive production is assumed to be of small or medium scale of operation and to make 'light' consumer goods, while capital-intensive production is identified with large-scale industrial production of 'heavy' or capital goods. It is sufficient here to remark that these are general concepts; the mutual relation-ships lack statistical proof, mainly because such data are scarce.

In many underdeveloped lands there is no shortage of labour, but the amount of capital likely to be available is limited. This is generally the reverse of conditions pertaining in the developed countries, where labour is scarce and capital more abundant. Industry there has become more and more capital-intensive; machines replace scarce labour, technology is introduced and an outlook quite un-suited to conditions in underdeveloped countries has developed. Here, then, we find considerable differences; it is clear that particular technologies in use in developed countries need not be taken over wholesale by underdeveloped countries, and in many cases they may be inappropriate. Where labour is plentiful it is extravagant to use capital as a substitute, although there is a case for it if machines can replace a dearth of skill (e.g. in textile, boot and shoe industries).

There is a strong body of opinion that where capital is limited it is better to spread it thinly in order to cover a greater labour force, in other words to place emphasis upon labour-intensive industries and methods. Here low labour costs can exert their maximum effects on total costs. By these means there is more development and a wider distribution of purchasing power among those who will quickly spend it, mainly (it is hoped) on consumer goods. Much of the labour used might otherwise be unproductive, and capital saved by the use of this labour can be used for the production of other goods and the employment of yet more labour. As a result total production and income will be greater than if more highly mechanised methods had been used. These views favour small-scale undertakings, between the cottage handicraft unit and the large-scale factory in both size and techniques. Other advantages claimed are that the volume of production from such plants is more likely to accord with the restricted market for the products (a few days' production of a large modern shoe factory would serve to satisfy the present effective annual demand for shoes in a country such as Morocco). Also small-scale industries making use of electric power are less exacting in locational demands and can be widely distributed and thus help to avoid excessive agglomerations of people in large urban areas, necessitating high cost of housing, utilities and sanitation. There is also the view that establishing small-scale industries is a natural first step whereby skill, technique and markets may be developed for subsequent large-scale operations. These policies are supported by Dr Schumacher under the title 'intermediate technology'. He also cites an important social aspect, that the development of work-places where people live and not merely in metropolitan areas will help arrest the flood of unemployed to the towns.[1] These views, of course, do not rigidly bar large-scale industry, but put most emphasis upon medium and small-scale ones, believing that they give more employment per unit of invested capital. A real danger is that little

[1] E. F. Schumacher, *Rural Industries*, in M. W. Clark, *India at Midpassage*, O.D.I. (London, 1964) pp. 30–9. See Chapter 15 below.

of the surplus product is likely to be saved for reinvestment and industrial expansion will be slow.

2. *Capital-intensive policies*

The opposite case is also a strong one, and is based on the premise that a cumulative increase in production and national income stems from ever-increasing productivity of labour. This increasing productivity can only come about through the adoption of increasingly efficient techniques and appliances, requiring heavy application of capital. Far higher productivity per worker is possible with capital-intensive processes (although a smaller return per unit of capital than with labour-intensive ones) and, if the profits per worker are continually reinvested, the net product will grow at a faster rate than that of the less intensive ones. This means, in fact, that while employment will be lower in the early years it accelerates rapidly and soon outstrips the initially higher levels obtaining in labour-intensive industries.

Investment should take as its aim the raising of productive capacity rather than the provision of the greatest number of jobs; with the attainment of one the other will follow. Higher productivity begets higher surpluses, allowing yet more capital for investment; thus an upward spiral may be envisaged. To this end emphasis on the establishment of capital-goods industries rather than consumer-goods industries is a further logical step, and some experts favour massive capital-intensive investment in basic industries producing equipment goods which later make possible a more rapid increase of consumer goods. Labour-intensive production lacks this self-accelerating character and with it an economy is likely to stagnate. Early Egyptian industrial development between the wars demonstrates this feature, while modern Indian planned development leans much more upon capital-intensive methods.

It is clear that both policies are vulnerable at some points and also that in any actual country (as opposed to theoretical models for planning purposes) the real decision concerns the proportion of the limited resources to be employed one way and the other. It is here that economic arguments may become subordinated to social and political policies. Thus we find the following industrial activities recommended by a mission to a heavily populated Asian country, their view clearly favouring labour-intensive industrialisation: rice milling, coir-fibre manufacture, cotton textiles by small-scale production ('The mission recognises that a fairly large and vertically integrated spinning and weaving mill would produce cloth more cheaply ... nevertheless other economic as well as social reasons make it imperative to encourage the development ... of small-scale production'), manufacture of footwear, metal-working industries including hardware, brass and aluminium products, ceramics, agricultural implements, building materials, galvanising and electro-plating.[1]

The influence of a social policy designed to avoid the creation of an industrial proletariat undoubtedly influenced the recommendations of other experts to a Middle East country. They urged the establishment of an integrated complex of small-scale and handicraft activities, and recommended that spinning, dyeing and finishing of cotton be carried out by factory techniques and that sizing, weaving and knitting be done by handicraft, cottage-industrial methods. To avoid the social effects of big agglomerations of industrial working population they suggested the building of three or four small textile units in villages some 15–20 km apart. With modern communications it was contended that they could be run as one big factory by one management and one technical service.[2]

Another expert to a different Asian country recommended capital-intensive industrialisation with particular emphasis upon large-scale capital goods and heavy machinery industries, and cited the country's economic position as justification. There was a satisfactory foreign trade position and no balance of payments difficulties, a high level of food production and a large reserve of manpower allowing development of basic industries without reducing production in other sectors. He rejected proposals for the expansion of cottage industries on the score that it merely disguised unemployment by means of social relief, since differences in the efficiency of production would involve subsidies to the cottage industries and output quotas on competing products of large-scale industries.[3]

Efficiency or output per worker cannot be taken entirely as a reflection of capital investment or size of plant, although a general correlation is discernible. Professor Mukerjee, for instance, has shown that from 1946 to 1949 there was an increase in capital intensity

[1] United Nations, *Industrialisation and Productivity*, Bulletin 1 (New York, 1958) p. 13.
[2] Ibid., p. 14.
[3] Ibid., p. 15.

in a number of India's manufacturing industries, in most cases accompanied by a rise in output per worker.[1] Studies to discover optimum techniques (capital- or labour-intensive) in various industries are only slowly being carried out, but it is clear that in some there may be room for combinations of methods. Further, it is not always necessary to introduce the latest European or American machinery or equipment, often very complicated and designed for very different settings where labour costs are very high. It may be uneconomic to take the newest machines; simple models – even second-hand – may give a better return.

Industrial advisers to underdeveloped countries are concerned with overcoming the technical problems involved in raising productivity in industrial plants, and it has been remarked that a general pattern emerging from their recommendations shows a ready resort to mechanisation. To technicians from industrialised countries faced with the task of improving volume, quality and uniformity of output and in reducing unit costs, this recommendation is in keeping with their experience. They are far less concerned with the social problems surrounding unemployment. However, as a rule modifications are possible and, while techniques may be up to date, the size, degree of capitalisation and specialisation in a wide range of industries will not for some time match those in developed countries. Some heavy industries, however, must be accepted with very little change: iron and steel works, chemical industries producing sulphuric acid, caustic soda, nitrogenous fertiliser need much capital and cannot be operated economically on a small scale.

THE ROLE OF GOVERNMENTS

This discussion has been designed to demonstrate the variety of conflicting interests involved in determining development targets, and the choice of means to achieve them. Social, economic, technical and strategic factors must be evaluated and governments must decide upon the tempo of development by means of their power of controls and emphasis upon long-term or short-term measures. To mobilise and employ all the forces available in the struggle for development requires that each government of underdeveloped countries prepares and puts into effect a general economic plan.

[1] K. Mukerjee, 'Employment and substitution of capital for labour', *Indian Econ. Journal*, 1956, p. 105.

The heart of such a plan is to procure the necessary capital in order to raise the amount of investment and so to increase productivity; utilising both internal and external sources. Given the capital, the plan should allocate proportions of it to the various sectors of the economy: transport, communications, power production; manufacturing industry, both 'heavy' and 'light', agriculture, health and education. In turn, detailed proposals for these should be made.

No underdeveloped country can hope to raise anything like the total capital it needs entirely from external sources; increasing quantities must come from investments and savings of its own population, and governmental policies become shaped to encourage and often to enforce this. The discipline of an underdeveloped population becomes most tried after the first fruits of development gradually appear. Expanding incomes lead to an increasing demand for consumer goods, and government measures designed to encourage saving and reinvestment attempt to damp down this demand in order to keep control over the development process. There is the further advantage that keeping demand for consumer goods in check allows for more investment and for the growth of the more expensive capital-goods industries. Some of the enhanced demand will be for imported goods, and this has the added disadvantage of affecting the foreign exchange position. Consequently underdeveloped countries invariably impose import restrictions in one form or another, and these have the further effect of working to protect home manufactures.

Policies of protection are frequently criticised, yet if an underdeveloped country is ruthlessly determined to dedicate its powers to development, such a policy becomes necessary. While the aim that new industries should pay their way is laudable, it should also be clear that these standards have less immediate application in underdeveloped lands where investments are being made that for a long period may be unprofitable, yet are necessary to create external economies for subsequent industries. Much early investment in manufacturing industry is on a similar basis: it would not take place if some protection or inducement were not afforded, for the disincentives to manufacturing at that stage are too great, this being the reason why the investments were not made earlier.

New industries in underdeveloped countries take some time to become going concerns; they must train their labour, which will affect both quality and quantity of production; they may have to pay high rates for services and power; with few other industries operating there will be few external economies; they may find difficulty in breaking into the market, probably supplied by imported goods, and may work below capacity for a considerable period. Not surprisingly, costs of production are likely to be high during this initial period and these industries are in a competitively weak position. All these difficulties should lessen as development proceeds and, provided there is reasonable chance that the industry will duly pay its way, there is a good case for protection or some form of government help.

The main justification, however, is that the very existence of these young industries is giving a substantial return to the developing state beyond the mere value of their production. It is generally true that every new enterprise improves the external economies of other concerns. The more factories there are, the cheaper can be the supply of gas, electricity, oil fuel, repair facilities, and the greater the expansion of the industrial labour force. Concentration as opposed to dispersion of industry particularly permits further mutual advantages in the use of raw materials, by-products, transport and other services so that a cumulative reduction of cost may be envisaged as development proceeds. The system of protection deserves criticism if it is given in an unplanned economy to haphazard industrial promotions that never become competitive, for the higher prices are a burden on the consumer and contract rather than expand the market.

The range of government help and methods that can be employed are very great. Frequently tariffs are levied on selected categories of imported goods, roughly in the form nil on machinery, low on raw materials, moderate on semi-finished goods and heavy on finished manufactures. Internal freight rates to and from ports and factories also may be adjusted on similar lines, with especially favourable rates for moving indigenous raw materials. Other forms of help may be as loans at low interest rates; subsidies especially to goods seeking export markets; exemptions from certain taxes for a stated period and, in some countries, preferential treatment by government order departments.

15 Rural Industries

E. F. SCHUMACHER

INTRODUCTION[1]

THE programmes included in the Third Indian Five-Year Plan 'are expected to provide employment opportunities for about 14 million people'. Yet the labour force is expected to grow by over 17 million, and there is a backlog of unemployment of at least 9 million, not counting the tens of millions of people who are severely under-employed. It is said that there is therefore an urgent need 'for increasing employment opportunities further' and that 'this will be partly done by expanding the programmes for village and small industries and agriculture'. It is thus immediately obvious that when talking of rural industries the authors are thinking in terms of very large numbers of people – millions rather than thousands; and it is equally obvious that this cannot be implemented by expanding existing programmes but only by a radically new approach.

The total employment effect of all programmes designed to help village and small industries, while an essential contribution to the rural areas, has so far been of negligible proportions when put against the country's needs. In the Third Plan there is the hope that 'small industries' will offer at the end of the period 900,000 additional jobs, not counting part-time employment. But there is nothing in current policies and practice to encourage the expectation that more than a small proportion of these new jobs will be in rural areas. Even if the proportion were 50 per cent, what is the significance of less than half a million new jobs in five years for a rural population whose labour force is growing at nearly 3 million a year?

Why has there been so little success in rural industrialisation?

The problem is obviously a peculiarly difficult one; but I have come to the conclusion that the difficulties might have been less formidable if policies had been based on a more realistic diagnosis. Even today,

---

[1] This paper was originally presented to the Planning Commission in New Delhi.

it seems to me, the nature of the task and of its difficulties is not sufficiently understood.

In short, there is a twofold need which, so far, has not been met:

(1) the need for a suitable technology; and
(2) the need for a suitable 'set-up' or organisational form.

TECHNOLOGY

None of the developed countries has ever had to face the problems which are posed in India today and *which arise from the existence and partial infiltration of a foreign technology which is at once vastly superior and vastly expensive.*

If this foreign – i.e. Western – technology were merely superior, without being vastly expensive, the difficulties would still be great, yet small in comparison with those actually encountered. Being so very expensive, the new technology is in fact out of reach for a poor country like India; yet it appears to be within reach because even in a poor country there are some concentrations of wealth whereby the superior technology can be 'afforded'.

No consistent thought seems to have been given to the fundamental question of what level of technology India can afford. It seems to have been assumed that what is 'best' in a developed country must be 'best' in a developing country also. Instead of asking: 'How much can we afford to pay for each workplace?' (capital investment per person in continuing employment), it was thought to be a matter of objective ascertainment to find the amount of capital *required* in various industries. In the report on 'The Third Five-Year Plan', the only references to this subject are in Appendix C; but their purpose is merely to calculate the employment effect of the capital allocations under the Plan:

> For small-scale industries employment of one person would mean an investment on the average of Rs 5,000 (£370); for handicrafts the estimate is Rs 1,500 (£111); for coir and sericulture it is roughly Rs 1,000 (£74).
>
> Under large and medium industries there will be different norms of continuing employment. The following Table, which is essentially illustrative, indicates the amount of capital required per person in a number of important industries:

	Capital required per person	
	Rs	£
Steel	160,000	11,900
Fertilisers	40,000	3,000
Machine tools (graded)	25,000	1,900
Heavy machine building plant	100,000	7,400
Foundry (forge plant)	100,000	7,400
Coal-mining machinery	60,000	4,400
Heavy electricals	50,000	3,700

It should, however, be stated that the data on which the calculations given above are based, are on the whole very meagre. The conclusions which are drawn are, therefore, intended to suggest broad dimensions. Indeed, precision in this field can only come from prolonged study.

These are the only references to the all-important matter of 'capital per workplace' which I have been able to find, and it is clear that they do not indicate any consciousness of the problem of finding a *suitable* level of technology.

Not that this problem is an unfamiliar one in daily life. Every person has to find the 'level of technology' he can afford – in his kitchen and other household arrangements, his office, his transport, his garden, etc. Every farmer, artisan, shopkeeper, etc., is faced with the same problem; he cannot simply take the 'best', or the 'most efficient', or the most modern equipment; what he can afford stands in some relation to

(*a*) what he possesses already, i.e. his total capital worth; and
(*b*) his past and current income.

It requires no lengthy argument to agree that India is 'long' in labour and 'short' in capital. This means that she requires a level of technology, or 'capital investment per workplace', that is likely to be very different from that current in the Western countries, which are 'long' in capital and 'short' in labour. At present, in India as in all other developing countries, the most primitive exists side by side with the most advanced – an artisan employing seven shillings' worth of tools, and workers minding machines worth £4,000. But the intermediate industrial technology which would really suit India's conditions does not exist in an articulated form except perhaps accidentally. The situation in agriculture and related fields (e.g. bee-keeping) is much easier, partly because the technological gap between the traditional and the modern is much narrower than in industry, and partly, I think, because there has been more understanding that development must be organic, step by step, and cannot be fruitful if there are excessive jumps.

Under the Second and Third Five-Year Plans the employment effect of the massive investment of £3,000 million in 'industries and minerals' (excluding 'small industries') is 1·5 million in ten years, or an average of 150,000 new jobs a year. It is obvious that a poor country cannot create large numbers of industrial jobs at a level of technology which requires roughly £2,000 per workplace. As the technology, moreover, is essentially a foreign one, it also requires a large expenditure in foreign exchange, amounting to an average of £1,000 per workplace in the Third Plan.

If, therefore, it is intended to create millions of jobs in industry, and not just a few hundred thousands, a technology must be evolved which is cheap enough to be accessible to a larger sector of the community than the very rich and can be applied on a mass scale without making altogether excessive demands on the savings and foreign exchange resources of the country.

I believe that it is not very difficult, from an engineering point of view, to devise such a technology, provided the engineers can be told in fairly precise terms what is wanted. It is no use simply asking for 'an intermediate technology', nor does it suffice to say: 'We want a technology that employs the minimum of capital', for the minimum is zero. If one specified 'the minimum of capital consistent with profitable production at a wage of at least two rupees a day', one would, I think, be asking the engineer to go beyond his competence and become a businessman. The simpler the specifications, the better will be the results, and the simplest would be a statement of the amount of money to be spent on the equipment of each workplace. As a start, I should therefore suggest that the *average* investment per workplace in manufacturing enterprise, suitable for widespread rural industrialisation, would be of the order of Rs 1,000, not counting the cost of building. In some cases, no doubt, Rs 2,000 per workplace could be fully justified; in other cases, a much smaller amount might suffice.

What is needed, I suggest, is that detailed design studies should be undertaken on this basis for all industries envisaged for establishment in rural areas. The studies themselves will disclose whether this average of Rs 1,000 is realistic and what variations from the average might be required by different industries. All that the figure of Rs 1,000 per workplace is meant to do is to indicate an order of magnitude and to provide a starting point for design studies.

What can be said in favour of this choice? First, that the cost of a workplace would be fairly close to the amount a man can earn in a year; as people normally can cope with money matters if the sums involved are not greatly in excess of what they can earn in a year, this level of capitalisation would appear to be 'within reach' of any able man who wants to become, or remain, his own master; second, that at this average level of capitalisation the central government can stand ready to finance any number of workplaces that can be organised – Rs 1,000 crores would be enough to equip 10 million workplaces – so that unrestricted use could be made of the free, spontaneous organising power of the people; third, that the foreign exchange content of equipment at this level of technology would be so small as not to constitute a significant problem; and fourth, that the type of equipment involved would, in general, be so simple that it could itself be produced in small-scale industry.

It may well be that these arguments would still hold good at the level of Rs 2,000 per workplace. Only detailed design studies can settle the point.

Industrialisation on a mass basis is possible when there is a fairly high degree of self-sufficiency in equipment, so that the repair, maintenance, and replacement of equipment can be done largely from nearby resources. If in this sense 'the circle can be closed', then, and only then, can there be self-sustained growth. It is the structure of real things, not the appearance of symbols (like the rate of saving), which decides these matters.

With democratic decentralisation and the introduction of *Panchayati Raj*, it is expected that the people's institutions will take over more and more responsibilities for the establishment of village industries and small industries in rural areas. But how could they succeed unless a suitable technology is available for them? I believe, therefore, that a most determined, centrally directed effort towards the establishment of such a technology is now most urgently required.

The 'intermediate technology' is required in two versions, with electrification and without. Even by the end of the Third Plan the number of towns and villages electrified is likely to be only 43,000, although this will include all towns and villages with 5,000 inhabitants or more and about half of the 100,000 villages with a population between 2,000 and 5,000. A large part of the population will have to carry on without electricity. It is moreover uncertain whether the installation of new capacity will be able to keep step with the growth of demand, and for many years to come there may be power cuts damaging to industry. 'The bulk of the increase in energy consumption over the next 20 years would go to the new and existing urban communities. By 1981, while 160 million people, forming one-fourth of the population, might come close to enjoying the benefits of energy equivalent of one ton of coal, the remaining three-fourths of the population, numbering 480 million, is likely to be consuming 0·28 tons of coal per capita per year.'[1]

Urgent attention has therefore to be given to the utilisation of such minor or scattered sources of energy as cow-dung methane, solar heat, wind power, peat, etc. Technical work on these subjects, I suggest, is of greater relevance to India's problems than work on nuclear energy – the most capital-intensive and costly source of energy ever tackled.

It is possible and even probable that far more of the 'intermediate technology' exists already than is known to any one person or authority. Proposals to create a 'Technological Information Service to serve rural needs' therefore deserves sympathetic consideration.

[1] J. C. Kapur, 'Socio-Economic Considerations in the Utilisation of Solar Energy in Underdeveloped Countries', vi 3 (July 1962).

16 The Economic Expansion of Jinja, Uganda

B. S. HOYLE

THE municipality of Jinja, second town of Uganda, with an estimated population of 30,000, stands at an altitude of 3,750 ft on the
east shore of the Victoria Nile (Fig. 16.1) at the point where the river
formerly issued from Lake Victoria in the Ripon Falls.[1] A century
ago John Hanning Speke, discoverer of the source of the Nile,[2]
recorded[3] that these falls constituted

> by far the most interesting sight I had seen in Africa ... that
> attracted one to it for hours – the roar of the waters, the thousands
> of passenger-fish, leaping at the falls with all their might, the
> Wasoga and Waganda fishermen coming out in boats and taking
> post on all the rocks with rod and hook, hippopotami and
> crocodiles lying sleepily on the water, the ferry at work above the
> falls, and cattle driven down to drink at the margin of the lake –
> made ... as interesting a picture as one could wish to see.
> The expedition had now performed its functions. I saw that old
> father Nile without any doubt rises in the Victoria N'yanza....

Thus 'the subject of so much speculation, and the object of so
many explorers'[4] was revealed to the outside world.[5]

The thick riverain forests have now been cleared, and the fauna
dispersed. The ferry to which Speke made reference – an ancient and

[1] *Jinja* is the Luganda word for 'stone'. This is taken to refer either to the
rocks of the Ripon and Owen Falls or, more probably, to a sacrificial stone on a
hilltop overlooking the town.

[2] The centenary of the discovery of the source of the Nile by John Hanning
Speke on 28 July 1862 was celebrated both in Speke's home town of Ilminster,
Somerset, and in Jinja, Uganda, where exhibitions and a trade fair provided
an appropriate prelude to the independence celebrations held throughout
Uganda in the following October. Speke named the Ripon Falls after the then
president of the Royal Geographical Society in London.

[3] John Hanning Speke, *Journal of the Discovery of the Source of the Nile*
(Edinburgh and London, 1863) pp. 466–7.

[4] John Hanning Speke, *What Led to the Discovery of the Source of the Nile*
(Edinburgh and London, 1864) p. 307.

[5] For a useful summary of earlier ideas and contributions towards the
solution of the Nile mystery, see B. W. Langlands, 'Concepts of the Nile',
Uganda Journ., XXVI (1962) 1–22.

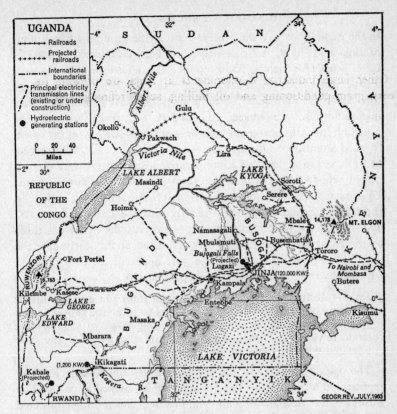

Fig. 16.1 Principal railroads and electric power lines in Uganda. The railroad between Gulu and Pakwach is now under construction. Transmission network is shown as of the end of 1963, when the Uganda Electricity Board's current development programme is scheduled for completion.

essential link between the rival states on the two shores, used at times by the Kabaka Mutesa's armies when raiding Busoga from the west[1] – has been replaced by a railway bridge and by a road that traverses the crest of the Owen Falls Dam. The Ripon Falls are submerged under the higher Nile waters behind the dam.

[1] Speke approached the Nile through Buganda from the Kabaka's court at Mengo (Kampala) and did not cross to the east, or Busoga, shore of the river. The first white man to visit the site of the present town of Jinja was Henry M. Stanley in 1875.

HISTORICAL BACKGROUND

In the earliest years of the present century the economic significance of Jinja was slight. A British post had been established in 1893 at Chief Luba's fort nearby (later rebuilt as Fort Thruston), but Iganga, a little way to the north-east, became the first headquarters of the then Central Province of Uganda in 1900. The establishment of a lake steamer service between Jinja and Port Florence (Kisumu), the port that in 1901 became the terminus of the railway from the coast, focused attention on the significance of Jinja's location with respect to transportation, and the administrative headquarters were accordingly opened at Jinja in that year. Two years later the newly formed Uganda Company introduced cotton into Uganda as a cash crop (first into Buganda, and subsequently into the Eastern Province), and in 1904 the first export of cotton was recorded; previous trade to the coast had been largely in ivory. Even at this early date the geographical potentialities of Jinja were apparent. In 1908 Winston Churchill wrote,[1] with considerable perspicacity:

> Jinja is destined to become a very important place in the future economy of Central Africa. . . . In years to come the shores of this splendid bay may be crowned with long rows of comfortable tropical villas and imposing offices, and the gorge of the Nile crowded with factories and warehouses.

The opening in 1912 of the sixty-one-mile-long Busuga Railway represented an important step forward, which helped to consolidate Busoga as a cotton-growing and ginning area; this railway connected Jinja with the Lake Kyoga steamer services at Namasagali and thus provided a link in the chain of north–south communications with the Sudan. The significance of Jinja as a transport focus was further emphasised by the completion in 1928 of a direct railway connection with Kenya and the coast. In 1931 this line was continued westward to Kampala and northward from Tororo to Soroti, and became a basic factor in the subsequent economic expansion of the country as a whole. The lake steamer services were, of course, adversely affected by these developments, but whereas in 1925 goods traffic of the port of Jinja amounted to only 15,000 tons, the total tonnage of goods handled at the Jinja railway station in 1961 reached 69,000.

[1] Winston Spencer Churchill, *My African Journey* (London, 1908) p. 119. A new edition of this fascinating book was published in 1962 by the Holland Press (Neville Spearman Ltd), London. The passages quoted occur on p. 80–1 of this new edition.

RECENT DEVELOPMENTS

The economic growth of Jinja, previously unspectacular and due almost entirely to the expansion of commercial activities, has been considerably accelerated during the past decade. The town has become a focus of modern manufacturing industry and the seat of Uganda's leading industrial concerns. The basis for these developments was the decision taken in 1947 to proceed with the construction of a dam and hydro-electric power station at the point where the Nile leaves Lake Victoria. With reference to this site, Churchill[1] had commented earlier that

> there is power enough to gin all the cotton and saw all the wood in Uganda, and it is here that one of the principal emporia of tropical produce will certainly be created. . . . It would be perfectly easy to harness the whole river and let the Nile begin its long and beneficent journey to the sea by leaping through a turbine. It is possible that nowhere else in the world could so enormous a mass of water be held up by so little masonry.

By providing large quantities of industrial power at economic rates (Fig. 16.2), the completion of the Owen Falls Dam at Jinja in 1954 marked a major turning point in the economic development of the town and of the country.[2] The dam has not raised the level of Lake Victoria, though it has caused the submergence of the Ripon Falls and the Owen Falls. The generating station has an installed capacity of 120,000 kilowatts (in eight sets of 15,000 kilowatts each), and space is provided for two additional turbines, which would increase the capacity to a maximum of 150,000 kilowatts. The scheme led to an unprecedented boom in building and commerce in Jinja and had many complex social repercussions. The provision of a basic power grid in southern Uganda opened up wide possibilities of industrial production. Considerable expansion has taken place, notably in Kampala, Jinja and Tororo. On the basis of United Kingdom and World Bank loans totalling £5·5 million, power lines are being extended, and by the end of 1963 electricity supplies from Owen Falls will be available in Fort Portal in the west, to Gulu in the north, beyond Masaka in the south, and beyond Mbale in the

---

[1] Ibid., pp. 119–20.
[2] David N. McMaster, 'Some effects of the Owen Falls scheme, Uganda', *Geography*, XL (1955) 123–6.

east. Valuable income is also derived from the export of bulk supplies
of power to western Kenya and Nairobi.[1] However, the present
potential output of the station (105,000 kilowatts, one set being
retained as spare capacity) greatly exceeds demands, which are
expected to rise to 84,000 kilowatts by the end of 1963. Proposals to
develop further hydro-electric power stations along the Victoria
Nile – for example, at the Bujagali Falls – have been investigated but
are not likely to be effected for many years unless new large industrial
consumers are found or unless it is decided that Kenya's expanding
demand can best be met by augmenting the present bulk-supply
contract rather than by building the projected Seven Forks scheme
in Kenya.

Most of the industrial establishments that have grown up in Jinja
and elsewhere in Uganda as a result of the stimulus provided by
electricity supplies have been promoted and largely financed by the
Uganda Government through the Uganda Development Corporation.
The largest single consumer of electricity is the smelter that treats
copper concentrates from Kilembe, in the foothills of the Ruwenzori
massif. An ore concentrator is situated at Kilembe and a roasting
plant eight miles away at Kasese. The development of the industry
was made possible by the 208-mile westward extension of the railway
from Kampala to Kasese in 1956. The copper smelter at Jinja came
into operation in the same year, and in 1962 production reached
15,231 tons of blister copper, which added almost £4 million to the
country's export earnings. Unfortunately, the prospects for further
expansion appear at the moment to be slight in spite of recent new
ore discoveries; at the present rate of working, ore reserves will
become exhausted in 1971–2. Moreover, there seems to be no likeli-
hood whatsoever that any other mineral will assume a major position
in the economy of Uganda. In assessing the prospects of the copper
industry, the members of the International Bank's economic mission
to Uganda commented in 1961 that 'the failure of Kilembe would
make it even more difficult to attract overseas capital to other mineral

---

[1] The rate at which this export takes place is highly favourable to Kenya.
In 1962, 42 per cent of the output of Owen Falls went to Kenya, but the
revenue derived from this sale accounted for only 13·4 per cent of the Uganda
Electricity Board's total income for that year. Nevertheless, the Kenya bulk
supply is an economic proposition; without it, tariffs in Uganda would be
much higher. Kenya is responsible for transmission costs from the Uganda–
Kenya border. The agreement between Uganda and Kenya under which this
sale takes place is under review.

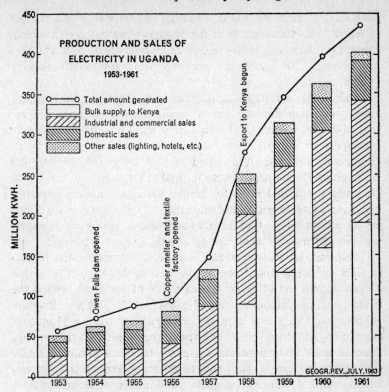

PRODUCTION AND SALES OF
ELECTRICITY IN UGANDA
1953-1961

○——○ Total amount generated
▢ Bulk supply to Kenya
▨ Industrial and commercial sales
▧ Domestic sales
▨ Other sales (lighting, hotels, etc.)

Export to Kenya begun

Copper smelter and textile factory opened

Owen Falls dam opened

MILLION KWH.

GEOGR.REV.,JULY,1963

*Fig. 16.2 Production and sales of electricity in Uganda, 1953–1961.
Data from Uganda Electricity Board and East African Statistical
Department.*

developments'.[1] in addition to intensifying labour problems and
resulting in a serious loss of national income.

A second major enterprise, which came into production at Jinja
in 1956, is a long-projected cotton-textile factory, which uses entirely
local raw material. Initially it proved difficult to sell cloth produced at
Jinja, since Africans preferred to buy cheaper Indian cloth and Asian
traders were reluctant to handle locally produced material; production costs were high at first as a result of the small output and the
relatively high level of industrial wages. These difficulties have now

[1] *The Economic Development of Uganda: Report of a Mission Organised by the
International Bank for Reconstruction and Development at the Request of the
Government of Uganda* (Baltimore, 1962) p. 269; (Entebbe, Uganda, 1961)
p. 212.

been largely overcome, and demand has increased to such an extent in recent years that the size of the original plant has been doubled. Present production is at the rate of 28 million yds of cotton cloth a year. Some 2,500 people are employed on a treble-shift working system.

Other large industrial developments at Jinja are brewing (of beer), grain conditioning and oil milling, sugar refining, and tea and coffee processing. Tobacco curing and cigarette manufacture represents an important undertaking, and there are several light-engineering concerns. A plywood factory and a steel rolling mill have recently been opened – both the first of their kind in East Africa. Recently announced plans for further expansion are considerable, requiring a total investment of more than £5 million. Plans are drawn up for a flour mill, a tool factory and a second textile plant; paper-making and match-making are among the projects envisaged.

These various developments have been accommodated in two distinct industrial zones: one on the west bank of the Nile, within Buganda, and the other on the east side of the river beyond the central commercial and residential zones (Fig. 16.3). The cultivation of cash crops such as cotton, coffee, sugar and tea is a prominent feature of the agricultural landscape in the Jinja area; the primary processing of these products has given rise to a group of major undertakings, largely in the hands of private enterprise. It is interesting to note that cash-crop production and processing remain concentrated in the areas served by the first railway link with the coast – a legacy from the earliest days of Uganda's economic development. Sugar, first planted near Jinja in 1921, has been highly successful; forty years later the extensive Lugazi and Kakira estates together produced a record crop of 95,000 tons. The Muljibhai Madhvani group of companies is founded on sugar cultivation and now employs more than 11,000 people; among its subsidiary developments are a farm boarding school, a commercial college, grain mills, soap and glass factories, and the new steel rolling mill mentioned earlier. The Madhvani organisation is also the basis of much of the planned development outlined above.

LOCATIONAL FACTORS

The Luganda phrase *Kiyira bwe bugagga*, inscribed on the coat of arms of the municipality of Jinja, signifies that 'the Nile is wealth',

and it is true that Speke's 'magnificent stream', harnessed to produce electricity and channelled into industry, is a prime factor in the
recent economic growth of the town. However, the precise extent to
which the availability of virtually unlimited supplies of electricity
has acted as an industrial locational factor for Jinja itself is open to
debate. The Uganda Electricity Board offers a special uniform tariff,
irrespective of distance from Owen Falls, to relatively small-scale
industrial consumers: the cost of power does not normally exceed
about 8 per cent of the total annual expenses of a small concern. But
although the availability of a good supply of electricity is clearly a
prime consideration for these industries, its cost is not a vital factor.
For large-scale industries, to whose manufacturing techniques
electricity provides a major contribution, power costs form a much
higher proportion of total expenses. There are distinct savings in
locating such consumers near Owen Falls; short, inexpensive private
power lines can be easily laid and are less susceptible to interruption
than long-distance lines. The policy of the Uganda Electricity Board
is therefore to consider special tariff arrangements, by private agreement, for any potential large-scale consumer of electricity in the
Jinja area; similar agreements may be concluded with consumers
farther afield – for example, at Tororo – but obviously in these cases
the transmission costs, and therefore the tariff charges, are higher.
It would appear that a definite financial incentive exists to attract
the larger industrial establishments to Jinja – the copper smelter, the
textile factory and the new steel rolling mill are cases in point –
but that this incentive does not extend to smaller industrial concerns.

Apart from electricity, the geographical basis for Jinja's 'miniature
economic revolution', which has 'telescoped into the space of a few
years processes which elsewhere have occurred only in decades',[1]
is to be found in the simultaneous occurrence in area of a number of
additional factors; these include the general situation of the town in a
highly productive agricultural area forming part of the economically
focal lake zone of Uganda,[2] the ready availability of a plentiful
supply of water and of land for industrial use, the presence of a large

[1] Cyril and Rhona Sofer, *Jinja Transformed: A Social Survey of a Multi-Racial
Township*, East African Studies No. 4 (East African Institute of Social Research,
Kampala, 1955) p. 113.

[2] An interesting examination of the comparative economic progress of
Buganda and the other three regions of Uganda is provided by A. M. O'Connor,
'Regional inequalities in economic development in Uganda', *East African
Geogr. Rev.*, no. 1 (Apr 1963) pp. 33–44.

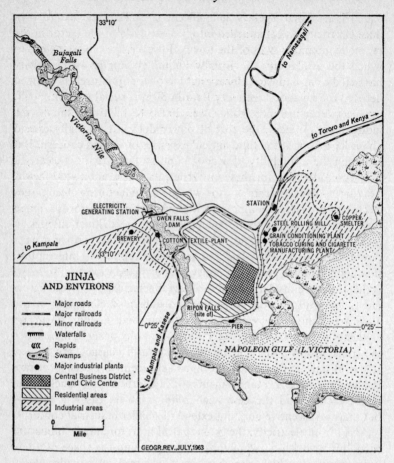

*Fig. 16.3   Urban regions and principal industrial establishments of Jinja.
Two distinct industrial areas have developed, one on each side of the
central commercial and residential core.*

and hard-working labour force, and the site of the town at a transport node where internal Busoga and Buganda routeways converge
and where the principal railway and road routes from Uganda to
Kenya and the coast cross the Nile route to the Sudan, a location
that facilitates both the collection of raw materials and the distribution of finished products. There is some evidence, however, to
show that in certain cases, notably that of the steel rolling mill, the
decisive locational factors are much more a matter of financial cir-

cumstance, government policy and administrative convenience than of geography.

PRESENT AND FUTURE PROSPECTS

The considerable industrial potential of Jinja has now been partly demonstrated, but industrialisation is still very much in its initial stages. Although Churchill's prophecies have been translated into reality, and although government encouragement has been both positive and continuous, the optimism engendered in 1954 by the provision of electricity has not been entirely justified by subsequent events, and the confidently expected industrial revolution has not taken place on the scale envisaged. The Owen Falls scheme has not yet become truly profitable, since the expected level of sales to large industrial consumers has not been attained; this is partly because a projected steel mill at Tororo was never built, and also because a railway, and not a power line, was built to the western region. Had these two early projects come to fruition, it is possible that the full capacity of Owen Falls would already have been absorbed. In contrast with the late 1940s and early 1950s, the past few years have been marked by relative economic stagnation in Uganda, shown particularly by a lack of confidence in the country on the part of overseas investors and, within Uganda, by a slight decline in per capita income. In common with most other African towns, Jinja has encountered social problems, rarely foreseen and always difficult of solution, as a result of the rapid intermixture of traditional African societies and the new urban culture, and in association with the essentially migratory character of industrial labour. Nevertheless, Jinja represents in some senses an epitome of the tremendous economic and social advances that have taken place in Uganda during the remarkable hundred years since Speke was at Mutesa's court and at the Ripon Falls.

17 An African Labour Force

W. ELKAN

LABOUR TURNOVER

THE Kampala factory of the East African Tobacco Company was built in 1937 and acquired by its present owners in 1948. It has in the past employed as many as 900 men. Since 1948, however, the number of employees has been gradually reduced to about 600 whilst at the same time output has increased.

This has been brought about principally by introducing more machines, but the contribution of careful labour management has not been insignificant. In some ways it is no doubt true that mechanisation facilitates good labour management, but conversely, unless attention had been paid to it, the introduction of the new machines might have proved disappointing in its results.

Employers in East Africa face two major problems: how to reduce labour turnover and how to improve the efficiency of their labour force. The two problems are of course related. Workers do not reach their maximum efficiency until they have done a job for some time, and to some extent the problem of how to improve efficiency resolves itself into one of getting people to stay longer in one job. In this chapter we shall be concerned with the first of these problems. We shall analyse the nature and extent of turnover and attempt to discuss some of its causes.

The tobacco factory did not begin to collect monthly turnover figures until 1952, and it was not until October 1953 that a distinction began to be made between men discharged in the ordinary sense and men who failed to turn up again although they had given no notice of their intention to leave. We cannot therefore estimate with any accuracy the success of different attempts to reduce labour turnover, but only outline the situation at the present time.

If we exclude men dismissed for major breaches of discipline, the average rate of turnover for the months of October 1953 to May 1954 was 7·6 per cent. Every month, in other words, seven or eight men in every 100 employed had left the factory either because they wanted to or, in a very few instances, because they had exhausted the patience of their supervisors by being continuously absent. This figure in itself, however, conceals a multitude of possibilities. It matters very much who are the ones who leave and to this an average of this sort provides no answer.

A study of the employment record cards of men who left the factory between September 1953 and June 1954 reveals two things of particular interest (see Table 1).

TABLE 1

Resignations and Voluntary Discharges, September 1953–June 1954 (Kampala)

Length of service	Ganda	Ankole	Ruanda	Luo	Other 12 Tribes	Total	%
Under 1 year	39	8	13	15	44	119	58
1 year and under 2 years	8	10	11	2	9	40	20
2 years and under 3 years	5	6	4	2	2	19	9
3 years and under 5 years	8	3	—	—	3	14	7
5 years and over	13	—	—	—	—	13	6
	73	27	28	19	58	205	100

A very high proportion of those who left did so in their first two years. Even within the first two years, the rate of leaving is a rapidly decreasing one: 58 per cent left in their first year, 20 per cent in their second year. Further, of the 119 men who left in their first year, 80 did so within the first two months, and 101 within the first six months. When we come to consider whether the causes of turnover amongst newcomers differ from those amongst men with longer service, the importance emerges of the background from which a man comes. The labour force is drawn from regions differing widely in their economic structure, and the ambitions and attitudes of men from backward areas are distinct from those of men who have grown up in the economically more advanced parts of East Africa. The figures of the table confirm that we should try to relate turnover to men's geographical origin, or more simply, to their tribe.

Let us take first the men who leave after a few months, and who constitute the major problem. A heavy loss of newcomers may appear to be less serious than one of well-trained men, but it too has its cost. Every new man has to be medically examined. His personal particulars have to be recorded and he has to be instructed in his job and in the factory rules. Even if he is given a job which requires no training, like keeping the compound clean, his cost to the firm during the first few months may well exceed the value of his services. This overhead cost becomes negligible only if it can be spread over a number of years.

Of those who in the months September 1953 to June 1954 left after less than one year's service, one-third were Ganda, although the Ganda only constituted one-eighth of those workers in the factory who had completed less than a year's service. In other words, the turnover amongst Ganda newcomers is very much higher than that amongst other tribes. This is illustrated by Table 2.

TABLE 2

Comparison of Newcomers[1] in the Labour Force with Newcomers who left between September 1953 and June 1954, by Tribe (Kampala)

	A Present employees (Newcomers)	B Voluntary leavers (Newcomers)	C[2] B as a percentage of A
Ganda	26	39	150
Ankole	46	8	17
Ruanda	35	13	37
Luo	27	15	56
Others	78	44	56
Total	212	119	56

[1] The term 'newcomer' is used for the sake of brevity to describe those with less than one year's service.

[2] This comparison is not strictly meaningful but gives some indication of the differential turnover of different tribes amongst newcomers.

The substantial number of Ganda who come to the factory seems at first sight to disprove the contention, which is often heard, that the Ganda will not enter unskilled employment; that so many leave so soon seems, on the contrary, to support it. The explanation to this apparent riddle may lie in the prospects which they find. A Ganda will stay if he sees before him a prospect of rapid increases in his earnings. Otherwise he leaves and goes from job to job. As I shall try to show later, the Ganda appear in increasing numbers to be accepting the status of permanent wage-earner (as opposed to independent farmer), and this is of course related to the keenness to get the best wage possible, even where this involves, as among the unskilled, frequent change of job.

Other causes of the heavy turnover among newcomers may be first, the method of selecting employees; second, ignorance of the wages paid; and third, the method of payment.

A great deal of the turnover in the early stages can be attributed to the method of selection. Men are picked out from a crowd which assembles outside the factory on the first day of each month, according to the impression created by their appearance. No questions were asked until recently, when the firm decided to give preference to men with some education. But even now no proof of education is required and it is luck alone if the firm in fact picks those with the longest spell at school. The result of this procedure is that men are frequently placed in jobs which they dislike or at which they are incompetent, and being new in the factory they leave sooner than ask to be transferred to other work.

The fact of immigrant labour, which is perhaps the most striking feature of African industrial life and which distinguishes it from European experience, is something over which the tobacco factory or any other firm has relatively little control. The habits and aspirations of the immigrant worker have, at least in the short run, to be taken as given, and are not likely to be modified by changes of labour policy on the part of individual employers.

It is, nevertheless, possible to say something about the methods by which the firm seeks to persuade men to stay in their jobs. It is hard to know by what criteria their success might be judged, since there is no other factory here of comparable size or nature; my impression is, however, that the firm does achieve a very creditable degree of stability. After all, nearly a third of its employees have a record of three or more years' service (see Table 3.)

TABLE 3

Present Employees by Tribe and Length of Service (Kampala)

Length of service	Ganda %	Ankole %	Ruanda %	Luo %	Others (23 Tribes) %	Total %
Under 1 year	18	40	45	50	48	38
1 year but under 2	18	29	16	16	13	18
2 years but under 3	11	21	25	16	12	15
3 years but under 5	22	7	10	8	7	12
5 years or more	31	3	4	10	20	17
	100	100	100	100	100	100

Again, what is interesting is that it is more successful with some groups of workers than with others. Although the Ganda figure most prominently amongst those who leave the factory within their first six months, over half of all Ganda now working in the factory have had a minimum of three years' service. In the case of the Ankole it is a tenth; in that of the Ruanda, a sixth. The firm's policy has been more successful in retaining its Ganda workers than in retaining others.

The firm's policy appears to be to reduce turnover in three ways. First, it seeks to pay wages which compare favourably with those paid elsewhere, and in addition men are given opportunities to increase their total earnings by working overtime and through production bonuses. In the month of June only 57 men received the bare minimum wage. Secondly, it provides a number of welfare services such as free medical attention, a free snack in the canteen, overalls and sick leave. Finally, it runs a Provident Fund to which the firm contributes on a 50–50 basis.

ATTRIBUTES OF THE LABOUR FORCE

To attempt to discuss all the difficulties which may arise in the employment of African workers would be beyond the scope of this essay; nor could I here deal adequately with the entire range of the Tobacco Company's policies towards its workers. In what follows, I have taken up certain problems, all more or less connected with labour turnover, and have tried to relate them to the differing economic backgrounds and also, when possible, to the practices of labour management in the factory.

It is important first of all to realise that much contemporary writing about labour efficiency has little relevance to conditions in Uganda. Before men can work efficiently, at least two conditions must obtain: an employer must know how to evoke the qualitities and abilities of his labour force effectively, but this in turn depends on whether the qualities and abilities, and in particular certain basic feelings about work, are there to be evoked. If much of current discussion is concerned with the first aspect of efficiency, it is mainly because in Western countries there exists now a labour force whose attitudes are appropriate to an industrial society. Uganda, however, resembles more the England of Robert Owen than that of the Institute of Personnel Management. It is often said that modern management began with Robert Owen.[1] This ignores his real contribution, which was not primarily to show how labour might be managed but how to create in workers qualities and aptitudes which are the peculiar requirements of industry and without which management in any positive sense can hardly begin. In England, the punctuality and discipline imposed on men by the machines with which they work may still be resented, but they have ceased to be wondered at and misunderstood. Two centuries of factory work have created new ways of thinking and of behaviour which take for granted the very aspects of factory life which, 150 years ago, men used to find most startling.

In Uganda, on the other hand, industry is still new and unfamiliar. The pattern of life which it imposes is seen only as the arbitrary tyranny of the employer. Qualities which single men out for praise or respect at home are not necessarily relevant in the factory and may be ignored there. The customary rhythm of work is the subject of derision on the employer's part, and is something for which he regards himself entitled to seek retribution. In these conditions the meaning of labour efficiency often must be the extent to which men have acquired the attitudes which make them effective industrial workers. It does not of course follow from this that once people begin to accept an industrial system of life and earnings, no more problems arise; rather one type of dissatisfaction gives way to another, as we shall see later.

Many causes contribute to the rather strained and dissatisfied condition of the immigrant factory worker, and prominent amongst these is the fact, generally overlooked by the men before they come to Kampala, that wages have to cover the cost of food. Few of those who come, attracted by seemingly high wages, have thought about the cost of food at all, for food is not something which one buys. Money one spends on tea and sugar perhaps, but not on flour or plantains. To 'eat one's wages' seems preposterous.

It is, of course, inevitable that industrial workers should pay for their food in cash. No English worker now resents it, though he may complain about the price of food. In Kampala men also complain about the price of food, but to imagine that they will be satisfied if prices of food could be reduced by simplifying the channels of distri-

[1] See for instance, L. Urwick and E. F. L. Brech, *The Making of Scientific Management*, II 40: 'Owen . . . was a very early exemplar of modern personnel management.'

bution is to overlook the basic resentment against the very fact that food should have a price at all.

This attitude towards food has an important bearing on efficiency. Since men resent having to spend money on food, they may sometimes spend less than is necessary to maintain health and strength. The effect of diet on working efficiency can be exaggerated, but it cannot be ignored. It is doubtful whether undernourishment is such as to leave men actually hungry. But it is probable that they are ill-nourished, i.e. they spend their money on food that satisfies hunger, to the exclusion of things which in the long run maintain health and energy. This has three consequences. In the first place, men will not go on doing it indefinitely, and it may therefore be regarded as a contributory factor to labour turnover. One English-speaking Ankole clerk put it like this. 'A man comes to Kampala to earn cash. If his wages allow him to eat the things to which he is accustomed, he will stay for a long time. But most men in order to save have to accept poor food and within a year they go back – they will not punish themselves for longer.' In the second place it makes men lethargic in their work, unable to summon the energy to work hard consistently or to make the occasional extra effort required to prevent some mishap or to do a job thoroughly. Even where industrial relations are at their best, one notices an atmosphere of 'I don't care', which may well be due more to the food in men's stomachs than to any native ill disposition in their minds.

The difficulty of combating absenteeism is enhanced by the fact that absences are sometimes very profitable. Granted that much absenteeism is connected with intemperate living, there is yet a proportion of men who take days off because the loss in wages which it entails is more than counterbalanced by gains of trade, harvest or inheritance. Kampala offers many opportunities to the occasional trader – to men who will peddle a load of fish sent them by relatives from across the lake or who have the occasional load of plantains for disposal. Men who have land nearby may gain more by taking days off during the planting and harvesting seasons than they lose in wages. Again, a man stands to gain more by being present at the division of a deceased relative's property than by being present at his place of work. Absenteeism due to these causes is naturally most common amongst those whose homes are nearby.

18 Planning and Industrial Developments in Apulia

ALAN B. MOUNTJOY

In July 1965, the life of the *Cassa per il Mezzogiorno* (The Southern Fund) was prolonged for fifteen years by the Italian Government, and nearly £1,000 million allotted to it for expenditure up to 1970. The *Cassa* was founded at the end of 1950 to co-ordinate the main lines of economic development in Italy's backward and impoverished South; to invest government and other public capital in these measures and, by infrastructure provision, to attract private capital into the region. Since the *Cassa* began operations in 1951, over £2,100 million has been poured into the Mezzogiorno (South). In many areas striking changes are becoming apparent, particularly in parts of the Molise, Apulia and Campania where effective land reform, irrigation developments and the successful establishment of co-operatives are transforming considerable areas of the rural landscape.

By the end of its first decade, the *Cassa* encountered some criticism for its widespread dispersion of investment. It was suggested that the available funds were being spread too thinly over too wide an area. Since 1959 new theories, following Hirschman's 'unbalanced growth' approach, prefer that, instead of widespread infrastructure invest-ment over the agricultural South, there should be a concentration of investment into those areas that have the greatest prospect of success-ful industrial growth. The intention is, by a discriminatory invest-ment programme and careful selection of suitable industries, to create what are termed 'poles of expansion' capable of transforming the local economy into one of dynamic growth. Earlier aims at a slower but more balanced growth have become outmoded. Neverthe-less, after a decade, great progress has been made in establishing, in Rostow terminology, the preconditions for 'take-off'. It is hoped that the new lines of investment and development will achieve, for the selected areas, take-off into full-scale industrialisation.

To facilitate the application of the new ideas, much greater use has been made of the Industrial Areas Law of 1957. This permits local authorities in designated industrial development zones to form a consortium to develop basic infrastructure works, to expropriate suitable land, to improve environmental conditions for industry and to offer varying inducements (such as buildings for sale or rent) to attract industrialists. By 1959 Bari, Brindisi and Taranto had been designated 'industrial development zones', and, more recently, the European Economic Commission designated this triangular part of Apulia as a pole for regional development. Another very effective law obliges state-controlled enterprises to locate 60 per cent of all new investment in the Mezzogiorno. This is having significant results by bringing into the South great industrial groups such as Italsider (iron and steel), E.N.I. (oil and gas) and Breda (mechanical engineering), and these (plus the discovery of natural gas at Ferrandina in the Basento valley, forty miles to the west of Taranto) in turn help to attract some of the larger private firms, such as Shell and Montecatini.

It was against this background that the E.E.C. in 1962 commissioned Italconsult, a Rome industrial management consulting firm, to prepare a pilot development scheme for industrial growth in the Bari–Brindisi–Taranto–Ferrandina area. Italy's Mezzogiorno is the Common Market countries' most underdeveloped area, and the preparation of this plan was the first major action taken by the E.E.C. to implement that part of the Treaty of Rome which calls for a reduction in the inequality in the economic development of different regions of the community. The proposals of Italconsult were made public in 1965 and are important, not only for Apulia but also for other 'depressed' or backward regions. That such areas need a concentration of public works and investment incentive is qualified by the view that such methods bring only long-term results (thirty to forty years is suggested): for short-term results much more detailed intervention is necessary. In fact, dynamic growth had not come to the South because, despite incentives, firms felt they would lack the external economies (the general benefits of an industrial environment) that they could count upon in the North.

A comprehensive input–output table of the region was constructed, to show the goods and services consumed and produced in all existing productive activities. These were then analysed and new industries that might find the region's resources advantageous were listed. Feasibility studies for each such industry were then carried out, and close consideration given to the needs of these industries within the spectrum of external economies. Upon examination, it was found that, for most industries, being surrounded by numerous other industries did not necessarily create adequate external economies, but that specialised auxiliary firms were required. Some of these provide components, others retooling and service activities. With ever-increasing specialisation and constant improvements in transport, it is becoming apparent that for some industries closeness to auxiliaries rather than to raw materials, etc., may now be considered vital.

Other factors were also taken into account. For example, the region's peripheral position does not favour strongly market-oriented industries; and where great scale was needed and strong specialism already existed in the North (such as in car and tractor manufacture), these industries were struck out, as were industries that required much skilled labour. These considerations reduced a list of over two hundred 'possibles' to thirty. Doubt regarding the gas reserves at Ferrandina and delay in completing the pipelines led the planners to shelve temporarily the schemes for expanding petrochemical activities at Ferrandina and Brindisi and to concentrate on mechanical industries at Bari and Taranto.

Here the planners started with some advantages, for the *Cassa* had done much to improve infrastructure facilities and definite industrial projects were under way. The E.E.C. plan, in fact, will give renewed momentum to these measures. Bari, the regional capital and a port with eastern connections, during the last five years has attracted 'forced' investment from a number of government-controlled firms and now has a small oil refinery and a variety of mechanical engineering enterprises, in particular the Breda plant for making pipeline valves and control systems. At Taranto, one response to the investment requirement of government-controlled firms has been the establishment since 1960 of Italy's largest single iron and steel plant. Well over £200 million have now been invested in this project, and production began in 1964. As Figure 18.1 shows, the site covers nearly three square miles of former olive groves at the edge of the town and only a mile from the sea. New jetties, wharves and overhead transporters are being constructed to deal with the substantial imports of iron ore (from Venezuela, North Africa, Liberia) and coal (from the U.S.A.), and the export of finished steel. The initial annual output of the new plant is 2 million tons; by 1970 this is to be trebled and the plant will be one of the largest in Europe.

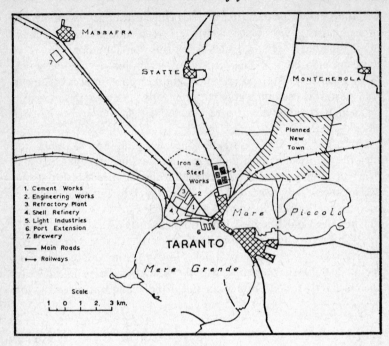

1. Cement Works
2. Engineering Works
3. Refractory Plant
4. Shell Refinery
5. Light Industries
6. Port Extension
7. Brewery

—— Main Roads
⊢——→ Railways

Fig. 18.1

The port of Taranto, under the instep of Italy, was formerly a naval port but is being expanded and is assuming commercial functions. It has a central situation in the Mediterranean, with markets of considerable potential on the North African shore and in the Levant. Orders for steel pipes for oil and gas pipelines are now being fulfilled for the U.S.S.R., Libya and the Argentine. Other newly established industries include a large cement works, a plant for the manufacture of refractories, a structural metal plant, and a large brewery at Massafra, seven miles to the north-west. Shell are now constructing an oil refinery (Fig. 18.1). In the past five years up to 25,000 new jobs have been provided in Taranto, which now has a growth rate exceeding that of Bari.

The E.E.C. plan aims at creating two development poles, at Bari and Taranto, by the relatively modest investment of *c.* £100 million and the establishment of some forty mechanical engineering firms. Nine main industries have been selected: they will produce pumps, agricultural machinery, mechanical excavators, cranes, machine-tools, structural steelwork, elevators and domestic appliances. They, in turn, require thirty auxiliary industries concerned with repairs, tooling, foundry-work, gear-cutting, pressing, moulding, galvanising. These, and the infrastructure established for them, are expected to promote the growth of allied and service industries and to provide non-agricultural jobs so much needed throughout the Mezzogiorno. Above all, it is expected that these carefully selected industries will be able to produce competitively for an integrated European market.

By 1970 a decade of industrial development in the Bari–Taranto areas is expected to have made marked changes in both the geography and the economy of these towns and their hinterlands. The planned development of Taranto, involving a new port area, large and small-scale industrial 'estates', and a new town (to be developed on the north of the Mare Piccolo) is shown on Fig. 18.1. Whether or not this refined planning exercise produces the catalyst needed to engender dynamic economic growth in Italy's far South, it will certainly be watched with great interest by those who are grappling with similar problems throughout the world.

19 The City in the Developing World and the Example of South-east Asia

D. J. DWYER

IN seeking to generalise about the city in the developing world, using examples drawn largely from South-east Asia, it is not the intention to adopt here the attitude which is becoming increasingly prevalent in geography: that if it cannot be graphed, reduced to an equation or put through a computer it is rather old-fashioned and intellectually suspect because of its lack of precision. Neither will there be exhibited, however, the traditional concern of the urban geographer with what Emrys Jones[1] has perceptively called 'the empty shell of the city', that is the examination of the site, situation and physical layout of the city and the evolution through time of its town plan. Despite this latter reservation, it is a useful starting point to call attention to the most fundamental distinction in physical form within the fabric of the South-east Asian city, namely the contrast between what might be called, albeit somewhat loosely, its Western and non-Western parts.

The Western parts usually comprise what perhaps, even in the developing world, can be called the Central Business District: though in few cases, it seems, is this district so specialised in its functions or as sparsely inhabited by permanent residents as would be the case in cities of a comparable size in Western Europe or the United States, nor indeed are the typical South-east Asian city's central activities so highly localised in one area. The Western parts comprise also the high-class residential suburbs, port facilities and, more recently, perhaps an area reserved for modern factory development as an industrial estate. It is in the non-Western areas of the city, however, that the majority of the population lives and still, to a surprising extent, circulates. In every South-east Asian city there is a considerable Chinatown composed of shophouses; indeed in population composition Singapore and Kuala Lumpur are basically Chinese cities. More surprising, perhaps, to the Western-

---

[1] E. Jones, *The City in Geography* (University of London, London, 1962) p. 9.

oriented eye is the existence of large urban areas indigenous in building form, the *kampong* areas as they are called in Malaya and Indonesia. Such areas interpenetrate the city and come close to its central core. They are characterised by the use of local constructional materials and by building forms remarkably similar to rural types. In marked contrast to the city's Western parts, they are also characterised by an almost complete lack of physical planning, and hence of regular layout, by gross overcrowding (as, indeed, are the China-towns), usually by a lack of even the most rudimentary community facilities and sometimes even by the absence of sanitation and safe water supply. In sum, considerable parts of the cities of South-east Asia are even today almost completely rural in building form, a veritable *rus in urbe* situation, as D. W. Fryer[1] has already remarked elsewhere. This generalisation applies equally well in many other parts of the developing world.

Such dichotomy in physical form has been a feature of most of the cities of South-east Asia from their very foundation. Seventeenth-century maps of Manila show clearly the marked contrast between the walled Spanish district of Intramuros, the Parian, where the Chinese were required to live, and the surrounding areas of indigenous building.[2] One could produce a series of similar maps for the other cities of the region; indeed, as late as the 1820s, Singapore was being laid out on a plan which provided for the separation of its districts on racial lines, a separation which in time tended to become confirmed in building types.[3]

Dichotomy in physical form is, in fact, only one of the many historical parallels traceable in the development of the cities of South-east Asia. In the first place all except Bangkok were essentially colonial creations, and though Bangkok was nominally the capital of an independent state, like the other cities its growth was very closely linked with the economic penetration of South-east Asia by the West which was a major motif of the colonial period. Except for Bangkok – created as a royal capital in 1782 – the great cities of South-east Asia arose essentially as the points from which the surge in development of the resources of South-east Asia which

[1] D. W. Fryer, 'The million city in South-east Asia', *Geographical Review*, XLIII (1953) 474–94.

[2] M. L. Diaz-Trechuelo, *Arquitectura Española en Filipinas* (Escuela de Estudios Hispano-Americanos de Sevilla, Seville, 1959).

[3] B. W. Hodder, 'Racial groupings in Singapore', *Malayan Journal of Tropical Geography*, I (1953) 25–36.

characterised the colonial period could be directed.[1,2,3,4] They grew up at points from which large productive areas tributary to them in the economic sense could be commanded, and mainly wherever access to the sea coincided with this requirement. In almost every case indigenous settlements upon the site were small before foreign entrepreneurs and colonial government officials created the cities as essential funnels, service points and administrative centres. Though this is not to say, of course, that there were no cities built in Southeast Asia before the colonial period: the magnificent ruins of Angkor alone are sufficient evidence of this.[5,6,7] As Murphey[8] has pointed out, the points chosen during the colonial period were those at which exportable products could be most conveniently assembled; the same access worked equally well in reverse for imports and, of course, for the needs of national administration. Major traditional lines of movement, especially the rivers of the mainland and sea lanes in the island realm, thus commonly focused upon the site choices of the colonial powers; modern transport services were introduced to reinforce these traditional lines of movement. The new cities became the seats of government. Hence they developed rapidly into the largest settlements in their respective countries.

Thus Manila, founded in 1571 by the Spaniards as an administrative, military and missionary centre, grew both as its hinterland in Luzon developed and as the sea connections between China and the Philippines, already in existence in pre-Spanish times,[9] were intensified during the early colonial period in the islands, and expanded to include trade between China and Acapulco in Mexico (and ultimately Spain) by means of the famous Manila galleons.[10] Later, a

[1] Fryer, op. cit.

[2] N. S. Ginsburg, 'The great city in South-east Asia', *American Journal of Sociology*, LX (1955) 455–62.

[3] R. Murphey, 'New capitals of Asia', *Economic Development and Cultural Change*, V (1957) 216–43.

[4] T. G. McGee, *The South-east Asian City* (Bell, London, 1967).

[5] G. Coedès, *Pour Mieux Comprendre Angkor* (Musée Guimet, Paris, 1947).

[6] W. Kirk, 'Some factors in the historical geography of Burma', *Journal of the Manchester Geographical Society*, LIV (1949) 16–26.

[7] L. Sternstein, 'Krung Kao, the old capital of Ayutthaya', *Journal of the Siam Society*, LIII (1965) 83–121.

[8] Murphey, op. cit., pp. 218–20.

[9] Ching-hong Wu, 'A study of references to the Philippines in Chinese sources from the earliest times to the Ming dynasty', *Philippines Social Sciences and Humanities Review*, XXIV (1959) 1–181.

[10] W. L. Schurz, *The Manila Galleon* (Dutton, New York, 1939).

further basis for growth was provided for the city, especially when it came under American rule, with the marked expansion of export crop production, principally sugar, tobacco and Manila hemp, which characterised the period after 1820 and for which Manila served both as the organisational headquarters and the main port of shipment.[1] Nearer the other end of the time scale for the colonial period in South-east Asia, Singapore's rapid growth after its foundation by Raffles in 1819 was based both upon its position at the point of overlap of world ocean lanes with the inner seas of the Indonesian archipelago and also upon the internal development of Malaya. Parts of the island, notably Java, reached a high level of export crop production under the Dutch, and interior Malaya was developed for tin and rubber by Chinese and British interests.[2] Rangoon[3] grew upon the general internal development which resulted from Burmese contact with the West, and especially upon the export trade in rice of the Irrawaddy delta, which was created during the colonial period. Saigon grew in sympathy with the French development of Indo-China, while Batavia, now Djakarta, was essentially the headquarters from which the Dutch ruled their possessions in the East Indies and from which radiated their official shipping line, collecting the commerce of the Outer Islands to that port.

Although there were from the beginning large areas indigenous in building form within their fabric, it is therefore primarily as centres of international trade that we must view the growth of the region's cities during the colonial period. The cities were much more international than local creations and perhaps, as Singer[4] has implied, in the economic sense they should be regarded more as outposts of the economies of the colonial powers than as intrinsic products of the internal evolution of the countries in which they were located. They were international too in their population composition, for they quickly became extremely cosmopolitan. Large numbers of Chinese flooded into South-east Asia to participate in the economic opportunities created there during the colonial period; Indians came also,

[1] E. Wickberg, *The Chinese in Philippine Life* (Yale University Press, New Haven and London, 1965) pp. 45–8.

[2] C. A. Fisher, 'South-east Asia: the Balkans of the Orient?', *Geography*, XLVII (1962) 347–67.

[3] O. H. K. Spate and L. W. Trueblood, 'Rangoon: a study in urban geography', *Geographical Review*, XXXII (1942) 56–73.

[4] H. W. Singer, 'The distribution of gains between investing and borrowing countries', *American Economic Review*, XL (2) (1950) 473–85.

especially into Burma. The impact of immigration was felt most in Malaya, where the highest level of economic development in the region was achieved only through significant inputs of immigrant labour, as the Deputy Registrar of Hong Kong University has shown.[1] A large proportion of the immigrants settled in the cities, with the result that today Singapore and Kuala Lumpur are largely Chinese, while the other cities of the region each contain sizeable alien minorities.

At this point it will be relevant to attempt to assess the economic contribution of the colonial system, which gave birth to the cities of South-east Asia, towards the development of the countries in which the cities were founded. Within the world economy, Europe's rising demand led to important explorations from the fifteenth century onwards,[2] at first often to search for and to control the sources of supply of condiments. This led to Portuguese and later Spanish penetration into South-east Asia and to the development of direct trade with the Spice Islands. Increasing European wealth, especially during the early part of the colonial period from the gold and silver of the Americas, led to the progressive increase of European demands, and these were later enormously enlarged both in variety and volume by the rapidity of economic development in both Europe and the U.S.A. which resulted from the Industrial Revolution. Certain tropical foods and beverages, notably sugar, coconut products, palm oil, coffee and tea, some minerals, for example tin, and a range of industrial raw materials, such as rubber, Manila hemp and tropical woods, found almost insatiable markets. The location of mineral production was, however, largely controlled by the occurrence of the deposits as was forest exploitation by access to communications. Agricultural production for external markets came to be organised on a highly localised system of estates or, failing this, within very restricted geographical areas in each country. The Malayan tin–rubber belt is a classic case of this pattern of development.

At the same time certain parts of the region such as the Irrawaddy delta, the Bangkok plain and parts of Cochin-China were developed for rice grown for export. This rice, however, circulated largely within South-east Asia and nearby India and China. Within the region it

[1] R. N. Jackson, *Immigrant Labour and the Development of Malaya* (Government Printer, Kuala Lumpur, 1961).

[2] M. A. P. Meilink-Roelofz, *Asian Trade and European Influence in the Indonesian Archipelago* (Nijhoff, The Hague, 1962).

went, for example, to Malayan rubber workers and tin miners, to Philippine sugar growers and to plantation workers in north Sumatra, as well as to the clerks, dock workers, runners, sweepers and the like who made up the rapidly growing populations of the cities. As Keyfitz[1] has pointed out, it could thus be thought of in large measure as a fuel consumed by the machine developed during the colonial period whose final products were tea, coffee, sugar, rubber, Manila hemp, tin, edible and inedible oils and a host of other primary products for export through the great cities to Europe and the U.S.A.

Today, however, the trading future of the final products of this machine is very much in question and, again to quote Keyfitz,[2] it is only now, when colonialism in South-east Asia has receded into history, that the full tragedy inherent in the classical colonial economic situation is being realised. The countries of South-east Asia have become highly specialised in the export of tropical foods and raw materials. For most of this century, however, the trend of world prices has been heavily against sellers of food and raw materials and in favour of sellers of manufactured articles. It appears that this is in part because in the case of manufactured commodities, which are by and large produced in the more developed countries, the fruits of technical progress have been distributed largely in the form of rising incomes within those countries rather than lower prices on world markets.[3] On the other hand, the fruits of technical progress in the production of raw materials and foods in the less developed nations have been generally shown in price reductions. The demand for primary products being notoriously inelastic, the fall in their relative prices has not been compensated by total revenue effects.

Perhaps it is possible to go even further than this in explaining the present dilemma of the less-developed nations. Only for a relatively short period did the rapid growth of industry in Europe and the United States take all the tropical raw-material products that could be obtained. The system had attained its height by the early 1920s. More recently several major tropical raw-material products have been facing severe competition from synthetic substitutes. It appears

[1] N. Keyfitz, 'Political-economic aspects of urbanisation in South and South-east Asia', in Philip Hauser and Leo F. Schnore, *The Study of Urbanisation* (Wiley, New York, 1965) pp. 265–309.

[2] N. Keyfitz, 'Indonesian population and the European Industrial Revolution', *Asian Survey*, v (1965) 503–14.

[3] Singer, op. cit., pp. 477–9.

that in this respect the near-completion of a cycle of Western industrial technology is being experienced.[1] Baeyer's synthesis of indigo in 1879 destroyed the value of many hundreds of square miles of British plantations in India. It was the first of a long series of new processes, undoubtedly not yet completed, which are making Western industry each year ecologically more self-contained. Petroleum is one of the few remaining products of the less-developed nations still vitally required by Western industry. Silk, kapok, quinine, rubber and a host of lesser products have gone, or will shortly go, the way of indigo.

A further complication is that the structural difficulties of the economies which today's independent states in South-east Asia inherited from the colonial powers have been compounded during the last twenty years by the relatively slow realisation of the goals of national developmental planning. Unfortunately Sinai's assessment of the Burmese situation has become all too typical. 'It soon became apparent', he has written, 'that it was easier to draw up vast plans than to realise them. When the time came to prepare a balance sheet of Burma's first forward-thrusting impulse, it was discovered that there was a wide and dangerous gap between promise and performance.'[2] For most of the countries of the region, the future as expressed in their development plans simply refuses to be born. As a result, the industrial estates and the steel mills in the cities, the prestige public buildings symbolising nationalism triumphant, the opulent new housing of the tiny minority of the rich, and the pre-war commercial symbols of the central business districts, are as islands which today seem about to be engulfed in a rising tide of migrants from the countryside, the most disturbing expression of the arrival of which is the squatter hut.

National economic development in South-east Asia during the colonial and post-colonial periods thus concerns present patterns of city form and function very directly. The impasse which has now been reached in economic progress in the countries of the region is the major determinant in current social, economic and, as we shall see, developmental conditions within the great cities and it is finding widespread expression in their physical make-up. Such internal conditions are worth looking at as they are considerably different

---

[1] Keyfitz, op. cit. (ref. 22).
[2] I. R. Sinai, *The Challenge of Modernisation* (Chatto & Windus, London, 1964) p. 159.

both from those prevailing today within the cities of the more developed nations and from the historical experience of urbanisation in Europe and the U.S.A.

In the absence of similar research work on South-east Asia, we must turn here to the example of India, though the general argument is no less valid for South-east Asia. Hoselitz[1] has compared the degree of urbanisation in India recorded in the 1951 census with that attained in certain European countries during the last two decades of the nineteenth century. In 1951, for example, 11·9 per cent of the population of India lived in cities of over 20,000 population. Austria was at this stage of urbanisation in 1890 as, broadly, were Norway and Switzerland. France had attained it somewhat earlier. But generally when these European countries had reached this stage of urbanisation, the proportion of the labour force engaged in manufacturing industry was substantially larger than that in India in 1951. In Austria for example, 30 per cent of the labour force was in manufacturing in 1890, compared with 11 per cent in India in 1951.

One important difference in the historical experience of urbanisation in the West and in the presently developing nations would therefore seem to lie in the relationship between urbanisation and industrial growth. While urbanisation in South-east Asia, in India, in other developing areas and in the Europe of an earlier date was built upon sizeable in-migration as well as upon natural increase within the urban areas, in Europe capital formation and social development proceeded with a rapidity such that new arrivals in the urban areas could sooner or later find employment in industry or associated occupations. In fact, as Hoselitz[2] has stated, '... in the long run the period of European industrialisation and urbanisation must be regarded as one characterised by shortage of labour'. At the same time the rationalisation and technical improvement of agriculture were proceeding apace in Europe. This meant not only that dramatic reductions in the rural population were possible, but also that those remaining on the land could participate in rising standards of living resulting from relatively rapid national economic growth.

[1] B. F. Hoselitz, 'The role of urbanisation in economic development: some international comparisons', in R. Turner (ed.), *India's Urban Future* (Univ. of California Press, Berkeley, 1962) pp. 157–81.

[2] Ibid., p. 168.

The contrast between this situation and that of present-day South-east Asia is extreme because in contemporary Asia a fragile and in-sufficient superstructure of modern industry is being erected, often behind high protective fiscal walls, upon a foundation of a largely stagnant agricultural sector. In these circumstances, even a small increase in industrial development may cause disproportionate urban growth. From smaller towns, in which the effect of establishing one factory or other modern enterprise is observable, it has been reported that the increment in employment resulting specifically from such a project may well be accompanied by an increase in unemploy-ment and in casual or irregular employment within the town.[1] This is because the new source of wealth attracts large numbers from the countryside seeking to obtain some benefit from it, usually indirectly in rendering some form of service to those employed in the new enterprise.

It is for reasons such as these that the proportion of the economi-cally active population recorded in 'service' occupations is charac-teristically so large in the Asian city. This tends to give a false picture of the prosperity of the cities because in the West a full tertiary sector is usually associated with a high level of economic development. In Asia the reverse tends to be the case. Many more persons are sup-ported in the cities than the economic base warrants through what is essentially a shared poverty system. The proposition here is quite simple and realistic. It is as Wertheim[2] puts it that 'If a great propor-tion of the urban population is not to starve, a much larger number of jobs has to be created than is reconcilable with efficient manage-ment'. For the masses of immigrants from the countryside who now crowd into the cities, the urban standard of living must remain only marginally above that which they can obtain in their home villages, an abysmally low level, in order to be acceptable. Hence street-sellers abound; there are many more pedicab drivers than are really needed; large numbers of domestic servants are kept; and there are far too many office employees. The process extends even into official admini-stration. There are many middlemen in commerce also, each taking a small share of the profit on the movement of goods.[3]

[1] United Nations, *Report on the World Social Situation* (New York, 1957) p. 126.

[2] W. F. Wertheim, *East–West Parallels: Sociological Approaches to Modern Asia* (van Hoeve, The Hague, 1964).

[3] C. Geertz, *Peddlers and Princes: Social Change and Economic Modernisation in Two Indonesian Towns* (Univ. of Chicago Press, Chicago, 1963) pp. 30–2, 45–6.

This type of city employment is an urban interpretation of an ethic originally created in response to purely agricultural demands, that is, an extension of the pattern of shared poverty of the countryside where complicated renting and sub-renting patterns have developed which allow a great number of people to claim a small portion of agricultural output from a single piece of land. It may well affect the progress of economic development. Wertheim and The Siauw Gap[1] explain the situation in the countryside of Java thus: 'A land-owner replacing the traditional rice knife (*ani-ani*, with which the stalks are cut ear by ear) with a scythe in order to save labour, would place himself outside of the village community. . . . The generally accepted value-system resisted any innovation or technical improvements, as this would mean misery and distress for a significant proportion of the villagers.' And the same is basically true of South-east Asia's urban areas. Geertz[2] has cited one example from a town in Indonesia:

> One of my informants [he states] set up a cigarette factory in a shed behind his house. He began with two workers – girls – rolling the cigarettes by hand in corn sheaths provided by the workers themselves. The factory grew to employ a work force of twenty girls, the number not being determined by economic considerations but by the entrepreneur's and the girls' notions of the 'correct' number which should be employed, given the work involved. The result was an extremely uneconomically operated factory. Unable to accumulate enough capital to provide sufficient tobacco to keep twenty girls working even six hours a day at full capacity, the entrepreneur merely apportioned out regulated quantities of the available tobacco to each girl each day, and the girls worked at a very slow speed, producing only 1,000 cigarettes in a working day where they might easily have produced 1,500–2,000. The outcome was typical: twenty workers and an entrepreneur made a semi-adequate living and no one made a good one, with the added consideration in this case that this economically inefficient operation reduced even further the opportunities to amass enough capital to increase output and hire more workers. As a matter of fact, the business failed after a while, and the Javanese entrepreneur fled his Chinese creditors.

Because of the prevalence of systems of shared poverty, the rudimentary state of most national statistical systems and the relative

---

[1] W. F. Wertheim and The Siauw Gap, 'Social change in Java, 1900–30', *Pacific Affairs*, xxxv (1962) 223–47, ref. p. 288.
[2] C. Geertz, 'Religious belief and economic behaviour in a central Javanese town: some preliminary considerations', *Economic Development and Cultural Change*, iv (1956) 134–58, ref. p. 143.

unimportance of labour exchanges in handling vacancies, recorded rates of unemployment (so beloved of economists in the Western world) give a completely misleading picture of the true economic state of the cities of South-east Asia today. Appalling and virtually unchanging poverty, still largely of a rural type, and itself, as we have just seen, a considerable anti-developmental factor, is a major characteristic of the urban areas. This mass poverty, coupled with heavy migration from the largely stagnant rural sector of the economy, results in a rash of squatter settlement wherever there are unoccupied and unprotected sites and, as in Kuala Lumpur and (until they were cleared from Intramuros in 1963) in Manila, in shanty towns almost adjacent to the commercial hearts of the cities as well as in extensive peripheral shack development.[1] A concomitant is the gross overcrowding of inner urban residential areas, especially the Chinatowns,[2] through their subdivision into cubicles and bed spaces.

With regard to the squatter problem and the general housing and social situation in most of the urban areas within its purview, a recent ECAFE report has stated that these are now 'assuming the proportions of a first-rate crisis'.[3] A further report reviewed urban employment opportunities in the region in some detail and concluded that the prospects for their expansion on any scale remotely comparable to need were very gloomy.[4] In housing, the fact is that the efforts of most countries in South-east Asia in this direction have fallen far short of meeting even the most basic needs. This failure has to date been at least in part due to national policies of capital allocation for the various developmental ends. The prevailing mass poverty of the cities means that throughout the developing world there is a wide gap between the economic rent for new dwellings and the social rent, or what the tenant can afford. It has been estimated in India, for example, that on average an industrial worker's family would be unable to pay more than 10 per cent of its earnings in rent, but this would meet only one-quarter of the annual economic rent

[1] D. J. Dwyer, 'The problem of in-migration and squatter settlement in Asian cities: two case studies, Manila and Victoria–Kowloon', *Asian Studies*, II (1964) 145–69.

[2] B. Kaye, *Upper Nankin Street, Singapore* (Univ. of Mayala Press, Singapore, 1960).

[3] United Nations, 'Review of the social situation in the ECAFE region', *Economic Bulletin for Asia and the Far East*, XVI (1965) 26–44, ref. p. 37.

[4] United Nations, 'Economic development and human resources', *Economic Survey of Asia and the Far East* 1965 (Bangkok, 1966) pp. 1–155.

of a dwelling built to adequate health and technical standards.[1] In all, only about 12 per cent of the urban population of India could bear the full economic rent even of workers' housing. In the face of statistics such as these, most Asian countries have avoided any large-scale commitment to the subsidisation of workers' urban housing. The general argument of the planners has been that housing is non-productive and therefore significant inputs of scarce capital into it cannot be justified.

It is, however, a well-recognised fact in urban geography that form often outlasts function. There are many examples of this, not the least those of the difficulties caused throughout the world by the funnelling of motor vehicles through street patterns laid out in the pre-automobile age. That form can outlast function merits careful consideration in respect of the current housing problems of the South-east Asian city. The normal manner of viewing the city in developing countries would be to assign to it a dynamic role. Urbanisation has usually been considered as the key factor in the race between increased productivity and population growth. The city has also been said to provide most of the political and economic leadership for national development. It has been seen as the point at which basic social transformation begins and spreads outward into the more conservative hinterland.[2,3,4]

Against this, let us consider Sinai's sensitive description of contemporary Rangoon:[5]

> Rangoon [he writes] is the modern heart of Burma, the government centre and the commercial centre, but the buildings which symbolise these European elements fit, one feels, only rather flimsily into the town. The European-created core looks solid, exists and functions. Business is transacted, the shops of foreign nations lie in the docks and telephone communications keep Burma, if only ineffectively, in touch with the world. The Burmese are still pulling the switches which the British introduced. But because of the weight of old, slow-moving Asia that is everywhere, what

[1] United Nations, 1965, op. cit., p. 38.

[2] C. Bauer, 'The pattern of urban and economic development: social implications', *Annals of the American Academy of Political and Social Science*, cccv (1956) 60–9.

[3] R. Crane, 'Urbanism in India', *American Journal of Sociology*, lx (1955) 463–70.

[4] B. F. Hoselitz, *Sociological Aspects of Economic Growth* (Free Press, Glencoe, Ill., 1962) p. 162.

[5] Sinai, *The Challenge of Urbanisation*, p. 166.

belongs to the modern world seems to have merged with the general, interminable stagnation of the old. The activities of modern civilisation go on but they have lost their inner drive – their inner life. There are no modern men to sustain them. ... All the motors and engines that impel a modern city merely keep on ticking, without actually driving the whole mechanism forward.

Who has lived recently for any length of time in a city in South-east Asia, except perhaps for Singapore, and has not on occasion shared these sentiments? In 1966, for example, Carroll wrote bitterly about the state of Manila:[1]

In the past twelve months Manila has had a water shortage in which some 70 per cent of the metropolitan area was without regular service ... it has had a garbage crisis ... there has been a school crisis, though a minor one this year ... electric services went through a bad period some months ago ... mail is in a continual state of crisis and in general it seems better to give up trying to use the telephone ... police and fire protection are unreliable ... the constantly increasing burden of traffic and the condition of the roads discourage one from venturing beyond walking distance. In other words, social organisation in the Manila area has not been able to maintain these services in the face of population increase and normal wear and tear on facilities; and at times it appears we are returning to *barrio* [village]-type of existence.

What Carroll did not mention, however, is what is perhaps the most crucial element of all in the make-up of contemporary Manila: the presence of approximately 300,000 urban squatters in the city as the visible representation in the urban fabric of a massive post-war rural–urban migration.

The existence of squatters in the urban fabric is re-emphasised here because the most central group of problems requiring evaluation in respect of the city in South-east Asia concerns the quality of life of today's urban dwellers. It seems that it can by no means be assumed that the innovating role played by cities in the earlier economic experience of the developed nations is currently being repeated in full in the developing world. This is in large measure due to currently massive rates of rural–urban migration, rates which appear to present the danger of the cities becoming infected with rural ideals and aspirations rather than the rural migrants themselves becoming urbanised, especially as all the evidence is that over the foreseeable future such rates will accelerate markedly.

[1] J. J. Carroll, 'Philippine social organisation and national development', *Philippine Studies*, XIV (1966) 573–90, ref. p. 585.

It is not possible here to demonstrate the evidence which exists concerning the growing transfer of rural characteristics and attitudes into South-east Asia's cities through in-migration. Some of this evidence has been outlined in another paper.[1] One point that is very well worth making in the present context, however, is that there is now a great deal of evidence that recent migrants to the city, and especially the squatters, throughout the developing world are tending wherever possible to group themselves in residential locations according to common rural origins. If the normal sociological approach to this kind of immigrant phenomenon is accepted – that is that residential dispersion is an important part of the group's incorporation into the dominant social structure of the city[2] – then possible national policies towards the provision of mass low-cost housing in which people of various origins can be mixed must obviously be considered in much more than a purely economic frame of reference. Viewed in the context of the developing world, Hong Kong is undoubtedly a pioneer in the field of mass low-cost housing. As of December 1967, the Resettlement Department alone had re-housed over one-quarter of the total population of 3·8 millions. It is of tremendous significance not only for future policy in Hong Kong but perhaps even more so to the future of the cities of the developing world in general that the re-housing programmes of Hong Kong, some of which have run for almost fifteen years, should now be scientifically assessed, especially in their possible contribution towards national economic growth.

There is a bright future for urban geography in participating in this kind of social research which is of vital importance in the developing world.

[1] D. J. Dwyer, 'Problems of urbanisation: the example of Hong Kong', in I.B.G., *Land Use and Resources: Studies in Applied Geography* (London, 1968).
[2] K. J. Myers, 'Assimilation to the economic and social systems of a community', *American Sociological Review*, xv (1950) 367–72.

20 The United Nations Development Decade at Mid-point

U THANT

MODERN technology, for the last hundred years or more, has un-locked the doors of skill and output, confounded the gloomy prophets of inherent physical limitation and so fantastically increased man's power to produce that, in developed economies, to sustain sufficient demand is more the problem than to mobilise sufficient supply. This technology is, naturally and inevitably, one of the developing nations' chief hopes for the successful achievement of modernisation and for any considerable bridging of the gap between rich and poor.

The poor nations are, in some ways, infinitely better placed than the pioneers of an earlier century. In the first place, they have a hundred years of other nations' experience upon which to draw with some degree of clarity. One forgets how much in earlier tech-nological advance was based on uncertain experiment and lucky guess. Above all, one forgets the mystery in which the whole pro-cess of modernisation was shrouded. The early entrepreneurs tried out new processes, tested the market, made a profit – or perhaps were ruined – and all the time they were unwittingly changing the face of the earth. The very phrase that was used, 'the Industrial Revolution', is a symbol of the inadequate estimate of what in fact was happen-ing. Industry played only one part in the remaking of a whole society by the uses of reason, calculation, analysis, cost-consciousness, improvement, experiment and feed-back. Today, with hindsight we can better interpret what has been happening. In fact, the whole idea of development as a *dynamic* process, the factors which make for transformation, the policies which can accelerate it lie at the very root of the concept of a 'Decade of Development'. It is therefore hardly surprising that the United Nations and the specialised agencies have undertaken special studies and experiments dealing with the process of development itself. An Economic Projections and Pro-gramming Centre has been established within the United Nations Secretariat, a United Nations Research Institute for Social Develop-ment began operations in Geneva last year, a United Nations

Institute for Training and Research has just been launched, the I.L.O. established an International Institute for Labour Studies in 1960 and UNESCO an International Institute for Educational Planning in 1963. The Special Fund, in co-operation with the regional commissions, has been active in setting up institutes of economic development and planning – in Latin America in 1962, in Africa in 1963, in Asia in 1964. The I.B.R.D. also has an Economic Development Institute and is extending its work in regional seminars. The United Nations has set up a Centre for Industrial Development. We shall come back to this concept of development as a process in later discussions of the types of aid available to the emergent nations. Here the point is simply to note the relative newness of the conscious idea of development as a coherent process.

A second advantage in the developing world is the sheer scale of information now available in every field connected with development. There is not an area of knowledge or action in which remarkable experiments have not been carried out – experiments which can be freely studied and may be of crucial help. In the critical field of agriculture, for instance, well-known and straightforward changes in the use of fertiliser, better seed, new tools and plant protection can as much as quadruple yields from the land. The developing world might well despair if it had used up all the available technology and was still undernourished. The vastness of potential innovation is the best guarantee of progress – and the task of transferring knowledge of it is correspondingly urgent.

Every branch of the United Nations family is profoundly involved in collecting, evaluating and disseminating the data essential for formulating development policy. The United Nations itself has become a prime source for statistical information about every aspect – economic and social – of the world society. Between 1960 and 1963, for instance, under the stimulus of the United Nations World Census Programme, 150 countries and territories carried out population censuses, nine of them for the first time, and in 1963 ninety-two countries undertook industrial censuses. Every organisation publishes papers and findings, holds conferences, organises seminars, expert committees and workshops and responds to countless requests for information. At a level which escapes the headlines and therefore takes place almost in anonymity, a phenomenal increase has occurred over the last fifteen years in the process of humanity educating itself. If the first change in any revolution is to change the way in which people think, the whole world today is mined with explosive change – change in the whole dimension and dissemination of human knowledge, in the power that goes with it, in the expectations to which it gives rise.

During the Development Decade, the tempo of all this exchange of information and experience has been increasing. So have the attempts of the United Nations family to look ahead and study its material dynamically. For instance, the United Nations itself has published its *Long-term Economic Projections for the World Economy*. The F.A.O. has put out projections for agricultural commodities up to 1970, and is engaged on an ambitious Indicative World Plan for Agriculture. Meanwhile its Third World Food Survey has made calculations of food needs up to the year 2000 which suggest that while food supplies in general must triple, the increase needed for the poor countries is over 200 per cent higher still.

A wide variety of papers studying the likely development of international trade to the end of the 1960s was prepared for the United Nations Conference on Trade and Development held in 1964. Thus, the developing governments are being offered more than simple contemporary data. If they wish to approach their plans with a sense of dynamic purpose and direction, they can gain some insight into the changing world context into which their own plans will have to fit.

Along with this increase in the fund of knowledge available has gone an increase in internationally aided research of all kinds and in the search for new sources of natural wealth. In promoting scientific research in a great variety of fields UNESCO has played a central role. In 1961 the United Nations convened a Conference on New Sources of Energy which provided the first world-wide exchange of existing knowledge and experience in solar energy, wind power, geothermal and tidal energy and considered means of bringing techniques relating to these types of energy into wider use. The United Nations has carried out extensive studies in the development of water resources. Panels on the use of nuclear energy in desalinisation are held by the International Atomic Energy Agency (I.A.E.A.) twice a year. The United Nations is holding an interregional seminar on the economic aspects of water desalinisation this year. It has also been actively engaged with other agencies in the investigation of ground-water resources for domestic, agricultural and industrial uses in regions where lack of water has been preventing economic development.

Yet the present position of the developing nations, confronted with the vast surge of modern technology, is not all gain. Since much of the technology has been designed for other soceities at other times, it does not always fit in with the present needs of emergent states. Worse it may even involve them in contradictions which more developed societies have avoided. The most notorious and difficult of these contradictions is the tendency of modern measures of health to bring about a very sharp increase in population before any other factor in the community – food production, educational development, savings, industrial development – has become really dynamic.

This is not the only contradiction. A very large part of today's productive technology is geared to the needs of societies in which labour tends to be scarce and capital abundant. A modern refinery can cost over $60 million, yet employ only 300 people. This is an extreme case but the trend is general. Automatic looms, combine harvesters, road-laying machinery, earth-movers, power shovels – the inventions of sophisticated technology dispense with the only resource which all the developing countries have in abundant, indeed over-abundant, supply – its manpower – and offers instead machines which swallow up its meagre savings. And just those areas of the economy which seem to promise the most certain road to growth, wealth and independence – the heavy industrial sector which, via the magnetic appeal of the United States and the U.S.S.R. fascinates the new economies – are precisely the sectors in which capital investments are highest and the returns longest to mature.

A similar disproportion bedevils other fields. For example, virtually the entire expenditure of the world in commercial research takes place in the developed nations. It is designed to cut costs and increase competitiveness in the developed sector. Some substitutes made possible by the chemical revolution – for instance plastics and rayon – are cheaper than natural substances. Where the difference in price only slightly favours primary producers, manufacturers in developed countries often prefer substitutes which are under their control and beyond the vicissitudes of politics and weather. A new cheaper chemical insecticide could ruin in a year one of the chief standbys of peasant farming in East Africa – pyrethrum. Binder twine made as a by-product of petrochemicals could threaten to knock out the other – sisal. There are no flows of research money on anything like the same scale to increase the competitiveness of primary products or to diversify their use. Technology, used overwhelmingly as a tool of *developed* societies, can turn into a potent instrument of disruption elsewhere.

These risks lay at the basis of the United Nations decision to summon a Conference, to be prepared and run with the co-operation of a number of the agencies, on the Application of Science and Technology for the Benefit of the Less Developed Areas. It met in Geneva in 1963 and decided both to follow up this first initiative and to take positive steps to get more brains and money into research oriented towards developing needs. An Advisory Committee was established which began to meet in 1964 with the aim of picking out, from the vast potential supply of problems and possibilities, the most urgent points for 'concerted attack'. It was naturally not difficult to define major areas of primary interest – more and better food, improved health, new techniques and education, urban planning, the better use of natural resources and methods of industrialisation. The trouble is that such a list tends to be virtually coterminous with human existence and it is now the Advisory Committee's more difficult task – on which it has, in fact, embarked – to pick out in each category points of 'attack' where the chances of a breakthrough are great and the advantages of making one very widespread. One such instance is clearly large-scale desalinisation of water for agriculture, for which the best hope lies in utilising nuclear energy; another is the provision, from a multitude of sources, of more protein in ordinary diets, both by producing synthetic protein and by conserving available proteins by a variety of methods ranging from cold-storage chains to food irradiation. But the Committee still lacks the staff and resources needed for a vigorous lead on any really wide scale.

The greatest task of the United Nations Decade of Development is to convince governments and peoples that they have the means to wipe out mass poverty with its attendant miseries and dangers, and to stir them to use those means to the full. We have seen how much remains to be done, at this mid-point of the Decade, to achieve even the modest targets which have been set. Who, then, can deny the compelling urgency of applying our efforts more purposefully, more vigorously and with a more coherent strategy? Whether we shall succeed is still doubtful, and in that measure so is the future of man. But there is no doubt whatever about what can be done. If we have courage and constancy of purpose, a better world for all is within our reach.